Scientific Computing with Python
Second Edition

D1573262

High-performance scientific computing with NumPy, SciPy, and pandas

Claus Führer
Jan Erik Solem
Olivier Verdier

BIRMINGHAM - MUMBAI

Scientific Computing with Python
Second Edition

Group Product Manager: Kunal Parikh
Publishing Product Manager: Ali Abidi
Senior Editor: Mohammed Yusuf Imaratwale
Content Development Editor: Sean Lobo
Technical Editor: Manikandan Kurup
Copy Editor: Safis Editing
Project Coordinator: Aparna Ravikumar Nair
Proofreader: Safis Editing
Indexer: Rekha Nair
Production Designer: Joshua Misquitta

First published: December 2016
Second edition: July 2021

Production reference: 2280721

Published by Packt Publishing Ltd.
Livery Place
35 Livery Street
Birmingham
B3 2PB, UK.

ISBN 978-1-83882-232-3

www.packt.com

Contributors

About the authors

Claus Führer is a professor of scientific computations at Lund University, Sweden. He has an extensive teaching record that includes intensive programming courses in numerical analysis and engineering mathematics across various levels in many different countries and teaching environments. Claus also develops numerical software in research collaboration with industry and received Lund University's Faculty of Engineering Best Teacher Award in 2016.

Jan Erik Solem is a Python enthusiast, former associate professor, and computer vision entrepreneur. He co-founded several computer vision startups, most recently Mapillary, a street imagery computer vision company, and has worked in the tech industry for two decades. Jan Erik is a World Economic Forum technology pioneer and won the Best Nordic Thesis Award 2005-2006 for his dissertation on image analysis and pattern recognition. He is also the author of *Programming Computer Vision with Python*.

Olivier Verdier began using Python for scientific computing back in 2007 and received a Ph.D. in mathematics from Lund University in 2009. He has held post-doctoral positions in Cologne, Trondheim, Bergen, and Ume and is now an associate professor of mathematics at Bergen University College, Norway.

About the reviewer

Helmut Podhaisky works in the Institute of Mathematics at the Martin Luther University Halle-Wittenberg, where he teaches mathematics and scientific computing. He has co-authored a book on numerical methods for time integration and several papers on numerical methods. For work and fun, he uses Python, Julia, Mathematica, and Rust.

Acknowledgement

We want to acknowledge the competent and helpful comments and suggestions by Helmut Podhaisky, Halle University, Germany. To have such a partner in the process of writing a book is big luck and chance for the authors.

A book has to be tested in teaching. And here, we had fantastic partners: the teaching assistants from the course "Beräkningsprogramering med Python" during the years, especially, Najmeh Abiri, Christian Andersson, Peter Meisrimel, Azahar Monge, Fatemeh Mohammadi, Tony Stillfjord, Peter Meisriemel, Lea Versbach, Sadia Asim and Anna-Mariya Otsetova, Lund University.

A lot of input to the book came from a didactic project in higher education leading to a Ph.D. thesis by Dara Maghdid. Together with him, the material of the book was tested and commented on by students from Soran University in Kurdistan Region, Iraq.

Most of the examples in the new chapter on GUI's in this second edition were inspired by our colleague Malin Christersson. Co-teaching this course with her, Alexandros Sopasakis, Tony Stillfjord, and Robert Klöfkorn were fun. Hopefully not only for the teaching team but also for our students—undergraduates and Ph.D. students. Special thanks also to Anne-Maria Persson, friend, director of studies, and supporter of Python in mathematics and physics higher education.

A book has not only to be written, but it also has to be published, and in this process, Sean Lobo and Gebin George, Packt Publishing, were always constructive, friendly, and helpful partners bridging different time zones and often quite challenging text processing tools. They gave this book project momentum in its final stage to be completed—even under hard Covid19 work conditions.

Claus Führer, Jan-Erik Solem, Olivier Verdier , 2021

Table of Contents

Preface

Python has tremendous potential in the scientific computing domain. This updated edition of *Scientific Computing with Python* features new chapters on graphical user interfaces, efficient data processing, and parallel computing to help you perform mathematical and scientific computing efficiently using Python.

This book will help you to explore new Python syntax features and create different models using scientific computing principles. The book presents Python alongside mathematical applications and demonstrates how to apply Python concepts in computing with the help of examples involving Python 3.8. You'll use pandas for basic data analysis to understand the modern needs of scientific computing and cover data module improvements and built-in features. You'll also explore numerical computation modules such as NumPy and SciPy, which enable fast access to highly efficient numerical algorithms. By learning to use the plotting module Matplotlib, you will be able to represent your computational results in talks and publications. A special chapter is devoted to SymPy, a tool for bridging symbolic and numerical computations. The book introduces also to the Python wrapper, mpi4py, for message passing parallel programming.

By the end of this Python book, you'll have gained a solid understanding of task automation and how to implement and test mathematical algorithms along within scientific computing.

Who this book is for

This book is for students with a mathematical background, university teachers designing modern courses in programming, data scientists, researchers, developers, and anyone who wants to perform scientific computation in Python. The book evolved from 13 years of Python teaching in undergraduate science and engineering programs, as special industry in-house courses and specialization courses for high school teachers. The typical reader has the need to use Python in areas like mathematics, big data processings, machine learning and simulation. Therefore a basic knowledge of vectors and matrices as well of notions like convergence and iterative processes is beneficial.

What this book covers

Chapter 1, *Getting Started*, addresses the main language elements of Python without going into detail. Here we will have a brief tour of everything. It is a good starting point for those who want to start directly. It is a quick reference for those readers who want to revise their basic understanding of constructs such as functions.

Chapter 2, *Variables and Basic Types*, presents the most important and basic types in Python. Float is the most important data type in scientific computing together with the special numbers nan and inf. Booleans, integers, complex data types, and strings are other basic data types that will be used throughout this book.

Chapter 3, *Container Types*, explains how to work with container types, mainly lists. Dictionaries and tuples will be explained as well as indexing and looping through container objects. Occasionally, we can even use sets as a special container type.

Chapter 4, *Linear Algebra - Arrays*, covers the most important objects in linear algebra – vectors and matrices. This book chooses the NumPy array as the central tool for describing matrices and even higher-order tensors. Arrays have many advanced features and also allow universal functions to act on matrices or vectors elementwise. The book focuses on array indexing, slices, and the dot product as the basic operations in most computing tasks. Some linear algebra examples are shown to demonstrate the use of SciPy's `linalg` submodule.

Chapter 5, *Advanced Array Concepts*, explains some more advanced aspects of arrays. The difference between array copies and views is explained extensively as views make programs that use arrays very fast but are often a source of errors that are hard to debug. The use of Boolean arrays to write effective, compact, and readable code is shown and demonstrated. Finally, the technique of array broadcasting – a unique feature of NumPy arrays – is explained by comparing it to operations being performed on functions.

Chapter 6, *Plotting*, shows how to make plots, mainly classical *x/y* plots but also 3D plots and histograms. Scientific computing requires good tools for visualizing the results. Python's `matplotlib` module is introduced, starting with the handy plotting commands in its `pyplot` submodule. Finetuning and modifying plots becomes possible by creating graphical objects such as axes. We will show how attributes of these objects can be changed and how annotations can be made.

Chapter 7, *Functions*, looks at functions, which form a fundamental building block in programming that is closely linked to some underlying mathematical concepts. Function definition and function calls are explained as the different ways to set function arguments. Anonymous lambda functions are introduced and used in various examples throughout the book.

Chapter 8, *Classes*, defines objects as instances of classes, which we provide with methods and attributes. In mathematics, class attributes often depend on each other, which requires special programming techniques for setter and getter functions. Basic mathematical operations such as addition can be defined for special mathematical data types. Inheritance and abstraction are mathematical concepts that are reflected by object-oriented programming. We demonstrate the use of inheritance using a simple solver class for ordinary differential equations.

Chapter 9, *Iterating*, presents iteration using loops and iterators. There is now a chapter in this book without loops and iterations, but here we will come to the principles of iterators and create our own generator objects. In this chapter, you will learn why a generator can be exhausted and how infinite loops can be programmed. Python's `itertools` module is a useful companion for this chapter.

Chapter 10, *Series and DataFrames – Working with pandas,* gives a brief introduction to pandas. This chapter will teach you how to work with various time series in Python, the concept of DataFrames, and how to access and visualize data. This chapter will also cover how the concept of NumPy arrays is extended to pandas DataFrames.

Chapter 11, *Communication by a Graphical User Interface,* shows the basic principles of GUI programming within
Matplotlib. The role of events, slider movements, or mouseclicks and their interaction with so-called callback functions is explained along with a couple of examples.

Chapter 12, *Error and Exception Handling,* covers errors and exceptions and how to find and fix them. An error or an exception is an event that breaks the execution of a program unit. This chapter shows what to do then, that is, how an exception can be handled. You will learn how to define your own exception classes and how to provide valuable information that can be used for catching these exceptions. Error handling is more than printing an error message.

Chapter 13, *Namespaces, Scopes, and Modules,* covers Python modules. What are local and global variables? When is a variable known and when is it unknown to a program unit? This is discussed in this chapter. A variable can be passed to a function by a parameter list or tacitly injected by making use of its scope. When should this technique be applied and when shouldn't it? This chapter tries to give an answer to this central question.

Chapter 14, *Input and Output*, covers some options for handling data files. Data files are used for storing and providing data for a given problem, often large-scale measurements. This chapter describes how this data can be accessed and modified using different formats.

Chapter 15, *Testing*, focuses on testing for scientific programming. The key tool is `unittest`, which allows automatic testing and parametrized tests. By considering the classical bisection algorithm in numerical mathematics, we exemplify different steps to designing meaningful tests, which as a side effect also deliver documentation of the use of a piece of code. Careful testing provides test protocols that can be helpful later when debugging complex code often written by many different programmers.

Chapter 16, *Symbolic Computations – SymPy*, is all about symbolic computations. Scientific computing is mainly numeric computations with inexact data and approximative results. This is contrasted with symbolic computations' often formal manipulation, which aims for exact solutions in a closed-form expression. In this chapter, we introduce this technique in Python, which is often used to derive and verify theoretically mathematical models and numerical results. We focus on high-precision floating-point evaluation of symbolic expressions.

Chapter 17, *Interacting with the Operating System*, demonstrates the interaction of a Python script with system commands. The chapter is based on Linux systems such as Ubuntu and serves only as a demonstration of concepts and possibilities. It allows putting scientific computing tasks in an application context, where often different software have to be combined. Even hardware components might come into play.

Chapter 18, *Python for Parallel Computing*, covers parallel computing and the `mpi4py` module. In this chapter, we see how to execute copies of the same script on different processors in parallel. The commands presented in this chapter are provided by the `mpi4py` Python module, which is a Python wrapper to realize the MPI standard in C. After working through this chapter, you will be able to work on your own scripts for parallel programming, and you will find that we described only the most essential commands and concepts here.

Chapter 19, *Comprehensive Examples*, presents some comprehensive and longer examples together with a brief introduction to the theoretical background and their complete implementation. These examples make use of all the constructs shown in the book so far and put them in a larger and more complex context. They are open to extension by the reader.

To get the most out of this book

This book is intended for beginners or readers who have some experience in programming. You can read the book either from the first page to the last, or by picking the bits that seem most interesting. Prior knowledge of Python is not mandatory.

Software/hardware covered in the book	OS requirements
Python 3.8	Windows/Linux/macOS

You'll need a system with Ubuntu (or any other Linux OS) installed for Chapter 17, *Interacting with the Operating System*.

If you are using the digital version of this book, we advise you to type the code yourself or access the code via the GitHub repository (link available in the next section). Doing so will help you avoid any potential errors related to the copying and pasting of code.

Download the example code files

You can download the example code files for this book from GitHub at https://github.com/PacktPublishing/Scientific-Computing-with-Python-Second-Edition. In case there's an update to the code, it will be updated on the existing GitHub repository.

We also have other code bundles from our rich catalog of books and videos available at https://github.com/PacktPublishing/. Check them out!

Download the color images

We also provide a PDF file that has color images of the screenshots/diagrams used in this book. You can download it here: https://static.packt-cdn.com/downloads/9781838822323_ColorImages.pdf.

Conventions used

There are a number of text conventions used throughout this book.

CodeInText: Indicates code words in the text, database table names, folder names, filenames, file extensions, pathnames, dummy URLs, user input, and Twitter handles. Here is an example: "The for statement has two important keywords: break and else."

A block of code is set as follows:

```
t=symbols('t')
x=[0,t,1]
# The Vandermonde Matrix
V = Matrix([[0, 0, 1], [t**2, t, 1], [1, 1,1]])
y = Matrix([0,1,-1]) # the data vector
a = simplify(V.LUsolve(y)) # the coefficients
# the leading coefficient as a function of the parameter
a2 = Lambda(t,a[0])
```

Get in touch

Feedback from our readers is always welcome.

General feedback: If you have questions about any aspect of this book, mention the book title in the subject of your message and email us at customercare@packtpub.com.

Errata: Although we have taken every care to ensure the accuracy of our content, mistakes do happen. If you have found a mistake in this book, we would be grateful if you would report this to us. Please visit www.packtpub.com/support/errata, selecting your book, clicking on the Errata Submission Form link, and entering the details.

Piracy: If you come across any illegal copies of our works in any form on the Internet, we would be grateful if you would provide us with the location address or website name. Please contact us at copyright@packt.com with a link to the material.

If you are interested in becoming an author: If there is a topic that you have expertise in and you are interested in either writing or contributing to a book, please visit authors.packtpub.com.

Reviews

Please leave a review. Once you have read and used this book, why not leave a review on the site that you purchased it from? Potential readers can then see and use your unbiased opinion to make purchase decisions, we at Packt can understand what you think about our products, and our authors can see your feedback on their book. Thank you!

For more information about Packt, please visit packt.com.

Getting Started 1

In this chapter, we will give a brief overview of the principal syntactical elements of Python. Readers who have just started learning programming are guided through the book in this chapter. Every topic is presented here in a *how-to* way and will be explained later in the book in a deeper conceptual manner and will also be enriched with many applications and extensions.

Readers who are already familiar with another programming language will, in this chapter, encounter the Python way of doing classical language constructs. This offers them a quick start to Python programming.

Both types of readers are encouraged to refer to this chapter as a brief guideline when zigzagging through the book. However, before we start, we have to make sure that everything is in place and that you have the correct version of Python installed together with the main modules for scientific computing and tools, such as a good editor and a shell, which helps in code development and testing.

In this chapter, we'll cover the following topics:

- Installation and configuration instructions
- Program and program flow
- Basic data types in Python
- Repeating statements with loops
- Conditional statements
- Encapsulating code with functions
- Understanding scripts and modules
- Python interpreter

Read the following section, even if you already have access to a computer with Python installed. You might want to adjust things to have a working environment that conforms to the presentation in this book.

1.1 Installation and configuration instructions

Before diving into the subject of the book, you should have all the relevant tools installed on your computer. We give you some advice and recommend tools that you might want to use. We only describe public domain and free tools.

1.1.1 Installation

There are currently two major versions of Python; the 2.*x* branch and the new 3.*x* branch. There are language incompatibilities between these branches and you have to be aware of which one to use. This book is based on the 3.*x* branch, considering the language is up to release 3.7.

For this book, you need to install the following:

- The interpreter: Python 3.7 (or later)
- The modules for scientific computing: SciPy with NumPy
- The module for the graphical representation of mathematical results: matplotlib
- The shell: IPython
- A Python-related editor: preferably, Spyder (see *Figure 1.1*).

The installation of these is facilitated by the so-called distribution packages. We recommend that you use Anaconda.

1.1.2 Anaconda

Even if you have Python pre-installed on your computer, we recommend that you create your personal Python environment that allows you to work without the risk of accidentally affecting the software on which your computer's functionality might depend. With a virtual environment, such as Anaconda, you are free to change language versions and install packages without the unintended side effects.

If the worst happens and you mess things up totally, just delete the Anaconda directory and start again. Running the Anaconda installer will install Python, a Python development environment and editor (Spyder), the shell (IPython), and the most important packages for numerical computations: SciPy, NumPy, and matplotlib.

You can install additional packages with `conda install` within your virtual environment created by Anaconda (see also the official documentation).

1.1.3 Spyder

The default screen of Spyder consists of an editor window on the left, a console window in the lower-right corner, which gives access to an IPython shell, and a help window in the upper-right corner, as shown in the following figure:

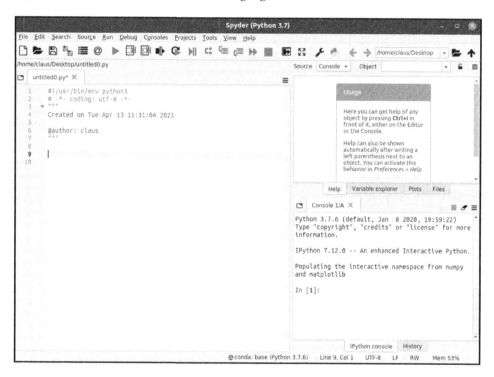

Figure 1.1: The default screen of Spyder

1.1.4 Configuration

Most Python codes will be collected in files. We recommend that you use the following header in all your Python files:

```
from numpy import *
from matplotlib.pyplot import *
```

With this, you make sure that all fundamental data types and functions used in this book for scientific computing purposes are imported. Without this step, most of the examples in the book would raise errors.

Spyder gives syntax warnings and syntax error indicators. Warnings are marked by a yellow triangle; see *Figure 1.2*.

Syntax warnings indicate statements that are correct but that you are discouraged from using for some reason. The preceding statement, `from`, causes such a warning. We will discuss the reasons for this later in this book. In this particular case, we ignore the warning.

```
  8
△ 9 from numpy import *
△ 10 from matplotlib.pyplot import *
 11
```

Figure 1.2: Warning triangles in Spyder

Many editors, such as Spyder, provide the possibility to create a template for your files. Look for this feature and put the preceding header into a template.

1.1.5 Python shell

The Python shell is good, but not optimal, for interactive scripting. We therefore recommend using IPython instead [25].

IPython can be started in different ways:

- In a terminal shell by running the following command: `ipython`

- By directly clicking on an icon called Jupyter QT Console:

- When working with Spyder, you should use an IPython console (see *Figure 1.1*).

1.1.6 Executing scripts

You often want to execute the contents of a file. Depending on the location of the file on your computer, it is necessary to navigate to the correct location before executing the contents of a file:

- Use the command `cd` in IPython in order to move to the directory where your file is located.
- To execute the contents of a file named `myfile.py`, just run the following command in the IPython shell:

```
run myfile
```

1.1.7 Getting help

Here are some tips on how to use IPython:

- To get help on an object, just type `?` after the object's name and then press the *Return* key.
- Use the arrow keys to reuse the last executed commands.
- You may use the *Tab* key for completion (that is, you write the first letter of a variable or method and IPython shows you a menu with all the possible completions).
- Use *Ctrl+D* to quit.
- Use IPython's magic functions. You can find a list and explanations by applying `%magic` on the command prompt.

You can find out more about IPython in its online documentation.

1.1.8 Jupyter – Python notebook

The Jupyter notebook is a fantastic tool for demonstrating your work. Students might want to use it to make and document homework and exercises and teachers can prepare lectures with it, even slides and web pages.

If you have installed Python via Anaconda, you already have everything for Jupyter in place. You can invoke the notebook by running the following command in the terminal window:

```
jupyter notebook
```

A browser window will open and you can interact with Python through your web browser.

1.2 Program and program flow

A program is a sequence of statements that are executed in top-down order. This linear execution order has some important exceptions:

- There might be a conditional execution of alternative groups of statements (blocks), which we refer to as branching.
- There are blocks that are executed repetitively, which is called looping (see *Figure 1.3*).
- There are function calls that are references to another piece of code, which is executed before the main program flow is resumed. A function call breaks the linear execution and pauses the execution of a program unit while it passes the control to another unit – a function. When this gets completed, its control is returned to the calling unit.

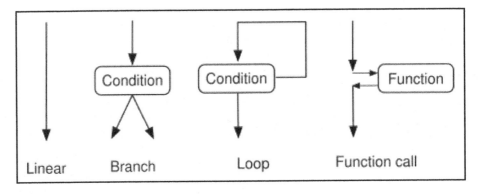

Figure 1.3: Program flow

Python uses a special syntax to mark blocks of statements: a keyword, a colon, and an indented sequence of statements, which belong to the block (see *Figure 1.4*).

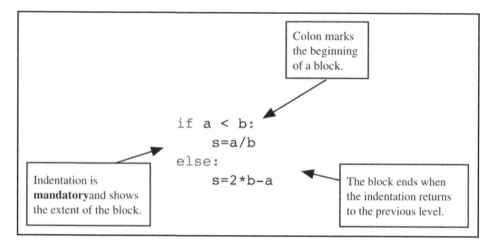

Figure 1.4: Block command

1.2.1 Comments

If a line in a program contains the symbol #, everything following on the same line is considered as a comment:

```
# This is a comment of the following statement
a = 3  # ... which might get a further comment here
```

1.2.2 Line joining

A backslash \ at the end of the line marks the next line as a continuation line, that is, *explicit line joining*. If the line ends before all the parentheses are closed, the following line will automatically be recognized as a continuation line, that is, *implicit line joining*.

1.3 Basic data types in Python

Let's go over the basic data types that you will encounter in Python.

1.3.1 Numbers

A number may be an integer, a real number, or a complex number. The usual operations are as follows:

- Addition and subtraction, + and –
- Multiplication and division, * and /
- Power, **

Here is an example:

```
2 ** (2 + 2) # 16
1j ** 2 # -1
1. + 3.0j
```

The symbol j denotes the imaginary part of a complex number. It is a syntactic element and should not be confused with multiplication by a variable.

1.3.2 Strings

Strings are sequences of characters, enclosed by single or double quotes:

```
'valid string'
"string with double quotes"
"you shouldn't forget comments"
'these are double quotes: ".." '
```

You can also use triple quotes for strings that have multiple lines:

```
"""This is
a long,
long string"""
```

1.3.3 Variables

A variable is a reference to an object. An object may have several references. You use the assignment operator = to assign a value to a variable:

```
x = [3, 4] # a list object is created
y = x # this object now has two labels: x and y
del x # we delete one of the labels
del y # both labels are removed: the object is deleted
```

The value of a variable can be displayed by the print function:

```
x = [3, 4] # a list object is created
print(x)
```

1.3.4 Lists

Lists are a very useful construction and one of the basic types in Python. A Python list is an ordered list of objects enclosed by square brackets. You can access the elements of a list using zero-based indexes inside square brackets:

```
L1 = [5, 6]
L1[0] # 5
L1[1] # 6
L1[2] # raises IndexError
L2 = ['a', 1, [3, 4]]
L2[0] # 'a'
L2[2][0] # 3
L2[-1] # last element: [3,4]
L2[-2] # second to last: 1
```

The indexing of the elements starts at zero. You can put objects of any type inside a list, even other lists. Some basic list functions are as follows:

- list(range(n))} creates a list with n elements, starting with zero:

  ```
  print(list(range(5))) # returns [0, 1, 2, 3, 4]
  ```

- len gives the length of a list:

  ```
  len(['a', 1, 2, 34]) # returns 4
  len(['a',[1,2]]) # returns 2
  ```

- append is used to append an element to a list:

  ```
  L = ['a', 'b', 'c']
  L[-1] # 'c'
  L.append('d')
  L # L is now ['a', 'b', 'c', 'd']
  L[-1] # 'd'
  ```

Operations on lists

- The operator + concatenates two lists:

```
L1 = [1, 2]
L2 = [3, 4]
L = L1 + L2 # [1, 2, 3, 4]
```

- As you might expect, multiplying a list by an integer concatenates the list with itself several times:

n*L is equivalent to making *n* additions:

```
L = [1, 2]
3 * L # [1, 2, 1, 2, 1, 2]
```

1.3.6 Boolean expressions

A Boolean expression is an expression that has the value True or False. Some common operators that yield conditional expressions are as follow:

- Equal: ==
- Not equal: !=
- Strictly less, less or equal: <, <=
- Strictly greater, greater or equal: >, >=

You combine different Boolean values with or and and. The keyword not gives the logical negation of the expression that follows. Comparisons can be chained so that, for example, x < y < z is equivalent to x < y and y < z. The difference is that y is only evaluated once in the first example. In both cases, z is not evaluated at all when the first condition, x < y, evaluates to False:

```
2 >= 4 # False
2 < 3 < 4 # True
2 < 3 and 3 < 2 # False
2 != 3 < 4 or False # True
2 <= 2 and 2 >= 2 # True
not 2 == 3 # True
not False or True and False # True!
```

The binary operators <, >, <=, >=, !=, and == have a higher precedence than the unary operator, not. The operators and and or have the lowest precedence. Operators with higher precedence rules are evaluated before those with lower precedence rules.

1.4 Repeating statements with loops

Loops are used to repetitively execute a sequence of statements while changing a variable from iteration to iteration. This variable is called the index variable. It is successively assigned to the elements of a list:

```
L = [1, 2, 10]
for s in L:
    print(s * 2) # output: 2 4 20
```

The part to be repeated in the `for` loop has to be properly indented:

```
my_list = [...] # define a list
for elt in my_list:
    ...    #do_something
    ...    #something_else
print("loop finished") # outside the for block
```

1.4.1 Repeating a task

One typical use of a `for` loop is to repeat a certain task a fixed number of times:

```
n = 30
for iteration in range(n):
    ... # a statement here  gets executed n times
```

1.4.2 break and else

The `for` statement has two important keywords: `break` and `else`. The keyword `break` quits the `for` loop even if the list we are iterating is not exhausted:

```
x_values=[0.5, 0.7, 1.2]
threshold = 0.75
for x in x_values:
    if x > threshold:
        break
    print(x)
```

The finalizing `else` checks whether the `for` loop was broken with the `break` keyword. If it was not broken, the block following the `else` keyword is executed:

```
x_values=[0.5, 0.7]
threshold = 0.75
for x in x_values:
```

```
    if x > threshold:
        break
else:
    print("all the x are below the threshold")
```

1.5 Conditional statements

This section covers how to use conditions for branching, breaking, or otherwise controlling your code.

A conditional statement delimits a block that will be executed if the condition is true. An optional block starting with the keyword `else` will be executed if the condition is not fulfilled (see *Figure 1.4*). We demonstrate this by printing, $|x|$, the absolute value of x:

$$|x| = \begin{cases} x & \text{if } x \geq 0 \\ -x & \text{otherwise} \end{cases}$$

The Python equivalent is as follows:

```
x = ...
if x >= 0:
    print(x)
else:
    print(-x)
```

Any object can be tested for the truth value, for use in an `if` or `while` statement. The rules for how the truth values are obtained are explained in Section 2.3.2, *Boolean casting*.

1.6 Encapsulating code with functions

Functions are useful for gathering similar pieces of code in one place. Consider the following mathematical function:

$$x \mapsto f(x) := 2x + 1$$

The Python equivalent is as follows:

```
def f(x):
    return 2*x + 1
```

In *Figure 1.5*, the elements of a function block are explained:

- The keyword `def` tells Python we are defining a function.
- `f` is the name of the function.
- `x` is the argument or input of the function.
- What is after `return` is called the output of the function.

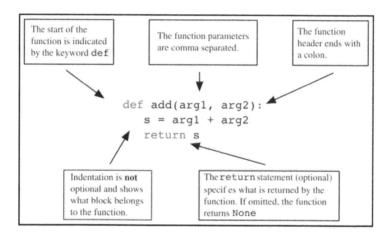

Figure 1.5: Anatomy of a function

Once the function is defined, it can be called using the following code:

```
f(2)  # 5
f(1)  # 3
```

1.7 Understanding scripts and modules

A collection of statements in a file (which usually has a `py` extension) is called a script.
Suppose we put the contents of the following code into a file named `smartscript.py`:

```
def f(x):
    return 2*x + 1
z = []
for x in range(10):
    if f(x) > pi:
        z.append(x)
    else:
        z.append(-1)
print(z)
```

In a Python or IPython shell, such a script can then be executed with the `exec` command after opening and reading the file. Written as a one-liner, it reads as follows:

```
exec(open('smartscript.py').read())
```

The IPython shell provides the magic command `%run` as a handy alternative way to execute a script:

```
%run smartscript
```

1.7.1 Simple modules – collecting functions

Often, you collect functions in a script. This creates a module with additional Python functionality. To demonstrate this, we create a module by collecting functions in a single file, for example, `smartfunctions.py`:

```
def f(x):
    return 2*x + 1
def g(x):
    return x**2 + 4*x - 5
def h(x):
    return 1/f(x)
```

- These functions can now be used by any external script or directly in the IPython environment.
- Functions within the module can depend on each other._
- Grouping functions with a common theme or purpose gives modules that can be shared and used by others.

Again, the command `exec(open('smartfunctions.py').read())` makes these functions available to your IPython shell (note that there is also the IPython magic function, `run`). In Python terminology, you say that they are put into the actual namespace.

1.7.2 Using modules and namespaces

Alternatively, the modules can be imported by the command `import`. This creates a namespace named after the filename. The command `from` puts the functions into the general namespace without creating a separate namespace:

```
import smartfunctions
print(smartfunctions.f(2))      # 5
```

```
from smartfunctions import g     #import just this function
print(g(1)) # 0
from smartfunctions import *     #import all
print(h(2)*f(2))                 # 1.0
```

Import the commands `import` and `from`. Import the functions only once into the respective namespace. Changing the functions after the import has no effect on the current Python session.

1.8 Python interpreter

The Python interpreter executes the following steps:

1. First, it checks the syntax.
2. Then it executes the code line by line.
3. The code inside a function or class declaration is *not* executed, but its syntax is checked:

```
def f(x):
    return y**2
a = 3   # here both a and f are defined
```

You can run the preceding program because there are no syntactical errors. You get an error only when you call the function `f`.

In that case, we speak about a *runtime error*:

```
f(2) # error, y is not defined
```

Summary

In this chapter, we briefly addressed the main language elements of Python without going into detail. You should now be able to start playing with small pieces of code and test different program constructs. All this is intended as an appetizer for the chapters to follows, where we will provide you with the details, examples, exercises, and more background information.

Variables and Basic Types

2

In this chapter, we will present the most important and basic types in Python. What is a type? It is a set consisting of data content, its representation, and all possible operations. Later in this book, we will make this definition much more precise when we introduce the concepts of a class in `Chapter 8`: *Classes*.

In this chapter, we'll cover the following topics:

- Variables
- Numeric types
- Booleans
- Strings

2.1 Variables

Variables are references to Python objects. They are created by assignments, for example:

```
a = 1
diameter = 3.
height = 5.
cylinder = [diameter, height] # reference to a list
```

Variables take names that consist of any combination of capital and small letters, the underscore _, and digits. A variable name must not start with a digit. Note that variable names are case sensitive. A good naming of variables is an essential part of documenting your work, so we recommend that you use descriptive variable names.

Python has 33 *reserved keywords*, which cannot be used as variable names (see *Table 2.1*). Any attempt to use such a keyword as a variable name would raise a syntax error:

and	as	assert	break	class	continue	def	del
elif	else	except	exec	False	finally	for	from
global	if	import	in	is	lambda	None	nonlocal
not	or	pass	raise	return	True	try	while
yield							

Table 2.1: Reserved Python keywords

As opposed to other programming languages, variables require no type declaration in Python. The type is automatically deduced:

```
x = 3 # integer (int)
y = 'sunny' # string (str)
```

You can create several variables with a multiple assignment statement:

```
a = b = c = 1 # a, b and c get the same value 1
```

Variables can also be altered after their definition:

```
a = 1
a = a + 1 # a gets the value 2
a = 3 * a # a gets the value 6
```

The last two statements can be written by combining the two operations with an assignment directly by using increment operators:

```
a += 1 # same as a = a + 1
a *= 3 # same as a = 3 * a
```

2.2 Numeric types

At some point, you will have to work with numbers, so we start by considering different forms of numeric types in Python. In mathematics, we distinguish between natural numbers ($\mathbb{N}$), integers ($\mathbb{Z}$), rational numbers ($\mathbb{Q}$), real numbers ($\mathbb{R}$), and complex numbers ($\mathbb{C}$). These are infinite sets of numbers. Operations differ between these sets and may even not be defined. For example, the usual division of two numbers in $\mathbb{Z}$ might not result in an integer — it is not defined on $\mathbb{Z}$.

In Python, like many other computer languages, we have numeric types:

- The numeric type, `int`, which is at least theoretically the entire $\mathbb{Z}$
- The numeric type, `float`, which is a finite subset of $\mathbb{R}$
- The numeric type, `complex`, which is a finite subset of $\mathbb{C}$

Finite sets have a smallest and a largest number and there is a minimum spacing between two numbers; see `Section 2.2.2`, *Floating-point numbers*, for further details.

2.2.1 Integers

The simplest numeric type is the integer type `int`.

Plain integers

The statement `k = 3` assigns the variable `k` to an integer.

Applying an operation such as +, –, or * to integers returns an integer. The division operator, //, returns an integer, while / returns a `float`:

```
6 // 2  # 3  an integer value
7 // 2  # 3
7 / 2   # 3.5  a float value
```

The set of integers in Python is unbounded; there is no largest integer. The limitation here is the computer's memory rather than any fixed value given by the language.

 If the division operator (/) in the preceding example returns 3, you have not installed the correct Python version.

2.2.2 Floating-point numbers

If you execute the statement a = 3.0 in Python, you create a floating-point number (Python type: float). These numbers form a finite subset of rational numbers, $\mathbb{Q}$.

Alternatively, the constant could have been given in exponent notation as a = 30.0e-1 or simply a = 30.e-1. The symbol e separates the exponent from the mantissa, and the expression reads in mathematical notation as $a = 30.0 \times 10^{-1}$. The name *floating-point number* refers to the internal representation of these numbers and reflects the floating position of the decimal point when considering numbers over a wide range.

Applying elementary mathematical operations, such as +, -, *, and /, to two floating-point numbers, or to an integer and a floating-point number, returns a floating-point number.

Operations between floating-point numbers rarely return the exact result expected from rational number operations:

```
0.4 - 0.3 # returns 0.10000000000000003
```

This fact matters when comparing floating-point numbers:

```
0.4 - 0.3 == 0.1 # returns False
```

The reason for this becomes apparent when looking at the internal representation of floating-point numbers; see also Section 15.2.6, *Float comparisons*.

Floating-point representation

A floating-point number is represented by three quantities: the sign, the mantissa, and the exponent:

$$\text{sign}(x)\left(x_0 + x_1\beta^{-1} + \ldots + x_{t-1}\beta^{-(t-1)}\right)\beta^e$$

with $\beta \in \mathbb{N}$ and $x_0 \neq 0, \ 0 \leq x_i < \beta$.

$x_0 \ldots x_{t-1}$ is called the mantissa, β the basis, and e the exponent, with $1 - e_{\max} \leq e \leq e_{\max}$. t is called the mantissa length. The condition $x_0 \neq 0$ makes the representation unique and saves, in the binary case ($\beta = 2$), one bit.

Two-floating point zeros, $+0$ and -0, exist, both represented by the mantissa 0.

On a typical Intel processor, $\beta = 2$. To represent a number in the `float` type, 64 bits are used, namely, 1 bit for the sign, $t = 52$ bits for the mantissa, and 11 bits for the exponent e. The upper bound e_{max} for the exponent is consequently $2^{10} - 1 = 1023$.

With this data, the smallest positive representable number is

$$\text{fl}_{min} = 1.0 \times 2^{-1023} \approx 10^{-308}$$, and the largest $\text{fl}_{max} = 1.11\ldots1 \times 2^{1023} \approx 10^{308}$.

Note that floating-point numbers are not equally spaced in $[0, \text{fl}_{max}]$. There is, in particular, a gap at zero (see also [29]). The distance between 0 and the first positive number is 2^{-1023}, while the distance between the first and the second is smaller by a factor $2^{-52} \approx 2.2 \times 10^{-16}$. This effect, caused by the normalization $x_0 \neq 0$, is visualized in *Figure 2.1*:

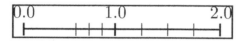

Figure 2.1: The floating-point gap at zero. Here $t = 3, e_{max} = 1$

This gap is filled equidistantly with *subnormal* floating-point numbers to which such a result is rounded. Subnormal floating-point numbers have the smallest possible exponent and do not follow the normalization convention, $x_0 \neq 0$.

Infinite and not a number

There are, in total, $2(\beta - 1)\beta^{t-1}(2e_{max} + 1) + 1$ floating-point numbers. Sometimes, a numerical algorithm computes floating-point numbers outside this range.

This generates number overflow or underflow. In NumPy, the special floating-point number `inf` is assigned to overflow results:

```
exp(1000.)  # inf
a = inf
3 - a  # -inf
3 + a  # inf
```

Working with `inf` may lead to mathematically undefined results. This is indicated in Python by assigning the result another special floating-point number, `nan`. This stands for *not-a-number*, that is, an undefined result of a mathematical operation. To demonstrate this, we continue the previous example:

```
a + a  # inf
a - a  # nan
a / a  # nan
```

There are special rules for operations with `nan` and `inf`. For instance, `nan` compared to anything (even to itself) always returns `False`:

```
x = nan
x < 0 # False
x > 0 # False
x == x # False
```

See *Exercise 4* for some surprising consequences of the fact that `nan` is never equal to itself.

The float `inf` behaves much more as expected:

```
0 < inf      # True
inf <= inf   # True
inf == inf   # True
-inf < inf   # True
inf - inf    # nan
exp(-inf)    # 0
exp(1 / inf) # 1
```

One way to check for `nan` and `inf` is to use the functions `isnan` and `isinf`. Often, you want to react directly when a variable gets the value `nan` or `inf`. This can be achieved by using the NumPy command `seterr`. The following command

```
seterr(all = 'raise')
```

would raise a `FloatingPointError` if a calculation were to return one of those values.

Underflow – Machine epsilon

Underflow occurs when an operation results in a rational number that falls into the gap at zero; see *Figure 2.1*.

The *machine epsilon*, or rounding unit, is the largest number ε such that $\text{float}(1.0 + \varepsilon) = 1.0$.

Note that $\varepsilon \approx \beta^{-t} = 2.2204 \times 10^{-16}$ on most of today's computers. The value that applies on the actual machine you are running your code on is accessible using the following command:

```
import sys
sys.float_info.epsilon # 2.220446049250313e-16
```

The variable `sys.float_info` contains more information on the internal representation of the float type on your machine.

The function `float` converts other types to a floating-point number, if possible. This function is especially useful when converting an appropriate string to a number:

```
a = float('1.356')
```

Other float types in NumPy

NumPy also provides other float types, known from other programming languages as double-precision and single-precision numbers, namely, `float64` and `float32`:

```
a = pi            # returns 3.141592653589793
a1 = float64(a)   # returns 3.141592653589793
a2 = float32(a)   # returns 3.1415927
a - a1            # returns 0.0
a - a2            # returns -8.7422780126189537e-08
```

The second last line demonstrates that a and a1 do not differ in accuracy. A difference in accuracy exists between a and its single-precision counterpart, a2.

The NumPy function `finfo` can be used to display information on these floating-point types:

```
f32 = finfo(float32)
f32.precision    # 6 (decimal digits)
f64 = finfo(float64)
f64.precision    # 15 (decimal digits)
f = finfo(float)
f.precision      # 15 (decimal digits)
f64.max          # 1.7976931348623157e+308 (largest number)
f32.max          # 3.4028235e+38 (largest number)
help(finfo)      # Check for more options
```

2.2.3 Complex numbers

Complex numbers are an extension of the real numbers frequently used in many scientific and engineering fields.

Complex numbers in mathematics

Complex numbers consist of two floating-point numbers, the real part, a, of the number, and its imaginary part, b. In mathematics, a complex number is written as $z = a + b\text{i}$, where i defined by $\text{i}^2 = -1$ is the *imaginary unit*. The conjugate complex counterpart of z is $\bar{z} = a - b\text{i}$.

If the real part a is zero, the number is called an imaginary number.

The j notation

In Python, imaginary numbers are characterized by suffixing a floating-point number with the letter j, for example, z = 5.2j. A complex number is formed by the sum of a real number and an imaginary number, for example, z = 3.5 + 5.2j.

While in mathematics the imaginary part is expressed as a product of a real number b with the imaginary unit i, the Python way of expressing an imaginary number is not a product: j is just a suffix to indicate that the number is imaginary.

This is demonstrated by the following small experiment:

```
b = 5.2
z = bj # returns a NameError
z = b*j # returns a NameError
z = b*1j # is correct
```

The method conjugate returns the conjugate of z:

```
z = 3.2 + 5.2j
z.conjugate() # returns (3.2-5.2j)
```

Real and imaginary parts

You may access the real and imaginary parts of a complex number z using the real and imag attributes. Those attributes are read-only; in other words, they cannot be changed:

```
z = 1j
z.real # 0.0
z.imag # 1.0
z.imag = 2 # AttributeError: readonly attribute
```

It is not possible to convert a complex number to a real number:

```
z = 1 + 0j
z == 1 # True
float(z) # TypeError
```

Interestingly, the `real` and `imag` attributes as well as the conjugate method work just as well for complex arrays; see also `Section 4.3.1`, *Array properties*. We demonstrate this by computing the Nth roots of unity, which are $z_k = e^{i2\pi k/N}$ $k = 0, \ldots, N-1$, that is, the N solutions of the equation $z^N = 1$:

```
from matplotlib.pyplot import *
N = 10
# the following vector contains the Nth roots of unity:
unity_roots = array([exp(1j*2*pi*k/N) for k in range(N)])
# access all the real or imaginary parts with real or imag:
axes(aspect='equal')
plot(unity_roots.real, unity_roots.imag, 'o')
allclose(unity_roots**N, 1) # True
```

The resulting figure shows the 10 roots of unity. In *Figure 2.2*, it is completed by a title and axes labels and shown together with the unit circle. (For more details on how to make plots, see `Chapter 6`: *Plotting*.)

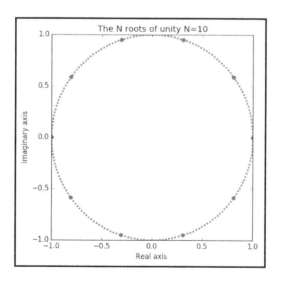

Figure 2.2: Roots of unity together with the unit circle

It is, of course, possible to mix the previous methods, as illustrated by the following examples:

```
z = 3.2+5.2j
(z + z.conjugate()) / 2. # returns (3.2+0j)
((z + z.conjugate()) / 2.).real # returns 3.2
(z - z.conjugate()) / 2. # returns 5.2j
((z - z.conjugate()) / 2.).imag # returns 5.2
sqrt(z * z.conjugate()) # returns (6.1057350089894991+0j)
```

2.3 Booleans

Boolean is a data type named after *George Boole* (1815-1864). A Boolean variable can take only two values, `True` or `False`. The main use of this type is in logical expressions. Here are some examples:

```
a = True
b = 30 > 45 # b gets the value False
```

Boolean expressions are often used in conjunction with `if` statements:

```
x= 5
if x > 0:
 print("positive")
else:
 print("nonpositive")
```

2.3.1 Boolean operators

Boolean operations are performed using the keywords and, or, and not:

```
True and False # False
False or True # True
(30 > 45) or (27 < 30) # True
not True # False
not (3 > 4) # True
```

The operators follow some precedence rules (see also Section 1.3.5, *Boolean expressions*) which would make the parentheses in the third and in the last line obsolete. Nevertheless, it is a good practice to use them in any case to increase the readability of your code.

Note, the `and` operator is implicitly chained in the following Boolean expressions:

```
a < b < c       # same as: a < b and b < c
a < b <= c      # same as: a < b and b <= c (less or equal)
a == b == c     # same as: a == b and b == c
```

2.3.2 Boolean casting

Most Python objects may be converted to Booleans; this is called *Boolean casting*. The built-in function `bool` performs that conversion. Note that most objects are cast to `True`, except 0, the empty tuple, the empty list, the empty string, or the empty array. These are all cast to `False`.

bool	False	True
string	`' '`	`'notempty'`
number	0	$\neq 0$
list	[]	[...] (not empty)
tuple	()	(..,..) (not empty)
array	`array([])`	`array([a])` ($a \neq 0$)
array	`array([0])`	
array	Exception raised if array contains more than one element	

Table 2.2: Casting rules for Booleans

It is *not* possible to cast arrays into Booleans unless they contain no or only one element; this is explained further in `Section 5.2.1`, *Boolean arrays*. The previous table (see Table 2.2: *Casting rules for Booleans*) contains summarized rules for Boolean casting.

We demonstrate this by means of some usage examples:

```
bool([]) # False
bool(0) # False
bool(' ') # True
bool('') # False
bool('hello') # True
bool(1.2) # True
bool(array([1])) # True
bool(array([1,2])) # Exception raised!
```

Automatic Boolean casting

Using an `if` statement with a non-Boolean type will cast it to a Boolean. In other words, the following two statements are always equivalent:

```
if a:
    ...
if bool(a): # exactly the same as above
    ...
```

A typical example is testing whether a list is empty:

```
# L is a list
if L:
    print("list not empty")
else:
    print("list is empty")
```

An empty list, or tuple, will return `False`.

You can also use a variable in the `if` statement, for example, an integer:

```
# n is an integer
if n % 2:            # the modulo operator
    print("n is odd")
else:
    print("n is even")
```

Note that we used % for the *modulo operation*, which returns the remainder of an integer division. In this case, it returns 0 or 1 as the remainder after modulo 2.

In this last example, the values 0 or 1 are cast to `bool`; see also `Section 2.3.4`, *Booleans and integers*.

The Boolean operators `or`, `and`, and `not` will also implicitly convert some of their arguments to a Boolean.

2.3.3 Return values of and and or

Note that the operators `and` and `or` do not necessarily produce Boolean values. This can be explained by the fact that the expression x `and` y is equivalent to:

```
def and_as_function(x,y):
    if not x:
        return x
```

```
else:
    return y
```

Correspondingly, the expression x or y is equivalent to:

```
def or_as_function(x,y):
    if x:
        return x
    else:
        return y
```

Interestingly, this means that when executing the statement True or x, the variable x need not even be defined! The same holds for False and x.

Note that, unlike their counterparts in mathematical logic, these operators are no longer commutative in Python. Indeed, the following expressions are not equivalent:

```
1 or 'a' # produces 1
'a' or 1 # produces 'a'
```

2.3.4 Booleans and integers

In fact, Booleans and integers are the same. The only difference is in the string representations of 0 and 1, which, in the case of Booleans, is False and True, respectively. This allows constructions such as this:

```
def print_ispositive(x):
    possibilities = ['nonpositive or zero', 'positive']
    return f"x is {possibilities[x>0]}"
```

The last line in this example uses string formatting, which is explained in Section 2.4.3, *String formatting*.

We note for readers already familiar with the concept of subclasses that the type bool is a subclass of the type int (see Chapter 8: *Classes*). Indeed, all four inquiries – isinstance(True, bool), isinstance(False, bool), isinstance(True, int), and isinstance(False, int) return the value True (see Section 3.7, *Checking the type of a variable*).

Even rarely used statements such as True+13 are correct.

2.4 Strings

The type `string` is a type used for text:

```
name = 'Johan Carlsson'
child = "Åsa is Johan Carlsson's daughter"
book = """Aunt Julia
        and the Scriptwriter"""
```

A string is enclosed either by single or double quotes. If a string contains several lines, it has to be enclosed by three double quotes """ or three single quotes '''.

Strings can be indexed with simple indexes or slices (see `Chapter 3`: *Container Types*, for a comprehensive explanation on slices):

```
book[-1] # returns 'r'
book[-12:] # returns 'Scriptwriter'
```

Strings are immutable; that is, items cannot be altered. They share this property with tuples. The command `book[1] = 'a'` returns:

```
TypeError: 'str' object does not support item assignment
```

2.4.1 Escape sequences and raw strings

The string `'\n'` is used to insert a line break and `'\t'` inserts a horizontal tabulator (TAB) into the string to align several lines:

```
print('Temperature\t20\tC\nPressure\t5\tPa')
```

These strings are examples of *escape sequences*. Escape sequences always start with a backslash, \. A multiline string automatically includes escape sequences:

```
a="""
A multi-line
example"""
a # returns '\nA multi-line \nexample'
```

A special escape sequence is "\\", which represents the backslash symbol in text:

```
latexfontsize="\\tiny"
print(latexfontsize) # prints \tiny
```

The same can be achieved by using a *raw string* instead:

```
latexfs=r"\tiny" # returns "\tiny"
latexfontsize == latexfs # returns True
```

Note that in raw strings, the backslash remains in the string and is used to escape some special characters:

```
print(r"\"") # returns \"
print(r"\\") # returns \
print(r"\") # returns an error (why?)
```

A raw string is a convenient tool to construct strings in a readable manner. The result is the same:

```
r"\"" == '\\"'
r"She: \"I am my dad's girl\"" == 'She: \\"I am my dad\'s girl\\"'
```

2.4.2 Operations on strings and string methods

The addition of several strings results in their concatenation:

```
last_name = 'Carlsson'
first_name = 'Johanna'
full_name = first_name + ' ' + last_name
  # returns 'Johanna Carlsson'
```

Consequently, multiplication by an integer is repeated addition:

```
game = 2 * 'Yo' # returns 'YoYo'
```

Multiplication by floating-point or complex numbers is undefined and results in a `TypeError`.

When strings are compared, lexicographical order applies and the uppercase form precedes the lowercase form of the same letter:

```
'Anna' > 'Arvi' # returns false
'ANNA' < 'anna'  # returns true
'10B' < '11A'    # returns true
```

Among the variety of string methods, we will mention here only the most important ones:

- **Splitting a string**: This method generates a list from a string by using a single or multiple blanks as separators. Alternatively, an argument can be given by specifying a particular substring as a separator:

```
text = 'quod erat demonstrandum'
text.split() # returns ['quod', 'erat', 'demonstrandum']
table = 'Johan;Carlsson;19890327'
table.split(';') # returns ['Johan','Carlsson','19890327']
king = 'CarlXVIGustaf'
king.split('XVI')  # returns ['Carl','Gustaf']
```

- **Joining a list to a string**: This is the reverse operation of splitting:

```
sep = ';'
sep.join(['Johan','Carlsson','19890327'])
# returns 'Johan;Carlsson;19890327'
```

- **Searching in a string**: This method returns the first index in the string, where a given search substring starts:

```
birthday = '20101210'
birthday.find('10') # returns 2
```

If the search string is not found, the return value of the method is −1.

- **String formatting:** This method inserts values of variables or results of expressions into a string. It is so important that we devote the following subsection to it.

2.4.3 String formatting

String formatting is the process of inserting values into a given string and determining the way in which they are displayed. This can be done in various ways. We first describe the related string method, format, and the more modern alternative, the so-called *f-string*.

Here is an example regarding the use of the format method:

```
course_code = "NUMA01"
print("Course code: {}".format(course_code))     # Course code: NUMA01
```

And here is an example of the variant by using an *f-string*:

```
course_code = "NUMA01"
print(f"Course code: {course_code}")              # Course code: NUMA01
```

The function `format` is a string method; it scans the string for the occurrence of placeholders, which are enclosed by curly brackets. These placeholders are replaced in a way specified by the argument of the format method. How they are replaced depends on the format specification defined in each `{}` pair. Format specifications are indicated by a colon, `":"`, as their prefix.

The format method offers a range of possibilities to customize the formatting of objects depending on their types. Of particular use in scientific computing are the formatting specifiers for the `float` type. You may choose either the standard fixed-point notation with `{:f}` or the exponential notation with `{:e}`:

```
quantity = 33.45
print("{:f}".format(quantity)) # 33.450000
print("{:1.1f}".format(quantity)) # 33.5
print("{:.2e}".format(quantity)) # 3.35e+01
```

Similarly, format specifiers can be used also in f-strings:

```
quantity = 33.45
print(f"{quantity:1.1f}")              # 33.5
```

The format specifiers allow specifying the rounding precision (digits following the decimal point in the representation). Also, the total number of symbols, including leading blanks, to represent the number can be set.

In this example, the name of the object that gets its value inserted is given as an argument to the format method. The first `{}` pair is replaced by the first argument, and the following pairs by the subsequent arguments. Alternatively, it may also be convenient to use the key-value syntax:

```
print("{name} {value:.1f}".format(name="quantity",value=quantity))
# prints "quantity 33.5"
```

Here, two values are processed – a string `name` without a format specifier, and a float `value` that is printed in fixed-point notation with one digit after the decimal point. (Refer to the complete reference documentation for more details on *string formatting*.)

Braces in the string

Sometimes, a string might contain a pair of curly braces, which should not be considered as placeholders for a `format` method. In that case, double braces are used:

```
r"we {} in LaTeX \begin{{equation}}".format('like')
```

This returns the following string: `'we like in LaTeX \\begin{equation}'`.

2.5 Summary

In this chapter, you met the basic data types in Python and saw the corresponding syntax elements. We will work mostly with numeric types such as integers, floats, and complex.

Booleans are needed for setting conditions, and by using strings, we often communicate results and messages.

2.6 Exercises

Ex. 1: Check whether $x = 2.3$ is a zero of the function:

$$f(x) = x^2 - 0.25x + 5$$

Ex. 2: According to de Moivre's formula, the following holds:

$$(\cos x + \mathrm{i}\sin x)^n = \cos nx + \mathrm{i}\sin nx \quad n \in \mathbb{Z}, x \in \mathbb{R}$$

Choose numbers *n* and *x* and verify that formula in Python.

Ex. 3: Complex numbers. Verify Euler's formula in the same way:

$$e^{\mathrm{i}x} = \cos x + \mathrm{i}\sin x \quad x \in \mathbb{R}$$

Ex. 4: Suppose we are trying to check the convergence of a diverging sequence (here, the sequence is defined by the recursive relation $u_{n+1} = 2u_n$ and $u_0 = 1.0$):

```
u = 1.0 # you have to use a float here!
uold = 10.
for iteration in range(2000):
    if not abs(u-uold) > 1.e-8:
        print('Convergence')
        break # sequence has converged
    uold = u
    u = 2*u
else:
    print('No convergence')
```

1. Since the sequence does not converge, the code should print the `No convergence` message. Execute it to see what happens.

2. What happens if you replace the line

    ```
    if not abs(u-uold) > 1.e-8:
    ```

    with

    ```
    if abs(u-uold) < 1.e-8:
    ```

    It should give exactly the same result, shouldn't it? Run the code again to see what happens.

3. What happens if you replace `u=1.0` with `u=1` (without a decimal point)? Run the code to check your predictions.

4. Explain the unexpected behavior of this code.

Ex. 5: An implication $C = (A \Rightarrow B)$ is a Boolean expression that is defined as

- C is `True` if A is `False`, or A and B are both `True`
- C is `False` otherwise

    Write a Python function `implication(A, B)`.

Ex. 6: This exercise is to train Boolean operations. Two binary digits (bits) are added by using a logical device called a **half adder**. It produces a carry bit (the digit of the next higher value) and the sum as defined by the following table, and half adder circuit:

p	q	sum	carry
1	1	0	1
1	0	1	0
0	1	1	0
0	0	0	0

Definition of the half adder operation:

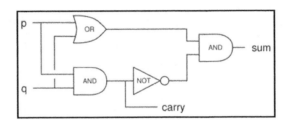

Figure 2.3: A half adder circuit

A full adder consists of two half adders and sums two bits and an additional carry bit on the input (see also the following figure):

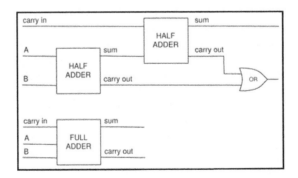

Figure 2.4: A full adder circuit

Write a function that implements a half adder and another that implements a full adder. Test these functions.

3
Container Types

Container types are used to group objects together. The main difference between the different container types is the way individual elements are accessed and how operations are defined. In this chapter, we discuss container types such as lists, tuples, dictionaries, and sets and related concepts such as indexing techniques. More specialized containers such as pandas DataFrames will be presented in Chapter 4: *Linear Algebra – Arrays*, Chapter 5: *Advanced Array Concepts*, and Chapter 10: *Series and DataFrames*.

In particular, we will cover the following topics:

- Lists
- Arrays
- Tuples
- Dictionaries
- Sets

3.1 Lists

In this section, we introduce lists – the most frequently used container datatype in Python. With lists, we can refer to several, even totally different, Python objects together.

A list is, as the name hints, a list of objects of any kind:

```
L = ['a', 20.0, 5]
M = [3,['a', -3.0, 5]]
```

The first list in this example contains a string, a float, and an integer object. The second list in this example, M, contains another list as its second item.

The individual objects are enumerated by assigning each element an index. The first element in the list gets index 0. This *zero-based indexing* is frequently used in mathematical notation. Consider as an example for zero-based indexing the usual indexing of coefficients of a polynomial.

The index allows us to access the following objects from the two lists defined in the preceding example:

```
L[1]  # returns 20.0
L[0]  # returns 'a'
M[1]  # returns ['a',-3.0,5]
M[1][2]  # returns 5
```

The bracket notation here corresponds to the use of subscripts in mathematical formulas. L is a simple list, while M itself contains a list so that you need two indexes to access an element of the inner list.

A list containing subsequent integers can easily be generated by the command range:

```
L=list(range(4))
# generates a list with four elements: [0, 1, 2 ,3]
```

A more general use is to provide this command with start, stop, and step parameters:

```
L=list(range(17,29,4))
# generates [17, 21, 25]
```

The command len returns the length of the list:

```
len(L) # returns 3
```

3.1.1 Slicing

Like cutting a slice from a loaf of bread, lists can be cut into slices. Slicing a
list between i and j creates a new list containing the elements starting at index i and
ending just before j.

For slicing, a range of indexes has to be given. L[i:j] means create a list by taking all
elements from L starting at L[i] until L[j-1]. In other words, the new list is obtained by
removing the first i elements from L and taking the next j-i elements $^{(\text{for } j > i \geq 0)}$.

Here, L[i:] means remove the i first elements and L[:i] means take only the first i
elements:

```
L = ['C', 'l', 'o', 'u', 'd', 's']
L[1:5] # remove one element and take four from there:
# returns ['l', 'o', 'u', 'd']
```

You may omit the first or last bound of the slicing:

```
L = ['C', 'l', 'o', 'u', 'd', 's']
L[1:] # ['l', 'o', 'u', 'd', 's']
L[:5] # ['C', 'l', 'o', 'u', 'd']
L[:] # the entire list
```

Python allows the use of negative indexes for counting from the right. In particular, the
element L[-1] is the last element in the list L. Similarly, L[:-i] means remove the
last i elements, and L[-i:] means take only the last i elements. This may be combined
in L[i:-j] to remove the first i and the last j elements.

Here is an example:

```
L = ['C', 'l', 'o', 'u', 'd', 's']
L[-2:] # ['d', 's']
L[:-2] # ['C', 'l', 'o', 'u']
```

Omitting one index in the range corresponds to half-open intervals in ℝ. The half-open interval (∞, *a*) means take all numbers strictly lower than *a*; this is similar to the syntax L[:j] ; see *Figure 3.1* for more examples:

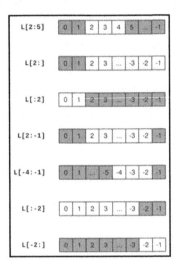

Figure 3.1: Some typical slicing situations

Notice that you never get index errors with *out-of-bound slices*. Possibly, you may obtain empty lists:

```
L = list(range(4)) # [0, 1, 2, 3]
L[4] # IndexError: list index out of range
L[1:100] # same as L[1:]
L[-100:-1] # same as L[:-1]
L[-100:100] # same as L[:]
L[5:0] # empty list []
L[-2:2] # empty list []
```

Be careful when using variables in indexing that may become negative, since it changes the slice completely. This might lead to unexpected results:

```
a = [1,2,3]
for iteration in range(4):
    print(sum(a[0:iteration-1]))
```

The result is 3, 0, 1, 3 while you expect 0, 0, 1, 3.

Let's sum up the use of slices:

- `L[i:]` amounts to taking all elements except the first *i* ones.
- `L[:i]` amounts to taking the first *i* elements.
- `L[-i:]` amounts to taking the last *i* elements.
- `L[:-i]` amounts to taking all elements except the last *i* ones.

Strides

When computing slices, you may also specify a stride, which is the length of the step from one index to the other. The default stride is `1`.

Here is an example:

```
L = list(range(100))
L[:10:2] # [0, 2, 4, 6, 8]
L[::20] # [0, 20, 40, 60, 80]
L[10:20:3] # [10, 13, 16, 19]
```

Note that the stride may also be negative:

```
L[20:10:-3] # [20, 17, 14, 11]
```

It is also possible to create a new list that is reversed, using a negative stride:

```
L = [1, 2, 3]
R = L[::-1] # L is not modified
R # [3, 2, 1]
```

Alternatively, you might want to use the method `reverse`, which is explained in `Section 3.1.4`: *List methods.*

3.1.2 Altering lists

Typical operations on lists are the insertion and deletion of elements and list concatenation. With the slicing notation, list insertion and deletion become obvious; deletion is just replacing a part of a list with an empty list [ ] :

```
L = ['a', 1, 2, 3, 4]
L[2:3] = [] # ['a', 1, 3, 4]
L[3:] = [] # ['a', 1, 3]
```

Insertion means replacing an empty slice with the list to be inserted:

```
L[1:1] = [1000, 2000] # ['a', 1000, 2000, 1, 3]
```

Two lists are concatenated by the plus operator + :

```
L = [1, -17]
M = [-23.5, 18.3, 5.0]
L + M # gives [1, -17, 23.5, 18.3, 5.0]
```

Concatenating a list n times with itself motivates the use of the multiplication operator *:

```
n = 3
n * [1.,17,3] # gives [1., 17, 3, 1., 17, 3, 1., 17, 3]
[0] * 5 # gives [0,0,0,0,0]
```

There are no arithmetic operations on a list, such as elementwise summation or division. For such operations, we use arrays; see Section 3.2: A quick glance at the concept of arrays.

3.1.3 Belonging to a list

You may use the keywords in and not in to determine whether an element belongs to a list or not, which is similar to $\in$ and $\notin$ in mathematics:

```
L = ['a', 1, 'b', 2]
'a' in L # True
3 in L # False
4 not in L # True
```

3.1.4 List methods

Some useful methods of the `list` type are collected in the following *Table 3.1*:

Command	Action
list.append(x)	Add x to the end of the list.
list.extend(L)	Extend the list by the elements of the list L.
list.insert(i,x)	Insert x at position i.
list.remove(x)	Remove the first item from the list whose value is x.
list.sort()	Sort the items of the list.
list.reverse()	Reverse the elements of the list.
list.pop()	Remove the last element of the list.

Table 3.1: In-place methods of the datatype list

These methods are in-place operations, that is, they change the list directly.

Other methods, such as those given in *Table 3.2*, do not alter the list, but return some information or create a new list object:

Command	Action
list.count(x)	Count how often x appears in the list.
list.copy()	Create a copy of the list.

Table 3.2: Methods of the datatype list that return a new object

In-place operations

Most methods that result in a list are in-place operations. These are operations that change a Python object directly without creating a new object of the same type. They can be best explained by looking at the following example, `reverse`:

```
L = [1, 2, 3]
L.reverse() # the list L is now reversed
L # [3, 2, 1]
```

Be aware of in-place operations. You might be tempted to write:

```
L=[3, 4, 4, 5]
newL = L.sort()
```

This is correct Python. But in-place operations return the value `None` and alter the list. Therefore, using the variable `newL` as if it was a (sorted) list, for example, as

```
print(newL[0])
```

causes an error:

```
TypeError: 'NoneType' object is not subscriptable
```

Here, we demonstrate in-place list operations:

```
L = [0, 1, 2, 3, 4]
L.append(5)  # [0, 1, 2, 3, 4, 5]
L.reverse()  # [5, 4, 3, 2, 1, 0]
L.sort()  # [0, 1, 2, 3, 4, 5]
L.remove(0)  # [1, 2, 3, 4, 5]
L.pop()  # [1, 2, 3, 4]
L.pop()  # [1, 2, 3]
L.extend(['a','b','c'])  # [1, 2, 3, 'a', 'b', 'c']
```

`L` is altered. The method `count` is an example of a method that generates a new object:

```
L.count(2)  # returns 1
```

3.1.5 Merging lists – zip

A particularly useful function for lists is `zip`. It can be used to merge two given lists into a new list by pairing the elements of the original lists. The result is a list of tuples (see `Section 3.3`: *Tuples*):

```
ind = [0,1,2,3,4]
color = ["red", "green", "blue", "alpha"]
list(zip(color,ind))
# gives [('red', 0), ('green', 1), ('blue', 2), ('alpha', 3)]
```

This example also demonstrates what happens if the lists have different lengths: the length of the zipped list is the shorter of the two input lists.

The function `zip` creates a special iterable object that can be turned into a list by applying the function `list`, as in the preceding example. See `Section 9.3`: *Iterable objects* for more details on iterable objects.

3.1.6 List comprehension

A convenient way to build up lists is by using the list comprehension construct, possibly with a condition inside. The syntax of a list comprehension is:

```
[<expr> for <variable> in <list>]
```

or more generally:

```
[<expr> for <variable> in <list> if <condition>]
```

Here are some examples:

```
L = [2, 3, 10, 1, 5]
L2 = [x*2 for x in L] # [4, 6, 20, 2, 10]
L3 = [x*2 for x in L if 4 < x <= 10] # [20, 10]
```

It is possible to have several `for` loops inside a list comprehension:

```
M = [[1,2,3],[4,5,6]]
flat = [M[i][j] for i in range(2) for j in range(3)]
# returns [1, 2, 3, 4, 5, 6]
```

This is of particular interest when dealing with arrays; see `Section 3.2`: *A quick glance at the concept of arrays*.

List comprehension is closely related to the mathematical notation for sets. Compare $L_2 = \{2x : x \in L\}$ and `L2 = [2*x for x in L]`. One big difference though is that lists are ordered while sets aren't; see `Section 3.5`: *Sets*.

As we complete our understanding of lists, we'll now move on to the next section, where we will learn about arrays.

3.2 A quick glance at the concept of arrays

The NumPy package offers arrays, which are container structures for manipulating vectors, matrices, or even higher-order tensors in mathematics. In this section, we point out the similarities between arrays and lists. But arrays deserve a broader presentation, which will be given in `Chapter 4`: *Linear Algebra – Arrays*, and `Chapter 5`: *Advanced Array Concepts*.

Arrays are constructed from lists by the function `array`:

```
v = array([1.,2.,3.])
A = array([[1.,2.,3.],[4.,5.,6.]])
```

To access an element of a vector, we need one index, while an element of a matrix is addressed by two indexes:

```
v[2]      # returns 3.0
A[1,2]    # returns 6.0
```

At first glance, arrays are similar to lists, but be aware that they are different in a fundamental way, which can be explained by the following points:

- Access to array data corresponds to that of lists, using square brackets and slices. But for arrays representing matrices, a double index is used. Lists assigned to a slice of an array can be used to alter the array:

```
M = array([[1.,2.],[3.,4.]])
v = array([1.,  2.,  3.])
v[0]  # 1
v[:2] # array([1.,2.])
M[0,1] # 2
v[:2] = [10, 20] # v is now array([10., 20., 3.])
```

- The number of elements in a vector, or the number of rows of a matrix, is obtained by the function `len`:

```
len(v)  # 3
```

- Arrays store only elements of the same numeric type
  (usually `float` or `complex` but also `int`).
- The operations +, *, /, and – are all elementwise. The function `dot` and, in Python versions ≥ 3.5, the infix operator @ are used for the scalar product and the corresponding matrix operations.
- Unlike lists, there is no `append` method for arrays. Nevertheless, there are special methods to construct arrays by stacking smaller size arrays; see `Section 4.7`: *Stacking*. A related point is that arrays are not as elastic as lists; you cannot use slices to change their length.
- Vector slices are views, that is, they may be used to modify the original array; see `Section 5.1`: *Array views and copies*.

We gave you in this section a quick glance at the container type `array`. It is so central in scientific computing with Python that we will devote two entire chapters to it with many more aspects to be presented and discussed; see `Chapter 4`: *Linear Algebra – Arrays*, and `Chapter 5`: *Advanced Array Concepts*.

3.3 Tuples

A tuple is an immutable list. Immutable means that it cannot be modified. A tuple is written as a comma-separated sequence of objects (a list without brackets). To increase readability, you often enclose a tuple in a pair of parentheses:

```
my_tuple = 1, 2, 3      # our first tuple
my_tuple = (1, 2, 3)    # the same
my_tuple = 1, 2, 3,     # again the same
len(my_tuple) # 3, same as for lists
my_tuple[0] = 'a'    # error! tuples are immutable
```

Omitting parentheses can have side effects; see the following example:

```
1, 2 == 3, 4 # returns (1, False, 4)
(1, 2) == (3, 4) # returns False
```

The comma indicates that the object is a tuple:

```
singleton = 1,    # note the comma
len(singleton)    # 1
singleton = (1,) # this creates the same tuple
```

Tuples are useful when a group of values goes together; for example, they are used to return multiple values from functions. See Section 7.3: *Return values*.

3.3.1 Packing and unpacking variables

You may assign several variables at once by unpacking a list or tuple:

```
a, b = 0, 1 # a gets 0 and b gets 1
a, b = [0, 1] # exactly the same effect
(a, b) = 0, 1 # same
[a,b] = [0,1] # same thing
```

Use packing and unpacking to swap the contents of two variables:

```
a, b = b, a
```

3.4 Dictionaries

Lists, tuples, and arrays are ordered sets of objects. Individual objects are inserted, accessed, and processed according to their place in the list. On the other hand, dictionaries are unordered sets of pairs. You access dictionary data by keys.

3.4.1 Creating and altering dictionaries

For example, we may create a dictionary containing the data of a rigid body in mechanics, as follows:

```
truck_wheel = {'name':'wheel','mass':5.7,
               'Ix':20.0,'Iy':1.,'Iz':17.,
               'center of mass':[0.,0.,0.]}
```

A key/data pair is indicated by a colon, :. These pairs are comma-separated and listed inside a pair of curly brackets, { }.

Individual elements are accessed by their keys:

```
truck_wheel['name']   # returns 'wheel'
truck_wheel['mass']   # returns 5.7
```

New objects are added to the dictionary by creating a new key:

```
truck_wheel['Ixy'] = 0.0
```

Dictionaries are also used to provide parameters to a function (refer to Section 7.2: *Parameters and arguments* in Chapter 7, *Functions*, for further information).

Keys in a dictionary can be, among others, strings, functions, tuples with immutable elements, and classes. Keys cannot be lists or arrays.

The command dict generates a dictionary from a list with key/value pairs:

```
truck_wheel = dict([('name','wheel'),('mass',5.7),
                    ('Ix',20.0), ('Iy',1.), ('Iz',17.),
                    ('center of mass',[0.,0.,0.])])
```

The zip function may come in handy in this context; see Section 3.15: *Merging lists – zip.*

3.4.2 Looping over dictionaries

There are mainly three ways to loop over dictionaries:

- By keys:

```
for key in truck_wheel.keys():
    print(key) # prints (in any order) 'Ix', 'Iy', 'name',...
```

  or equivalently:

```
for key in truck_wheel:
    print(key) # prints (in any order) 'Ix', 'Iy', 'name',...
```

- By value:

```
for value in truck_wheel.values():
    print(value)
    # prints (in any order) 1.0, 20.0, 17.0, 'wheel', ...
```

- By item, that is, key/value pairs:

```
for item in truck_wheel.items():
    print(item)
    # prints (in any order) ('Iy', 1.0), ('Ix, 20.0),...
```

Please consult `Section 14.4`: *Shelves* for a special dictionary object for file access.

3.5 Sets

The last container object we introduce in this section is defined by the data type `set`.

Sets are containers that share properties and operations with sets in mathematics. A mathematical set is a collection of distinct objects. Like in mathematics, in Python the elements of a set are also listed within a pair of braces.

Here are some mathematical set expressions:

$$A = \{1, 2, 3, 4\}, \; B = \{5\}, \; C = A \cup B \; D = A \cap C, \; E = C \backslash A, \; 5 \in C$$

And here are their Python counterparts:

```
A = {1,2,3,4}
B = {5}
C = A.union(B)    # returns{1,2,3,4,5}
D = A.intersection(C)    # returns {1,2,3,4}
E = C.difference(A)    # returns {5}
5 in C    # returns True
```

Sets contain an element only once, corresponding to the aforementioned definition:

```
A = {1,2,3,3,3}
B = {1,2,3}
A == B # returns True
```

Moreover, a set is unordered; that is, the order of the elements in the set is not defined:

```
A = {1,2,3}
B = {1,3,2}
A == B # returns True
```

Sets in Python can contain all kinds of immutable objects, that is, numeric objects, strings, and Booleans.

There are the methods `union` and `intersection` for the corresponding mathematical operations:

```
A={1,2,3,4}
A.union({5})
A.intersection({2,4,6}) # returns {2, 4}
```

Also, sets can be compared using the methods `issubset` and `issuperset`:

```
{2,4}.issubset({1,2,3,4,5}) # returns True
{1,2,3,4,5}.issuperset({2,4}) # returns True
```

An empty set is defined in Python by `empty_set=set([])` and not by `{}`, which would define an empty dictionary!

3.6 Container conversions

We summarize in the following *Table 3.3* the most important properties of the container types presented so far. (Arrays will be treated separately in `Chapter 4`: *Linear Algebra – Arrays*):

Type	Access	Order	Duplicate Values	Mutability
List	By index	Yes	Yes	Yes
Tuple	By index	Yes	Yes	No
Dictionary	By key	No	Yes	Yes
Set	No	No	No	Yes

Table 3.3: Container types

As you can see in the previous table, there is a difference in accessing container elements, and sets and dictionaries are not ordered.

Due to the different properties of the various container types, we frequently convert one type to another (see *Table 3.4*):

Container Types	Syntax
List → Tuple	`tuple([1, 2, 3])`
Tuple → List	`list((1, 2, 3))`
List, Tuple → Set	`set([1, 2]), set((1, ))`
Set → List	`list({1, 2 ,3})`
Dictionary → List	`{'a':4}.values()`
List → Dictionary	-

Table 3.4: Conversion rules for container types

We saw in this section how to convert container types. In Chapter 2: *Variables and Basic Types*, we saw how to convert more elementary datatypes such as numbers. So, it is time now to consider how to actually check which datatype a variable has, which is the topic of the next section.

3.7 Checking the type of a variable

The direct way to see the type of a variable is to use the command type:

```
label = 'local error'
type(label) # returns str
x = [1, 2] # list
type(x) # returns list
```

However, if you want to test for a variable to be of a certain type, you should use isinstance (instead of comparing the types with type):

```
isinstance(x, list) # True
```

The reason for using isinstance becomes apparent after having read about the concept of subclassing and inheritance in Section 8.5: *Subclassing and inheritance*. In short, often different types share some common properties with some basic type. The classical example is the type bool, which is derived by subclassing from the more general type int. In this situation, we see how the command isinstance can be used in a more general way:

```
test = True
isinstance(test, bool) # True
isinstance(test, int) # True
type(test) == int # False
type(test) == bool # True
```

So, in order to make sure that the variable test can be used as if it were an integer – the particular type may be irrelevant – you should check that it is an instance of int:

```
if isinstance(test, int): print("The variable is an integer")
```

Python is not a typed language. That means that objects are identified by what they can do rather than what they are. For instance, if you have a string manipulating function that acts on an object by using the `len` method, then your function will probably be useful for any objects implementing the `len` method.

So far, we have come across different datatypes: `float`, `int`, `bool`, `complex`, `list`, `tuple`, `module`, `function`, `str`, `dict`, and `array`.

3.8 Summary

In this chapter, you learned how to work with container types, mainly lists. It is important to know how to fill these containers and how to access and manage their content. We saw that there is access by position or by keyword.

We will meet the important concept of slicing again in the next chapter on arrays. These are specially designed containers for mathematical operations.

3.9 Exercises

Ex. 1: Execute the following statements:

```
L = [1, 2]
L3 = 3*L
```

1. What is the content of `L3`?
2. Try to predict the outcome of the following commands:

   ```
   L3[0]
   L3[-1]
   L3[10]
   ```

3. What does the following command do?

   ```
   L4 = [k**2 for k in L3]
   ```

4. Concatenate `L3` and `L4` to a new list `L5`.

Ex. 2: Use the `range` command and a list comprehension to generate a list with 100 equidistantly spaced values between 0 and 1.

Ex. 3: Assume that the following signal is stored in a list:

```
L = [0,1,2,1,0,-1,-2,-1,0]
```

What is the outcome of:

```
L[0]
L[-1]
L[:-1]
L + L[1:-1] + L
L[2:2] = [-3]
L[3:4] = []
L[2:5] = [-5]
```

Do this exercise by inspection only, that is, without using your Python shell.

Ex. 4: Consider the Python statements:

```
L = [n-m/2 for n in range(m)]
ans = 1 + L[0] + L[-1]
```

and assume that the variable m has been previously assigned an integer value. What is the value of `ans`? Answer this question without executing the statements in Python.

Ex. 5: Consider the recursion formula:

$$u_{n+3} = u_{n+2} + ha\left(\frac{23}{12}u_{n+2} - \frac{4}{3}u_{n+1} + \frac{5}{12}u_n\right) \text{ with } n = 0,\ldots,1000, h = 0.001, \text{ and } a = -0.5.$$

1. Create a list u. Store in its first three elements the three values e^0, e^{ha}, and e^{2ha}. These represent the starting values u_0, u_1, and u_2 in the given formula. Build up the complete list from the recursion formula.
2. Construct a second list, td, in which you store the values nh, with $n = 0,\ldots,1000$. Plot td versus u (see Section 6.1: *Making plots*). Make a second plot in which you plot the difference, that is, $|e^{at_n} - u_n|$, where t_n represents the values inside the vector td. Set axis labels and a title.

The recursion is a multistep formula to solve the differential equation $u' = au$ with the initial value $u(0) = u_0 = 1$.

u_n approximates $u(nh) = e^{anh} u_0$.

Ex. 6: Let A and B be sets. The set $(A \backslash B) \cup (B \backslash A)$ is called the symmetric difference of the two sets. Write a function that performs this operation. Compare your results to the result of the command:

```
A.symmetric_difference(B).
```

Ex. 7: Verify in Python the statement that the empty set is a subset of any set.

Ex. 8: Study other operations on sets. You can find a complete list of those by using the command completion feature of `IPython`. In particular, study the `update` and `intersection_update` methods. What is the difference between `intersection` and `intersection_update`?

Linear Algebra - Arrays

4

Linear algebra is one of the essential building blocks of computational mathematics. The objects of linear algebra are vectors and matrices. The package NumPy includes all the necessary tools to manipulate those objects.

The first task is to build matrices and vectors or to alter existing ones by slicing. The other main task is the dot operation, which embodies most linear algebra operations (scalar product, matrix-vector product, and matrix-matrix product). Finally, various methods are available to solve linear problems.

The following topics will be covered in this chapter:

- Overview of the array type
- Mathematical preliminaries
- The array type
- Accessing array entries
- Functions to construct arrays
- Accessing and changing the shape
- Stacking
- Functions acting on arrays
- Linear algebra methods in SciPy

4.1 Overview of the array type

For the impatient, here is how to use arrays in a nutshell. Be aware though that the behavior of arrays may be surprising at first, so we encourage you to read on after this introductory section.

Note again, the presentation in this chapter assumes like everywhere else in this book that you have the module NumPy imported:

```
from numpy import *
```

By importing NumPy, we give access to the datatype `ndarray`, which we'll describe in the next sections.

4.1.1 Vectors and matrices

Creating vectors is as simple as using the function `array` to convert a list into an array:

```
v = array([1.,2.,3.])
```

The object `v` is now a vector that behaves much like a vector in linear algebra. We have already emphasized the differences with the list object in Python in `Section 3.2`: *A quick glance at the concept of arrays*.

Here are some illustrations of the basic linear algebra operations on vectors:

```
# two vectors with three components
v1 = array([1., 2., 3.])
v2 = array([2, 0, 1.])

# scalar multiplications/divisions
2*v1 # array([2., 4., 6.])
v1/2 # array([0.5, 1., 1.5])

# linear combinations
3*v1 # array([ 3., 6., 9.])
3*v1 + 2*v2 # array([ 7., 6., 11.])

# norm
from numpy.linalg import norm
norm(v1) # 3.7416573867739413
# scalar product
dot(v1, v2) # 5.0
v1 @ v2 # 5.0 ; alternative formulation
```

Note that all basic arithmetic operations are performed elementwise:

```
# elementwise operations:
v1 * v2 # array([2., 0., 3.])
v2 / v1 # array([2.,0.,.333333])
v1 - v2 # array([-1., 2., 2.])/
v1 + v2 # array([ 3., 2., 4.])
```

Some functions act elementwise on arrays as well:

```
cos(v1) # cosine, elementwise: array([ 0.5403, -0.4161, -0.9899])
```

This subject will be covered in `Section` 4.8: *Functions acting on arrays*.

A matrix is created in a similar way to a vector, but from a list of lists instead:

```
M = array([[1.,2],[0.,1]])
```

Note, vectors are not column or row matrices. An n vector, an $n \times 1$, and a $1 \times n$ matrix are three different objects even if they contain the same data.

To create a row matrix containing the same data as the vector `v = array([1., 2., 1.])`, we apply the method `reshape`:

```
R = v.reshape((1,3))
shape(R)                    # (1,3): this is a row matrix
```

The corresponding column matrix is obtained by `reshape` in a corresponding manner:

```
C = v.reshape((3, 1))
shape(C) # (3,1): this is a column matrix
```

After having learned how to create arrays and after having seen basic array operations, we will study now how array elements and subarrays can be addressed by indexing and slicing.

4.1.2 Indexing and slices

Indexing and slicing are similar to the corresponding operations for lists. The main difference is that there may be several indexes or slices when the array is a matrix. The subject will be covered in depth in `Section 4.4.1`: *Basic array slicing*; here, we just give some illustrative examples of indexing and slicing:

```
v = array([1., 2., 3])
M = array([[1., 2], [3., 4]])
```

```
v[0] # works as for lists
v[1:] # array([2., 3.])

M[0, 0] # 1.
M[1:] # returns the matrix array([[3., 4]])
M[1] # returns the vector array([3., 4.])

# access
v[0] # 1.
v[0] = 10

# slices
v[:2] # array([10., 2.])
v[:2] = [0, 1] # now v == array([0., 1., 3.])
v[:2] = [1, 2, 3] # error!
```

As arrays are the basic datatype for all tasks in computational linear algebra, we now present in this overview section some examples, the dot product and the solution of linear equation systems.

4.1.3 Linear algebra operations

The essential operator that performs most of the usual operations of linear algebra is the Python function dot. It is used for matrix-vector multiplications (see Section 4.2.4: *The dot operations* for more details):

```
dot(M, v) # matrix vector multiplication; returns a vector
M @ v # alternative formulation
```

It may be used to compute a scalar product between two vectors:

```
dot(v, w)
# scalar product; the result is a scalar
v @ w # alternative formulation
```

Lastly, it is used to compute matrix-matrix products:

```
dot(M, N) # results in a matrix
M @ N # alternative formulation
```

Solving a linear system

If A is a matrix and b is a vector, you can solve the linear equation system

$$Ax = b$$

by using the function `solve` from the linear algebra submodule `numpy.linalg`:

```
from numpy.linalg import solve
x = solve(A, b)
```

For example, to solve

$$\begin{cases} x_1 + 2x_2 & = 1 \\ 3x_1 + 4x_2 & = 4 \end{cases}$$

the following Python statements are executed:

```
from numpy.linalg import solve
A = array([[1., 2.], [3., 4.]])
b = array([1., 4.])
x = solve(A, b)
allclose(dot(A, x), b) # True
allclose(A @ x, b) # alternative formulation
```

The command `allclose` is used here to compare two vectors. If they are close enough to each other, this command returns `True`. Optionally a tolerance value can be set. For more methods related to linear equation systems, see `Section` 4.9: *Linear algebra methods in SciPy*.

Now, you have seen the first and essential way of how to use arrays in Python. In the following sections, we'll show you more details and the underlying principles.

4.2 Mathematical preliminaries

In order to understand how arrays work in NumPy, it is useful to understand the mathematical parallel between accessing tensor (matrix and vector) elements by indexes and evaluating mathematical functions by providing arguments. We also cover in this section the generalization of the dot product as a reduction operator.

4.2.1 Arrays as functions

Arrays may be considered from several different points of view. If you want to approach the concept from a mathematical point of view, you might benefit from understanding arrays through an analogy of functions of several variables. This view will later be taken again, when explaining the concept of broadcasting in `Section` 5.5: *Broadcasting*.

For instance, selecting a component of a given vector in $\mathbb{R}^n$ may just be considered a function from the set of $\mathbb{N}_n$ to $\mathbb{R}$, where we define the set:

$$\mathbb{N}_n = \{0, 1, \ldots, n-1\}$$

Here the set $\mathbb{N}_n$ has n elements. The Python function `range` generates $\mathbb{N}_n$.

Selecting an element of a given matrix, on the other hand, is a function of two parameters, taking its value in $\mathbb{R}$. Picking a particular element of an $m \times n$ matrix may thus be considered a function from $\mathbb{N}_m \times \mathbb{N}_n$ to $\mathbb{R}$.

4.2.2 Operations are elementwise

NumPy arrays are essentially treated as mathematical functions. This is in particular true for operations. Consider two functions, f and g, defined on the same domain and taking real values. The product $f \cdot g$ of those two functions is defined as the pointwise product, that is,

$$(f \cdot g)(x) = f(x) \cdot g(x)$$

Note that this construction is possible for any operation between two functions. For an arbitrary operation defined on two scalars, which we denote here by $*$, we could define $f * g$ as follows:

$$(f * g)(x) = f(x) * g(x)$$

This innocuous remark allows us to understand NumPy's stance on operations; all operations are elementwise in arrays. For instance, the product between two matrices, M and N, is defined, as with functions, as follows:

$$(MN)_{ij} := M_{ij} N_{ij}$$

4.2.3 Shape and number of dimensions

There is a clear distinction between a:

- *Scalar:* A function with no arguments
- *Vector:* A function with one argument
- *Matrix:* A function with two arguments
- *Higher-order tensor:* A function with more than two arguments

In what follows, the number of dimensions is the number of arguments of a function. The shape corresponds essentially to the domain of a function.

For instance, a vector of size n is a function from the set $\mathbb{N}_n$ to $\mathbb{R}$. As a result, its domain is $\mathbb{N}_n$. Its shape is defined as the singleton $(n,)$. Similarly, a matrix of size $m \times n$ is a function defined on $\mathbb{N}_m \times \mathbb{N}_n$. The corresponding shape is simply the pair (m, n). The shape of an array is obtained by the function `numpy.shape`, and the number of dimensions by the function `numpy.ndim`; see also `Section 4.6`: *Accessing and changing the shape.*

4.2.4 The dot operations

Treating arrays as functions, although very powerful, completely neglects the linear algebra structures we are familiar with, that is, matrix-vector and matrix-matrix operations. Fortunately, these linear algebra operations may all be written in a similar unified form:

The vector-vector operation:

$$s = \sum_i x_i y_i$$

The matrix-vector operation:

$$y_i = \sum_j A_{ij} x_j$$

The matrix-matrix operation:

$$C_{ij} = \sum_k A_{ik} B_{kj}$$

The vector-matrix operation:

$$y_j = \sum_i x_i A_{ij}$$

The essential mathematical concept is that of reduction. For a matrix-vector operation, the reduction is given by:

$$\sum_j A_{ij} x_j$$

In general, a reduction operation defined between two tensors, T and U, of respective number of dimensions m and n may be defined as:

$$(T \cdot U)_{i_1,\ldots,i_{m-1},j_2,\ldots,j_n} := \sum_k T_{i_1,\ldots,i_{m-1},k} U_{k,j_2,\ldots,j_n}$$

Clearly, the shapes of the tensors must be compatible with that operation to make any sense. This requirement is familiar for matrix-matrix multiplication. The multiplication MN of matrices M and N only makes sense if the number of columns of M equals the number of rows of N.

Another consequence of the reduction operation is that it produces a new tensor with $m + n - 2$ dimensions. In *Table 4.1*, we gather the output of the reduction operation for the familiar cases involving matrices and vectors:

$T_1 = \text{tensor}(ndim)$	$T_2 = \text{tensor}(ndim)$	$(T_1 T_2)(ndim)$
matrix(2)	vector(1)	vector(1)
matrix(2)	matrix(2)	matrix(2)
vector(1)	vector(1)	scalar(0)
vector(1)	matrix(2)	vector(1)

Table 4.1: Output of the reduction operation involving matrices and vectors

In Python, all reduction operations are performed using the dot function or alternatively the @ operator:

```
angle = pi/3
M = array([[cos(angle), -sin(angle)],
           [sin(angle), cos(angle)]])
v = array([1., 0.])
y = dot(M, v)
```

In Python version 3.5 or higher, the dot product can be written either in its operator form, dot(M, v), or by using the infix notation, M @ v. From now on we'll stick to the more handy infix notation; you can modify the examples if the other form is preferred. We note, however, that dot performs type casting to arrays if its arguments are of other types that can be cast to an array, such as list or float. The infix operator form with @ does not have this feature.

The multiplication operator * is always elementwise. It has nothing to do with the dot operation. Even if A is a matrix and v is a vector, A*v is still a legal operation. This will be explained in Section 5.5: *Broadcasting*.

In this section, we identified the use of arrays with matrices and vectors in mathematics and explained operations. In particular, the most central operation in scientific computation, the dot product, was explained. We turn now to the array datatype ndarray and its methods more generally.

4.3 The array type

The objects used to manipulate vectors, matrices, and more general tensors in NumPy are called ndarrays, or just arrays for short. In this section, we examine their essential properties, how to create them, and how to access their information.

4.3.1 Array properties

Arrays are essentially characterized by the three properties, described in *Table 4.2*:

Name	Description
shape	This describes how the data should be interpreted, as a vector, a matrix, or a higher-order tensor, and it gives the corresponding dimension. It is accessed with the attribute shape.
dtype	This gives the type of the underlying data (float, complex, integer, and so on).

strides	This attribute specifies in which order the data should be read. For instance, a matrix could be stored in memory contiguously column by column (FORTRAN convention), or row by row (C convention). The attribute is a tuple with the numbers of bytes that have to be skipped in memory to reach the next row and the number of bytes to be skipped to reach the next column. It even allows for a more flexible interpretation of the data in memory, which is what makes array views possible.

Table 4.2: The three characterizing properties of an array

Consider, for example, the following array:

```
A = array([[1, 2, 3], [3, 4, 6]])
A.shape    # (2, 3)
A.dtype    # dtype('int64')
A.strides  # (24, 8)
```

Its elements have the type `'int64'`; that is, they use 64 bits or 8 bytes in memory. The complete array is stored in memory row-wise. The distance from `A[0, 0]` to the first element in the next row `A[1,0]` is thus 24 bytes (three matrix elements) in memory. Correspondingly, the distance in memory between `A[0,0]` and `A[0,1]` is 8 bytes (one matrix element). These values are stored in the attribute `strides`.

4.3.2 Creating arrays from lists

The general way to create an array is by using the function `array`. The syntax to create a real-valued vector would be:

```
V = array([1., 2., 1.], dtype=float)
```

To create a complex vector with the same data, you use:

```
V = array([1., 2., 1.], dtype=complex)
```

When no type is specified, the type is guessed. The `array` function chooses the type that allows storing all the specified values:

```
V = array([1, 2]) # [1, 2] is a list of integers
V.dtype # int64
V = array([1., 2]) # [1., 2] mix float/integer
V.dtype # float64
V = array([1. + 0j, 2.]) # mix float/complex
V.dtype # complex128
```

NumPy silently casts floats into integers, which might give unexpected results:

```
a = array([1, 2, 3])
a[0] = 0.5
a # now: array([0, 2, 3])
```

The same, often unexpected array type casting happens from `complex` to `float`.

Array and Python parentheses

As we noticed in `Section 1.2.2`: *Line joining*, Python allows a line break when some opening brace or parenthesis is not closed. This allows a convenient syntax for array creation, which makes it more pleasing to the human eye:

```
# the identity matrix in 2D
Id = array([[1., 0.], [0., 1.]])
# Python allows this:
Id = array([[1., 0.],
            [0., 1.]])
# which is more readable
```

So far, you saw a lot of differences in the definition and use between arrays and lists. Accessing array elements, in contrast, seems quite similar to the way list elements are accessed. But especially the use of multiple indexes and the resulting objects from the slicing operations require that we look at these issues in more detail.

4.4 Accessing array entries

Array entries are accessed by indexes. In contrast to vector coefficients, two indexes are needed to access matrix coefficients. These are given in one pair of brackets. This distinguishes the array syntax from a list of lists. There, two pairs of brackets are needed to access elements.

```
M = array([[1., 2.],[3., 4.]])
M[0, 0] # first row, first column: 1.0
M[-1, 0] # last row, first column: 3.0
```

Let's look now in more detail at the use of double indexes and slices.

4.4.1 Basic array slicing

Slices are similar to those of lists (see also `Section 3.1.1`: *Slicing*) except that they might now be in more than one dimension:

- `M[i,:]` is a vector filled by the row i of M.
- `M[:,j]` is a vector filled by the column j of M.
- `M[2:4,:]` is a slice of `2:4` on the rows only.
- `M[2:4,1:4]` is a slice of rows and columns.

The result of matrix slicing is given in the following *Figure 4.1*:

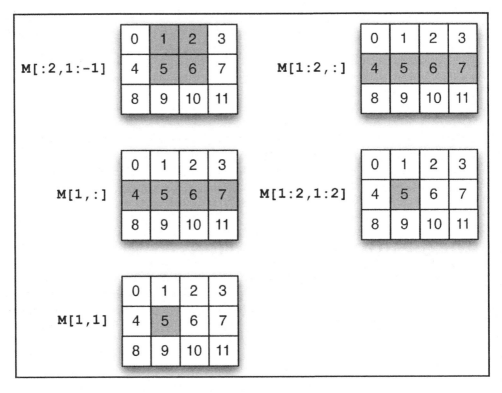

Figure 4.1: The result of matrix slicing

If you omit an index or a slice, NumPy assumes you are taking rows only. `M[3]` is a vector that is a view on the third row of M and `M[1:3]` is a matrix that is a view on the second and third rows of M.

Changing the elements of a slice affects the entire array (see also `Section 5.1`: *Array views and copies*):

```
v = array([1., 2., 3.])
v1 = v[:2] # v1 is array([1., 2.])
v1[0] = 0. # if v1 is changed ...
v # ... v is changed too: array([0., 2., 3.])
```

General slicing rules are given in *Table 4.3*:

Access	ndim	Kind
index, index	0	scalar
slice, index	1	vector
index, slice	1	vector
slice, slice	2	matrix

Table 4.3: General slicing rules

The results of slicing operations for an array M of shape *(4, 4)* are given in *Table 4.4*:

Access	Shape	ndim	Kind
M[:2, 1:-1]	(2,2)	2	matrix
M[1,:]	(4,)	1	vector
M[1,1]	()	0	scalar
M[1:2,:]	(1,4)	2	matrix
M[1:2, 1:2]	(1,1)	2	matrix

Table 4.4: Result of slicing operations for an array M of shape (4,4)

4.4.2 Altering an array using slices

You may alter an array using slices or by direct access. The following changes only one element in a 5×3 matrix M:

```
M[1, 2] = 2.0 # scalar
```

Also, we may change one full row of the matrix:

```
M[2, :] = [1., 2., 3.] # vector
```

Similarly, we may also replace a full submatrix:

```
M[1:3, :] = array([[1., 2., 3.],[-1.,-2., -3.]])
```

There is a distinction between a column matrix and a vector. The following assignment with a column matrix returns no error:

```
M[1:4, 1:2] = array([[1.],[0.],[-1.0]])
```

while the assignment with a vector returns a `ValueError`:

```
M[1:4, 1:2] = array([1., 0., -1.0]) #  error
```

The general slicing rules are shown in *Table 4.3*. The matrices and vectors in the preceding examples must have the right size to fit into matrix M. You may also make use of the broadcasting rules (see `Section 5.5`: *Broadcasting*) to determine the allowed size of the replacement arrays. If the replacement array does not have the right shape, a `ValueError` exception will be raised.

We saw how to construct arrays from other arrays by slicing. In the next section, we will consider special NumPy functions that are useful to directly create and initialize arrays.

4.5 Functions to construct arrays

The usual way to set up an array is via a list. But there are also a couple of convenient methods for generating special arrays, which are given in *Table 4.5*:

Methods	Shape	Generates
`zeros((n,m))`	(n,m)	Matrix filled with zeros
`ones((n,m))`	(n,m)	Matrix filled with ones
`full((n,m),q)`	(n,m)	Matrix filled with q
`diag(v,k)`	(n,n)	(Sub-, super-) diagonal matrix from a vector v
`random.rand(n,m)`	(n,m)	Matrix filled with uniformly distributed random numbers in `(0,1)`
`arange(n)`	$(n,)$	First n integers
`linspace(a,b,n)`	$(n,)$	Vector with n equispaced points between a and b

Table 4.5: Commands to create arrays

These commands may take additional arguments. In particular, the commands `zeros`, `ones`, `full`, and `arange` take `dtype` as an optional argument. The default type is `float`, except for `arange`. There are also methods such as `zeros_like` and `ones_like`, which are slight variants of the preceding ones. For instance, the command `zeros_like(A)` is equivalent to `zeros(shape(A))`.

The function `identity` constructs an identity matrix of a given size:

```
I = identity(3)
```

The command is identical to:

```
I = array([[ 1., 0., 0.],
           [ 0., 1., 0.],
           [ 0., 0., 1.]])
```

4.6 Accessing and changing the shape

The number of dimensions is what distinguishes a vector from a matrix. The *shape* is what distinguishes vectors of different sizes, or matrices of different sizes. In this section, we examine how to obtain and change the shape of an array.

4.6.1 The function shape

The shape of a matrix is the tuple of its dimensions. The shape of an $n \times m$ matrix is the tuple `(n, m)`. It can be obtained by the function `shape`:

```
M = identity(3)
shape(M)  # (3, 3)
```

or, simply by its attribute

```
M.shape   # (3, 3)
```

However, the advantage of using `shape` as a function and not as an attribute is that the function may be used on scalars and lists as well. This may come in handy when code is supposed to work with both scalars and arrays:

```
shape(1.) # ()
shape([1,2]) # (2,)
shape([[1,2]]) # (1,2)
```

For a vector, the shape is a singleton containing the length of that vector:

```
v = array([1., 2., 1., 4.])
shape(v) # (4,) <- singleton (1-tuple)
```

4.6.2 Number of dimensions

The number of dimensions of an array is obtained with the function `ndim` or using the array attribute `ndim`:

```
ndim(A) # 2
A.ndim # 2
```

Note that the number of dimensions, given by the function `ndim`, of a tensor `T` (a vector, matrix, or higher-order tensor) is always equal to the length of its shape:

```
T = zeros((2,2,3)) # tensor of shape (2,2,3); three dimensions
ndim(T) # 3
len(shape(T)) # 3
```

4.6.3 Reshape

The method `reshape` gives a new view of the array, with a new shape, without copying the data:

```
v = array([0,1,2,3,4,5])
M = v.reshape(2,3)
shape(M) # returns (2,3)
M[0,0] = 10 # now v[0] is 10
```

The various effects of `reshape` on an array defined by `arange(6)` are given in *Figure 4.2*:

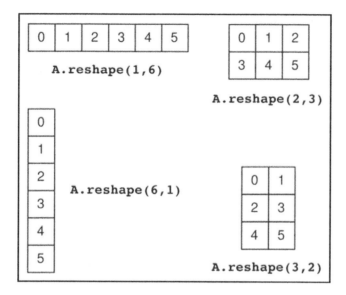

Figure 4.2: The various effects of `reshape` on an array

`reshape` does not create a new array. It rather gives a new view on the existing array. In the preceding example, changing one element of M would automatically result in a change in the corresponding element in v. When this behavior is not acceptable, you need to copy the data, as explained in `Section 5.1`: *Array views and copies*.

If you try to reshape an array with a shape that does not multiply to the original shape, an error is raised:

```
ValueError: total size of new array must be unchanged.
```

Sometimes, it is convenient to specify only one `shape` parameter and let Python determine the other in such a way that it multiplies to the original shape. This is done by setting the free `shape` parameter to −1:

```
v = array([1, 2, 3, 4, 5, 6, 7, 8])
M = v.reshape(2, -1)
shape(M) # returns (2, 4)
M = v.reshape(-1, 2)
shape(M) # returns (4,2 )
M = v.reshape(3,- 1) # returns error
```

Transpose

A special form of reshaping is *transposing*. It just switches the two shape elements of the matrix. The transpose of a matrix A is a matrix B such that

$$B_{ij} = A_{ji}$$

which is resolved in the following way:

```
A = ...
shape(A)  # (3,4)

B = A.T   # A transpose
shape(B)  # (4,3)
```

`transpose` does not copy: transposition is very similar to reshaping. In particular, it does not copy the data either and just returns a view on the same array:

```
A= array([[ 1., 2.],[ 3., 4.]])
B=A.T
A[1,1]=5.
B[1,1] # 5.0
```

Transposing a vector makes no sense since vectors are tensors of one dimension, that is, functions of one variable – the index. NumPy will, however, comply and return exactly the same object:

```
v = array([1., 2., 3.])
v.T # exactly the same vector!
```

What you have in mind when you want to transpose a vector is probably to create a row or column matrix. This is done using `reshape`:

```
v.reshape(-1, 1) # column matrix containing v
v.reshape(1, -1) # row matrix containing v
```

4.7 Stacking

The universal method to build matrices from a couple of (matching) submatrices is `concatenate`. Its syntax is:

```
concatenate((a1, a2, ...), axis = 0)
```

This command stacks the submatrices vertically (on top of each other) when `axis=0` is specified. With the argument `axis=1`, they are stacked horizontally, and this generalizes according to arrays with more dimensions. This function is called by several convenient functions, as follows:

- `hstack`: Used to stack arrays horizontally
- `vstack`: Used to stack arrays vertically
- `columnstack`: Used to stack vectors in columns

4.7.1 Stacking vectors

You may stack vectors row-wise or column-wise using `vstack` and `column_stack`, as illustrated in *Figure 4.3*:

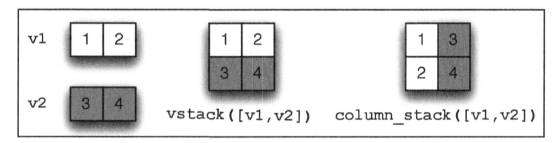

Figure 4.3: Difference between vstack and column_stack

Note that `hstack` would produce the concatenation of v1 and v2.

Let's consider the symplectic permutation as an example for vector stacking: we have a vector of size $2n$. We want to perform a symplectic transformation of a vector with an even number of components, that is, exchange the first half with the second half of the vector with sign change:

$$(x_1, x_2, \ldots, x_n, x_{n+1}, \ldots, x_{2n}) \mapsto (x_{n+1}, \ldots, x_{2n}, -x_1, \ldots, -x_n)$$

This operation is resolved in Python as follows:

```
# v is supposed to have an even length.
def symp(v):
    n = len(v) // 2 # use the integer division //
    return hstack([v[-n:], -v[:n]])
```

4.8 Functions acting on arrays

There are different types of functions acting on arrays. Some act elementwise, and they return an array of the same shape. Those are called *universal functions*. Other array functions return an array of a different shape. In this section, we will meet both types of functions and also learn how to convert scalar functions into *universal functions*.

4.8.1 Universal functions

Universal functions are functions that act elementwise on arrays. They thus have an output array that has the same shape as the input array. These functions allow us to compute the result of a scalar function on a whole array at once.

Built-in universal functions

A typical example is the cos function (the one provided by NumPy):

```
cos(pi) # -1
cos(array([[0, pi/2, pi]])) # array([[1, 0, -1]])
```

Note that universal functions work on arrays in a componentwise manner. This is also true for operators, such as multiplication or exponent:

```
2 * array([2, 4]) # array([4, 8])
array([1, 2]) * array([1, 8]) # array([1, 16])
array([1, 2])**2 # array([1, 4])
2**array([1, 2]) # array([2, 4])
array([1, 2])**array([1, 2]) # array([1, 4])
```

Creation of universal functions

Your function will automatically be universal if you use only universal functions in it. If, however, your function uses functions that are not universal, you might get scalar results, or even an error when trying to apply them on an array:

```
def const(x):
    return 1
const(array([0, 2])) # returns 1 instead of array([1, 1])
```

Another example is the following:

```
def heaviside(x):
    if x >= 0:
        return 1.
    else:
        return 0.

heaviside(array([-1, 2])) # error
```

The expected behavior would be that the heaviside function applied to a vector [a, b] would return [heaviside(a), heaviside(b)]. Alas, this does not work because the function always returns a scalar, no matter the size of the input argument. Besides, using the function with an array input would cause the statement if to raise an exception, as is explained in detail in Section 5.2.1: *Boolean arrays*.

The NumPy function vectorize allows us to quickly solve this problem:

```
vheaviside = vectorize(heaviside)
vheaviside(array([-1, 2])) # array([0, 1]) as expected
```

A typical application of this method is its use when plotting a function:

```
xvals = linspace(-1, 1, 100)
plot(xvals, vectorize(heaviside)(xvals))
axis([-1.5, 1.5, -0.5, 1.5])
```

Figure 4.4 shows the resulting graph:

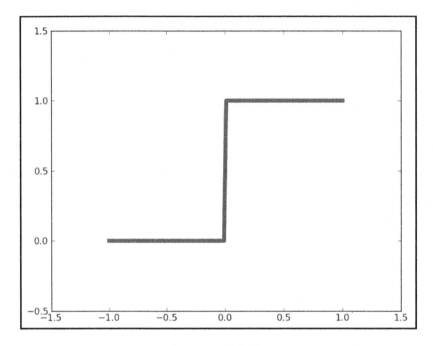

Figure 4.4: Heaviside function

The function `vectorize` provides a convenient way to quickly transform a function, so that it operates elementwise on lists and arrays.

`vectorize` can also be used as a decorator:

```
@vectorize
def heaviside(x):
    if x >= 0:
        return 1.
    else:
        return 0.
# and a call of this results in:
heaviside(array([-1, 2])) # array([0, 1])
```

Decorators will be introduced in `Section 7.8`: *Functions as decorators*.

4.8.2 Array functions

There are a number of functions acting on arrays that do not act componentwise. Examples of such functions are `max`, `min`, and `sum`. These functions may operate on the entire matrix, row-wise, or column-wise. When no argument is provided, they act on the entire matrix.

Suppose:

$$A = \begin{pmatrix} 1 & 2 & 3 & 4 \\ 5 & 6 & 7 & 8 \end{pmatrix}$$

The function `sum` acting on that matrix returns a scalar:

```
sum(A)  # 36
```

The command has an optional parameter, `axis`. It allows us to choose along which axis to perform the operation. For instance, if the axis is 0, it means that the sum should be computed along the first axis. The sum along axis 0 of an array of shape (m, n) will be a vector of length n.

Suppose we compute the sum of A along the axis 0:

```
sum(A, axis=0)  # array([ 6,  8,  10,  12])
```

This amounts to computing the sum on the columns:

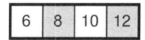

| 1 | 2 | 3 | 4 |
| 5 | 6 | 7 | 8 |

The result is a vector:

| 6 | 8 | 10 | 12 |

Now suppose we compute the sum along axis *1*:

```
A.sum(axis=1)  # array([10, 26])
```

This amounts to computing the sum on the rows:

1	2	3	4
5	6	7	8

The result is a vector:

After having seen in this section functions acting on arrays in general, we turn now to some functions solving tasks in basic scientific computing. We exemplify this by considering some standard tasks in linear algebra.

4.9 Linear algebra methods in SciPy

SciPy offers a large range of methods from numerical linear algebra in its module `scipy.linalg`. Many of these methods are Python wrapping programs from LAPACK, a collection of well-approved FORTRAN subroutines used to solve linear equation systems and eigenvalue problems, see [5]. Linear algebra methods are the core of any method in scientific computing, and the fact that SciPy uses wrappers instead of pure Python code makes these central methods extremely fast. We present in detail here how two linear algebra problems are solved with Scipy to give you a flavor of this module.

You met before some linear algebra functions taken from the module `numpy.linalg`. Both packages NumPy and SciPy are compatible, but Scipy has its focus on scientific computing methods and is more comprehensive, while NumPy's focus is on the array datatype and it provides only some linear algebra methods for convenience.

4.9.1 Solving several linear equation systems with LU

Let A be an $n \times n$ matrix and $b_1, b_2, \ldots, b_k$ be a sequence of n vectors. We consider the problem to find n vectors x_i such that:

$$Ax_i = b_i$$

We assume that the vectors b_i are not known simultaneously. In particular, it is quite a common situation that the ith problem has to be solved before b_{i+1} becomes available, for example in the context of the simplified Newton iteration, see [24].

LU factorization is a way to organize the classical Gauss elimination method in such a way that the computation is done in two steps:

- A factorization step of the matrix A to get matrices in triangular form
- A relatively cheap backward and forward elimination step that works on the instances of b_i and benefits from the more time-consuming factorization step

The method also uses the fact that if P is a permutation matrix such that PA is the original matrix with its rows permuted, the two systems $Ax = b$ and $PAx = Pb$ have the same solution.

LU factorization finds a permutation matrix P, a lower triangular matrix L, and an upper triangular matrix U such that:

$PA = LU$ or equivalently $A = PLU$.

Such a factorization always exists. Furthermore, L can be determined in such a way that $L_{ii} = 1$. Thus, the essential data from L that has to be stored is L_{ij} with $i > j$. Consequently, L and U can be stored together in an $n \times n$ array, while the information about the permutation matrix P just requires an n integer vector – the pivot vector.

In SciPy, there are two methods to compute the LU factorization. The standard one is `scipy.linalg.lu`, which returns the three matrices L, U, and P. The other method is `lu_factor`. That is the method we describe here, because it will be conveniently used later in combination with `lu_solve`:

```
import scipy.linalg as sl
[LU,piv] = sl.lu_factor(A)
```

Here, the matrix A is factorized and an array with the information about L and U is returned, together with the pivot vector. With this information, the system can be solved by performing row interchanges of the vectors b_i according to the information stored in the pivot vector, backward substitution using U, and finally, forward substitution using L. This is bundled in Python, in the method `lu_solve`. The following code snippet shows how the system $Ax_i = b_i$ is solved once the LU factorization is performed and its results stored in the tuple (LU, piv):

```
import scipy.linalg as sl
xi = sl.lu_solve((LU, piv), bi)
```

4.9.2 Solving a least square problem with SVD

A linear equation system $Ax = b$, with A being an $m \times n$ matrix and $m > n$, is called an overdetermined linear system. In general, it has no classical solution and you seek a vector $x^* \in \mathbb{R}^n$ with the property:

$$\underbrace{\|Ax^* - b\|_2}_{=:r} = \min_{x \in \mathbb{R}^n} \|Ax - b\|_2$$

Here, $\| \cdot \|_2$ denotes the Euclidean vector norm $\|x\|_2 = \sqrt{x_1^2 + \cdots + x_n^2}$.

This problem is called a least square problem. A stable method to solve it is based on factorizing $A = U\Sigma V^T$, with U being an $m \times m$ orthogonal matrix, V an $n \times n$ orthogonal matrix, and $\Sigma = (\sigma_{ij})$ an $m \times n$ matrix with the property $\sigma_{ij} = 0$ for all $i \neq j$. This factorization is called a **singular value decomposition** (SVD).

We write

$$\Sigma = \begin{bmatrix} \Sigma_1 \\ 0 \end{bmatrix}$$

with a diagonal $n \times n$ matrix Σ_1. If we assume that A has full rank, then Σ_1 is invertible and it can be shown that

$$x^* = V \begin{bmatrix} \Sigma_1^{-1} & 0 \end{bmatrix} U^{\mathrm{T}} b$$

holds.

If we split $U = \begin{bmatrix} U_1 & U_2 \end{bmatrix}$ with U_1 being an $m \times n$ submatrix, then the preceding equation can be simplified to:

$$x^* = V \Sigma_1^{-1} U_1^{\mathrm{T}} b$$

SciPy provides a function called `svd`, which we use to solve this task:

```
import scipy.linalg as sl
[U1, Sigma_1, VT] = sl.svd(A, full_matrices = False,
                            compute_uv = True)
xast = dot(VT.T, dot(U1.T, b) / Sigma_1)
r = dot(A, xast) - b # computes the residual
nr = sl.norm(r, 2) # computes the Euclidean norm of r
```

The keyword `full_matrices` tells whether the complete matrix U or only its submatrix U_1 should be computed. As you often use `svd` to compute only singular values, σ_{ii}, we have, in our case, to explicitly demand the computation of U and V by using the keyword `compute_uv`.

The SciPy function `scipy.linalg.lstsq` solves the least squares problem directly by internally using an SVD.

4.9.3 More methods

In the examples so far, you met a couple of methods for computational tasks in linear algebra, for example, `solve`. More methods are available after the command `import scipy.linalg as sl` is executed. The most common of them are listed in *Table 4.6*:

Methods	Description
sl.det	Determinant of a matrix
sl.eig	Eigenvalues and eigenvectors of a matrix
sl.inv	Matrix inverse
sl.pinv	Matrix pseudoinverse
sl.norm	Matrix or vector norm

`sl.svd`	Singular value decomposition
`sl.lu`	LU decomposition
`sl.qr`	QR decomposition
`sl.cholesky`	Cholesky decomposition
`sl.solve`	Solution of a general or symmetric linear system: $Ax = b$
`sl.solve.banded`	The same for banded matrices
`sl.lstsq`	Least squares solution

Table 4.6: Linear algebra functions of the module scipy.linalg

Execute `import scipy.linalg as sl` first.

4.10 Summary

In this chapter, we worked with the most important objects in linear algebra – vectors and matrices. For this, we learned how to define arrays and we met important array methods. A smaller section demonstrated how to use modules from `scipy.linalg` to solve central tasks in linear algebra.

In the following chapter, we consider more advanced and special aspects of arrays.

4.11 Exercises

Ex. 1: Consider a 4×3 matrix:

$$M = \begin{bmatrix} 1 & 2 & 3 \\ 4 & 5 & 6 \\ 7 & 8 & 9 \\ 10 & 11 & 12 \end{bmatrix}$$

1. Construct this matrix in Python using the function `array`.
2. Construct the same matrix using the function `arange` followed by a suitable `reshape`.
3. What is the result of the expression `M[2, :]`? What is the result of the similar expression `M[2:]`?

Ex. 2: Given a vector x, construct in Python the following matrix:

$$V = \begin{bmatrix} x_0^5 & x_0^4 & \cdots & x_0^1 & x_0^0 \\ x_1^5 & x_1^4 & \cdots & x_1^1 & x_1^0 \\ & & \vdots & & \\ x_5^5 & x_5^4 & \cdots & x_5^1 & x_5^0 \end{bmatrix}$$

Here, x_i are the components of the vector x (numbered from zero). Given a vector y, solve in Python the linear equation system $Va = y$. Let the components of a be denoted by a_i, $i = 0, \ldots, 5$. Write a function `poly`, which has a and z as input and computes the polynomial:

$$p(z) = \sum_{i=0}^{5} a_{5-i} z^i.$$

Plot this polynomial and depict in the same plot the points (x_i, y_i) as small stars. Try your code with the vectors:

$$x = (0.0, 0.5, 1.0, 1.5, 2.0, 2.5)$$
$$y = (-2.0, 0.5, -2.0, 1.0, -0.5, 1.0)$$

Ex. 3: The matrix V in *Ex. 2* is called a *Vandermonde matrix*. It can be set up in Python directly with the command `vander`. Evaluating a polynomial defined by a coefficient vector can be done with the Python command `polyval`. Repeat *Ex. 2* by using these commands.

Ex. 4: Let u be a one-dimensional array. Construct another array ξ with values $\xi_i = (u_i + u_{i+1} + u_{i+2})/3$. In statistics, this array is called the *moving average* of u. In approximation theory, it plays the role of the Greville abscissae of cubic splines. Try to avoid the use of `for` loops in your scrip t.

Ex. 5:

1. Construct from the matrix V given in *Ex. 2* a matrix A by deleting V's first column.
2. Form the matrix $B = (A^T A)^{-1} A^T$.

3. Compute $c = By$ with y from *Ex. 2*.

4. Use c and `polyval` to plot the polynomial defined by c. Plot in the same picture again the points (x_i, y_i).

Ex. 6: *Ex. 5* describes the least squares method. Repeat that exercise but use SciPy's `scipy.linalg.lstsq` method instead.

Ex. 7: Let v be a vector written in its coordinate form as a 3×1 matrix $[1 \quad -1 \quad 1]^T$. Construct the projection matrices:

$$P = \frac{vv^T}{v^T v} \text{ and } Q = I - P$$

Show experimentally that v is an eigenvector for both matrices P and Q. What are the corresponding eigenvalues?

Ex. 8: In numerical linear algebra the $m \times m$ matrix A with the property

$$A_{ij} = \begin{cases} 0 & \text{if } i < j \text{ and } j \neq m \\ 1 & \text{if } i = j \text{ or } j = m \\ -1 & \text{otherwise} \end{cases}$$

is used as an example for an extreme growth factor, when performing LU factorization, see [36, p. 165].

Set up this matrix in Python for various values of m, compute its LU factorization using the command `scipy.linalg.lu`, and derive experimentally a statement about the growth factor

$$\rho = \frac{\max_{ij} |U_{ij}|}{\max_{ij} |A_{ij}|}$$

in relation to m.

Advanced Array Concepts

5

In this chapter, we will explain some more advanced aspects of arrays. First, we will cover the notion of an array view – a concept that a NumPy programmer absolutely must be aware of to avoid hard-to-debug programming errors. Then, Boolean arrays will be introduced along with the ways to compare arrays. Furthermore, we will briefly describe indexing and vectorization, explaining special topics such as broadcasting and sparse matrices.

In this chapter, we will be covering the following topics:

- Array views and copies
- Comparing arrays
- Array indexing
- Performance and vectorization
- Broadcasting
- Sparse matrices

5.1 Array views and copies

In order to control precisely how memory is used, NumPy offers the concept of a view of an array. Views are smaller arrays that share the same data as a larger array. This works just like a reference to one single object.

5.1.1 Array views

The simplest example of a view is given by a slice of an array:

```
M = array([[1.,2.],[3.,4.]])
v = M[0,:] # first row of M
```

The preceding slice v is a view of M. It shares the same data as M. Modifying v will modify M as well:

```
v[-1] = 0.
v # array([[1.,0.]])
M # array([[1.,0.],[3.,4.]]) # M is modified as well
```

It is possible to access the object that owns the data using the array attribute base:

```
v.base # array([[1.,0.],[3.,4.]])
v.base is M # True
```

If an array owns its data, the attribute base is None:

```
M.base # None
```

5.1.2 Slices as views

There are precise rules on which slices will return views and which ones will return copies. Only basic slices (mainly index expressions with :) return views, whereas any advanced selections (such as slicing with a Boolean) will return a copy of the data. For instance, it is possible to create new matrices by indexing with lists (or arrays):

```
a = arange(4) # array([0.,1.,2.,3.])
b = a[[2,3]] # the index is a list [2,3]
b # array([2.,3.])
b.base is None # True, the data was copied
c = a[1:3]
c.base is None # False, this is just a view
```

In the preceding example, the array b is not a view, whereas the array c, obtained with a simpler slice, is a view.

There is an especially simple slice of an array that returns a view of the whole array:

```
N = M[:] # this is a view of the whole array M
```

5.1.3 Generating views by transposing and reshaping

Some other important operations return views. For instance, transposing an array returns a view:

```
M = random.random_sample((3,3))
N = M.T
N.base is M # True
```

The same applies to all reshaping operations:

```
v = arange(10)
C = v.reshape(-1,1) # column matrix
C.base is v # True
```

5.1.4 Array copies

Sometimes it is necessary to explicitly request that the data be copied. This is simply achieved with the NumPy function called `array`:

```
M = array([[1.,2.],[3.,4.]])
N = array(M.T) # copy of M.T
```

We can verify that the data has indeed been copied:

```
N.base is None # True
```

In this section, you saw the concept of array views. NumPy works with views instead of copies of a given array to save memory, which – especially for large arrays – can be crucial. On the other hand, unintentionally using views may cause programming errors that are hard to debug.

5.2 Comparing arrays

Comparing two arrays is not as simple as it may seem. Consider the following code, which is intended to check whether two matrices are close to each other:

```
A = array([0.,0.])
B = array([0.,0.])
if abs(B-A) < 1e-10: # an exception is raised here
    print("The two arrays are close enough")
```

This code raises the following exception when the `if` statement is executed:

```
ValueError: The truth value of an array with more than one element is
ambiguous. Use a.any() or a.all()
```

In this section, we'll explain why this is so and how to remedy this state of affairs.

5.2.1 Boolean arrays

Boolean arrays are useful for advanced array indexing (also see `Section 5.3.1`: Indexing with Boolean arrays). A Boolean array is simply an array for which the entries have the type `bool`:

```
A = array([True,False]) # Boolean array
A.dtype # dtype('bool')
```

Any comparison operator acting on arrays will create a Boolean array instead of a simple Boolean:

```
M = array([[2, 3],
           [1, 4]])
M > 2 # array([[False, True],
      #        [False, True]])
M == 0 # array([[False, False],
       #        [False, False]])
N = array([[2, 3],
           [0, 0]])
M == N # array([[True, True],
       #        [False, False]])
```

Note that because array comparison creates Boolean arrays, one cannot use array comparison directly in conditional statements, for example, `if` statements. The solution is to use the methods `all` and `any` to create a simple `True` or `False`:

```
A = array([[1,2],[3,4]])
B = array([[1,2],[3,3]])
A == B # creates array([[True, True], [True, False]])
(A == B).all() # False
(A != B).any() # True
if (abs(B-A) < 1e-10).all():
    print("The two arrays are close enough")
```

Here, the use of one of the methods `all` and `any` results in a "scalar" Boolean, which now allows array comparisons in `if` statements.

5.2.2 Checking for array equality

Checking the equality of two float arrays is not straightforward, because two floats may be very close without being equal. In NumPy, it is possible to check for equality with `allclose`. This function checks for the equality of two arrays up to a given precision:

```
data = random.rand(2)*1e-3
small_error = random.rand(2)*1e-16
data == data + small_error # False
allclose(data, data + small_error, rtol=1.e-5, atol=1.e-8)    # True
```

The tolerance is given in terms of a relative tolerance bound, `rtol`, and an absolute error bound, `atol`. The command `allclose` is a short form of:

```
(abs(A-B) < atol+rtol*abs(B)).all()
```

Note that `allclose` can be also applied to scalars:

```
data = 1e-3
error = 1e-16
data == data + error # False
allclose(data, data + error, rtol=1.e-5, atol=1.e-8)   #True
```

5.2.3 Boolean operations on arrays

You cannot use `and`, `or`, and `not` on Boolean arrays. Indeed, those operators force the casting from array to Boolean, which is not permitted. Instead, we can use the operators given in Table 5.1 for component-wise logical operations on Boolean arrays:

Logic operator	Replacement for Boolean arrays
A and B	A & B
A or B	A | B
not A	~ A

Table 5.1: Logical operators for component-wise logical array operations

Here is an example usage of logical operators with Boolean arrays:

```
A = array([True, True, False, False])
B = array([True, False, True, False])
A and B # error!
A & B # array([True, False, False, False])
A | B # array([True, True, True, False])
~A # array([False, False, True, True])
```

Suppose that we have a sequence of data that is marred with some measurement error. Suppose further that we run a regression and it gives us a deviation for each value. We wish to obtain all the exceptional values and all the values with a little deviation that are lower than a given threshold:

```
data = linspace(1,100,100) # data
deviation = random.normal(size=100) # the deviations
data = data + deviation
# do not forget the parentheses in the next statement!
exceptional = data[(deviation<-0.5)|(deviation>0.5)]
exceptional = data[abs(deviation)>0.5] # same result
small = data[(abs(deviation)<0.1)&(data<5.)] # small deviation and data
```

In this example, we first created a data vector and then we perturbed it with some deviations sampled from normally distributed random numbers. We demonstrated two alternative ways of finding elements of data with large perturbations in absolute values, and finally, we collected only small data values for small perturbations. Here, we used a Boolean array instead of indexes when working with the array `data`. This technique will be explained in the next section.

5.3 Array indexing

We have already seen that we can index arrays with combinations of slices and integers – this is a basic slicing technique. There are, however, many more possibilities that allow for a variety of ways to access and modify array elements.

5.3.1 Indexing with Boolean arrays

It is often useful to access and modify only parts of an array, depending on its value. For instance, you might want to access all the positive elements of an array. This turns out to be possible using Boolean arrays, which act like masks to select only some elements of an array. The result of such indexing is *always* a vector. For instance, consider the following example:

```
B = array([[True, False],
           [False, True]])
M = array([[2, 3],
           [1, 4]])
M[B] # array([2,4]), a vector
```

In fact, the command `M[B]` is equivalent to `M[B].flatten()`. You can then replace the resulting vector with another vector. For instance, you can replace all the elements with zero:

```
M[B] = 0
M # [[0, 3], [1, 0]]
```

Or you can replace all the selected values with others:

```
M[B] = 10, 20
M # [[10, 3], [1, 20]]
```

By combining the creation of Boolean arrays (`M > 2`), smart indexing (indexing with a Boolean array), and broadcasting, you can use the following elegant syntax:

```
M[M>2] = 0    # all the elements > 2 are replaced by 0
```

The expression broadcasting here refers to the tacit conversion of the scalar `0` to a vector of an appropriate shape (also see `Section 5.5`: *Broadcasting*).

5.3.2 Using the command where

The command `where` gives a useful construct that can take a Boolean array as a condition and either return the indexes of the array elements satisfying the condition or return different values depending on the values in the Boolean array.

The basic structure is:

```
where(condition, a, b)
```

This will return values from a when the condition is `True` and values from b when it is `False`.

For instance, consider a *Heaviside* function:

$$H(x) = \begin{cases} 0 & x < 0 \\ 1 & x \geq 0 \end{cases}$$

and its implementation with the command `where`:

```
def H(x):
    return where(x < 0, 0, 1)
x = linspace(-1,1,11)  # [-1. -0.8 -0.6 -0.4 -0.2 0. 0.2 0.4 0.6 0.8 1. ]
print(H(x))            # [0 0 0 0 0 1 1 1 1 1 1]
```

The second and third arguments can be either arrays of the same size as the condition (the Boolean array) or scalars. We'll give two more examples to demonstrate how to manipulate elements from an array or a scalar depending on a condition:

```
x = linspace(-4,4,5)
# [-4. -2.  0.  2.  4.]

print(where(x < 0, -x, x))
# [ 4., 2., 0, 2., 4.] ]
print(where(x > 0, 1, -1)) # [-1 -1 -1  1  1]
```

If the second and third arguments are omitted, then a tuple containing the indexes of the elements satisfying the condition is returned.

For example, consider the use of `where` with only one argument in the following code:

```
a = arange(9)
b = a.reshape((3,3))

print(where(a > 5))    # (array([6, 7, 8]),)
print(where(b > 5))    # (array([2, 2, 2]), array([0, 1, 2]))
```

This example demonstrates how to find out indexes of those elements of a Boolean array that are `True`. The command `where` is a very handy tool to search in an array for elements fulfilling a given condition.

In this section, you saw various use cases of Boolean arrays. Whenever your code contains `for` loops operating on conditions and arrays, check if the concept of Boolean arrays could help to remove unnecessary `for` loops and increase at least the readability of your code.

5.4 Performance and vectorization

When it comes to the performance of your Python code, it often boils down to the difference between interpreted code and compiled code. Python is an interpreted programming language and basic Python code is executed directly without any intermediate compilation to machine code. With a compiled language, the code needs to be translated to machine instructions before execution.

The benefits of an interpreted language are many but interpreted code cannot compete with compiled code for speed. To make your code faster, you can write some parts in a compiled language such as FORTRAN, C, or C++. This is what NumPy and SciPy do.

For this reason, it is best to use functions in NumPy and SciPy over interpreted versions whenever possible. NumPy array operations such as matrix multiplication, matrix-vector multiplication, matrix factorization, scalar products, and so on are much faster than any pure Python equivalent. Consider the simple case of scalar products. The scalar product is much slower than the compiled NumPy function `dot(a,b)` (more than 100 times slower for arrays with about 100 elements):

```
def my_prod(a,b):
    val = 0
    for aa, bb in zip(a,b):
        val += aa*bb
    return val
```

Measuring the speed of your functions is an important aspect of scientific computing. See `Section 15.3`: *Measuring execution time* for details on measuring execution times.

5.4.1 Vectorization

To improve performance, you have often to vectorize the code. Replacing `for` loops and other slower parts of the code with NumPy slicing, operations, and functions can give significant improvements.

For example, the simple addition of a scalar to a vector by iterating over the elements is very slow:

```
for i in range(len(v)):
    w[i] = v[i] + 5
```

But using NumPy's addition is much faster:

```
w = v + 5
```

Using NumPy slicing can also give significant speed improvements over iterating with `for` loops. To demonstrate this, let's consider forming the average of neighbors in a two-dimensional array:

```
def my_avg(A):
    m,n = A.shape
    B = A.copy()
    for i in range(1,m-1):
        for j in range(1,n-1):
            B[i,j] = (A[i-1,j] + A[i+1,j] + A[i,j-1] + A[i,j+1])/4
    return B

def slicing_avg(A):
    A[1:-1,1:-1] = (A[:-2,1:-1] + A[2:,1:-1] +
                    A[1:-1,:-2] + A[1:-1,2:])/4
    return A
```

These functions both assign each element the average of its four neighbors. The second version, using slicing, is much faster.

Besides replacing `for` loops and other slower constructions with NumPy functions, there is a useful function called `vectorized` (see `Section 4.8`: *Functions acting on arrays*). This takes a function and creates a vectorized version that applies the function on all elements of an array using functions wherever possible.

Consider the following function which we will use to demonstrate how to vectorize functions:

```
def my_func(x):
    y = x**3 - 2*x + 5
    if y>0.5:
        return y-0.5
    else:
        return 0def my_func(x):
    y = x**3 - 2*x + 5
    if y>0.5:
        return y-0.5
    else:
        return 0
```

Applying this function on elements of a vector v with 100 elements in a non-vectorized way:

```
[my_func(vk) for vk in v]
```

is nearly three times slower than using it in the vectorized way:

```
vectorize(my_func)(v)
```

In this section, we showed several examples of the vectorization of computations with NumPy arrays. An active use of this concept is recommended not only for speeding up the execution of your code but also for improving the readability of your code.

5.5 Broadcasting

Broadcasting in NumPy denotes the ability to guess a common, compatible shape between two arrays. For instance, when adding a vector (one-dimensional array) and a scalar (zero-dimensional array), the scalar is extended to a vector, in order to allow for the addition. The general mechanism is called broadcasting. We will first review that mechanism from a mathematical point of view, and then proceed to give the precise rules for broadcasting in NumPy. The mathematical view might give a mathematically trained reader easier access to broadcasting, while other readers might want to skip the mathematical details and directly continue reading Section 5.5.2: *Broadcasting arrays*.

5.5.1 Mathematical views

Broadcasting is often performed in mathematics, mainly implicitly. Examples are expressions such as $f(x) + C$ or $f(x) + g(y)$. We will give an explicit description of that technique in this section.

We have in mind the very close relationship between functions and NumPy arrays, as described in Section 4.2.1: *Arrays as functions*.

Constant functions

One of the most common examples of broadcasting is the addition of a function and a constant; if C is a scalar, we often write:

$$f := \sin + C$$

This is an abuse of notation since you should not be able to add functions and constants. Constants are, however, implicitly broadcast to functions. The broadcast version of the constant C is the function $\bar{C}$ defined by:

$$\bar{C}(x) := C \quad \text{for all } x$$

Now it makes sense to add two functions together:

$$f = \sin + \bar{C}$$

We are not being pedantic for the sake of it, but because a similar situation may arise for arrays, as in the following code:

```
vector = arange(4)  # array([0.,1.,2.,3.])
vector + 1.         # array([1.,2.,3.,4.])
```

In this example, everything happens as if the scalar `1.` had been converted to an array of the same length as `vector`, that is, `array([1.,1.,1.,1.])`, and then added to `vector`.

This example is exceedingly simple, so we'll proceed to show less obvious situations.

Functions of several variables

A more intricate example of broadcasting arises when building functions of several variables. Suppose, for instance, that we were given two functions of one variable, f and g, and that we want to construct a new function, F, according to the formula:

$$F(x, y) = f(x) + g(y)$$

This is clearly a valid mathematical definition. We would like to express this definition as the sum of two functions in two variables defined as

$$\begin{aligned} \bar{f}(x,y) &:= f(x) \quad \text{for all } y \\ \bar{g}(x,y) &:= g(y) \quad \text{for all } x \end{aligned}$$

and now we may simply write:

$$F := \bar{f} + \bar{g}$$

The situation is similar to that arising when adding a column matrix and a row matrix:

```
C = arange(2).reshape(-1,1)  # column
R = arange(2).reshape(1,-1)  # row
C + R                        # valid addition: array([[0.,1.],[1.,2.]])
```

This is especially useful when sampling functions of two variables, as shown in `Section 5.5.3`: *Typical examples*.

General mechanism

We have seen how to add a function and a scalar and how to build a function of two variables from two functions of one variable. Let's now focus on the general mechanism that makes this possible. The general mechanism consists of two steps: *reshaping* and *extending*.

First, the function g is *reshaped* to the function $\tilde{g}$, which takes two arguments. One of these arguments is a dummy argument, which we take to be zero, as a convention:

$$\tilde{g}(0, y) := g(y).$$

Mathematically, the domain of the definition of $\tilde{g}$ is now $\{0\} \times \mathbb{R}$. Then the function f is *reshaped* in a way similar to:

$$\tilde{f}(x, 0) := f(x).$$

Now both $\tilde{f}$ and $\tilde{g}$ take two arguments, although one of them is always zero. We proceed to the next step, *extending*. It is the same step that converted a constant into a constant function.

The function $\tilde{f}$ is *extended* to:

$$\bar{f}(x, y) := \tilde{f}(x, 0) \qquad \text{for all } y$$

The function $\tilde{g}$ is extended to:

$$\bar{g}(x, y) := \tilde{g}(0, y) \qquad \text{for all } x$$

Now the function of two variables, F, which was sloppily defined by $F(x, y) = f(x) + g(y)$, may be defined without reference to its arguments:

$$F := \bar{f} + \bar{g}$$

For example, let's describe the preceding mechanism for constants. A constant is a scalar, that is, a function of zero arguments. The *reshaping step* is thus to define the function of one (empty) variable:

$$\tilde{C}(0) := C.$$

Now the *extension step* proceeds simply with:

$$\overline{C}(x) := \widetilde{C}(0).$$

Conventions

The last ingredient is the convention for how to add the extra arguments to a function, that is, how the reshaping is automatically performed. By convention, a function is automatically reshaped by adding zeros on the left.

For example, if a function g of two arguments has to be reshaped to three arguments, the new function will be defined by:

$$\tilde{g}(0, x, y) := g(x, y)$$

After having seen a more mathematical motivation for broadcasting, we now show how this applies to NumPy arrays.

5.5.2 Broadcasting arrays

We'll now repeat the observation that arrays are merely functions of several variables (see `Section` 4.2: *Mathematical preliminaries*). Array broadcasting thus follows exactly the same procedure as explained above for mathematical functions. Broadcasting is done automatically in NumPy.

In Figure 5.1, we show what happens when adding a matrix of shape (4, 3) to a matrix of size (1, 3). The resulting matrix is of the shape (4, 3):

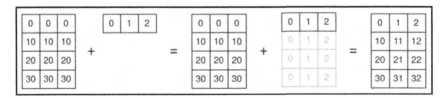

Figure 5.1: Broadcasting between a matrix and a vector

The broadcasting problem

When NumPy is given two arrays with different shapes and is asked to perform an operation that would require the two shapes to be the same, both arrays are broadcast to a common shape.

Suppose the two arrays have shapes s_1 and s_2. Broadcasting consists of the two steps:

1. If the shape s_1 is shorter than the shape s_2, that is, `len(s1) < len(s2)`, then ones are added on the left of the shape s_1. This is reshaping.
2. When the shapes have the same length, the first array is extended to match the shape s_2 (if possible).

Suppose we want to add a vector of shape $s_1 = (3,)$ to a matrix of shape $s_2 = (4, 3)$. The vector needs to be broadcast. The first operation is reshaping; the shape of the vector is converted from (3,) to (1, 3). The second operation is an extension; the shape is converted from (1, 3) to (4, 3).

For instance, suppose a vector v of size n is to be broadcast to the shape (m, n):

1. v is automatically reshaped to $(1, n)$.
2. v is extended to (m, n).

To demonstrate this, we consider a matrix defined by:

```
M = array([[11, 12, 13, 14],
           [21, 22, 23, 24],
           [31, 32, 33, 34]])
```

and a vector given by:

```
v = array([100, 200, 300, 400])
```

Now we may add M and v directly:

```
M + v # works directly
```

The result is this matrix:

$$\begin{bmatrix} 111 & 212 & 313 & 414 \\ 121 & 222 & 323 & 424 \\ 131 & 232 & 333 & 434 \end{bmatrix}$$

Shape mismatch

It is not possible to automatically broadcast a vector v of length n to the shape (n, m). This is illustrated in *Figure 5.2*.

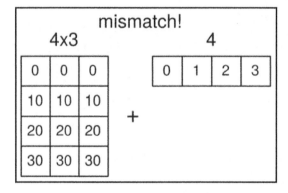

Figure 5.2: Failure of broadcasting due to shape mismatch

The broadcasting fails, because the shape (n,) may not be automatically broadcast to the shape (m, n). The solution is to manually reshape v to the shape (n, 1). The broadcasting will now work as usual (by extension only):

```
M + v.reshape(-1,1)
```

This is illustrated by the following example.

Define a matrix with:

```
M = array([[11, 12, 13, 14],
           [21, 22, 23, 24],
           [31, 32, 33, 34]])
```

and a vector with:

```
v = array([100, 200, 300])
```

Now automatic broadcasting will fail because automatic reshaping does not work:

```
M + v # shape mismatch error
```

The solution is thus to take care of the reshaping manually. What we want in that case is to add 1 on the right, that is, transform the vector into a column matrix. The broadcasting then works directly:

```
M + v.reshape(-1,1)
```

(For the shape parameter −1, see `Section 4.6.3`: *Reshape.*) The result is this matrix:

```
array([[111, 112, 113, 114],
       [221, 222, 223, 224],
       [331, 332, 333, 334]])
```

5.5.3 Typical examples

Let's examine some typical examples where broadcasting may come in handy.

Rescale rows

Suppose M is an $n \times m$ matrix and we want to multiply each row by a coefficient. The coefficients are stored in a vector `coeff` with n components. In that case, automatic reshaping will not work, and we have to execute:

```
rescaled = M*coeff.reshape(-1,1)
```

Rescale columns

The setup is the same here, but we would like to rescale each column with a coefficient stored in a vector `coeff` of length m. In this case, automatic reshaping will work:

```
rescaled = M*coeff
```

Obviously, we may also do the reshaping manually and achieve the same result with:

```
rescaled = M*coeff.reshape(1,-1)
```

Functions of two variables

Suppose u and v are vectors and we want to form the matrix W with elements $w_{ij} = u_i + v_j$. This would correspond to the function $F(x,y) = x + y$. The matrix W is merely defined by:

```
W=u.reshape(-1,1) + v
```

If the vectors u and v are $(1,2)$ and $(1,2,3)$ respectively, the result is:

```
array([[2, 3, 4],
       [3, 4, 5]])
```

More generally, suppose that we want to sample the function $w(x,y) = \cos(x) + \sin(2y)$. Supposing that the vectors x and y are defined, the matrix W of sampled values is obtained with:

```
W = cos(x).reshape(-1,1) + sin(2*y)
```

Note that this is very frequently used in combination with ogrid. The vectors obtained from ogrid are already conveniently shaped for broadcasting. This allows for the following elegant sampling of the function $\cos(x) + \sin(2y)$:

```
x,y = ogrid[0:1:3j,0:1:3j]
# x,y are vectors with the contents of linspace(0,1,3)
w = cos(x) + sin(2*y)
```

The syntax of ogrid needs some explanation: First, ogrid is not a function. It is an instance of a class with a __getitem__ method (see Section 8.1.5: *Special methods*). That is why it is used with brackets instead of parentheses.

The two commands are equivalent:

```
x,y = ogrid[0:1:3j, 0:1:3j]
x,y = ogrid.__getitem__((slice(0, 1, 3j),slice(0, 1, 3j)))
```

The stride parameter in the preceding example is a complex number. This is to indicate that it is the number of steps instead of the step size. The rules for the stride parameter might be confusing at first glance:

- If the stride is a real number, then it defines the size of the steps between start and stop and stop is not included in the list.

- If the stride is a complex number s, then the integer part of s.imag defines the number of steps between start and stop and stop is included in the list.

The output of ogrid is a tuple with two arrays, which can be used for broadcasting:

```
x,y = ogrid[0:1:3j, 0:1:3j]
```

This gives:

```
array([[ 0. ],
       [ 0.5],
       [ 1. ]])
array([[ 0. ,   0.5,   1. ]])
```

which is equivalent to:

```
x,y = ogrid[0:1.5:.5, 0:1.5:.5]
```

5.6. Sparse matrices

Matrices with a small number of nonzero entries are called *sparse matrices*. Sparse matrices occur, for example, in scientific computing when describing discrete differential operators in the context of numerically solving partial differential equations.

Sparse matrices often have large dimensions, sometimes so large that the entire matrix (with zero entries) would not even fit in the available memory. This is one motivation for a special datatype for sparse matrices. Another motivation is better performance of operations where zero matrix entries can be avoided.

There are only a very limited number of algorithms for general, unstructured sparse matrices in linear algebra. Most of them are iterative in nature and based on efficient implementations of matrix-vector multiplication for sparse matrices.

Examples of sparse matrices are diagonal or banded matrices. The simple pattern of these matrices allows straightforward storing strategies; the principal diagonal and the sub- and super-diagonals are stored in 1D arrays. Conversion from a sparse representation to the classical array type and vice versa can be done with the NumPy command diag.

In general, there is not such a simple structure and the description of sparse matrices requires special techniques and standards.

An example of such a matrix is shown in Figure 5.3. There, the pixels denote nonzero entries in the 1250 × 1250 matrix.

In this section, we present a row and a column-oriented type for sparse matrices, both available through the module `scipy.sparse`.

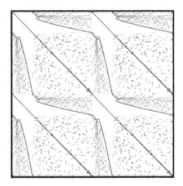

Figure 5.3: A stiffness matrix from a finite element model of an elastic plate.

5.6.1 Sparse matrix formats

The module `scipy.sparse` provides many different storing formats for sparse matrices. Here, we'll describe only the most important ones: CSR, CSC, and LIL. The LIL format should be used for generating and altering sparse matrices; CSR and CSC are efficient formats for matrix-matrix and matrix-vector operations.

Compressed sparse row format (CSR)

The **compressed sparse row (CSR)** format uses three arrays: `data`, `indptr`, and `indices`:

- The 1D array `data` stores all the nonzero values in order. It has as many elements as there are nonzero elements, often denoted by the variable `nnz`.

- The 1D array `indptr` contains integers such that `indptr[i]` is the index of the element in `data`, which is the first nonzero element of row i. If the entire row i is zero, then `indptr[i]==indptr[i+1]`. If the original matrix has m rows, then `len(indptr)==m+1`.

- The 1D array `indices` contains the column index information in such a way that `indices[indptr[i]:indptr[i+1]]` is an integer array with the column indexes of the nonzero elements in row i.
  Obviously, `len(indices)==len(data)==nnz`.

Let's see an example:

The CSR format of the matrix:

$$A = \begin{pmatrix} 1. & 0. & 2. & 0. \\ 0. & 0. & 0. & 0. \\ 3. & 0. & 0. & 0. \\ 1. & 0. & 0. & 4. \end{pmatrix}$$

is given by the three arrays:

```
data = array([1., 2., 3., 1., 4.])
indptr = array([0, 2, 2, 3, 5])
indices = array([0, 2, 0, 0, 3]
```

The module `scipy.sparse` provides a type, `csr_matrix`, with a constructor, which can be used in the following ways:

- With a 2D array as an argument
- With a matrix in one of the other sparse formats in `scipy.sparse`
- With a shape argument, `(m,n)`, to generate a zero matrix in CSR format
- By a 1D array for `data` and an integer array `ij` with the shape `(2,len(data))` such that `ij[0,k]` is the row index and `ij[1,k]` is the column index of `data[k]` of the matrix
- The three arguments, `data`, `indptr`, and `indices`, can be given to the constructor directly

The first two options are there for conversion purposes while the last two directly define the sparse matrix.

Consider the above example; in Python, it looks like:

```
import scipy.sparse as sp
A = array([[1,0,2,0],[0,0,0,0],[3.,0.,0.,0.],[1.,0.,0.,4.]])
AS = sp.csr_matrix(A)
```

Among others, the following attributes are provided:

```
AS.data        # returns array([ 1., 2., 3., 1., 4.])
AS.indptr      # returns array([0, 2, 2, 3, 5])
AS.indices     # returns array([0, 2, 0, 0, 3])
AS.nnz         # returns 5
```

Compressed sparse column format (CSC)

The CSR format has a column-oriented twin – the **compressed sparse column** (CSC) format. The only difference in it compared to the CSR format is the definition of the indptr and indices arrays, which are now column-related. The type for the CSC format is csc_matrix and its use corresponds to csr_matrix, explained previously in this subsection.

Continuing the same example in CSC format:

```
import scipy.sparse as sp
A = array([[1,0,2,0],[0,0,0,0],[3.,0.,0.,0.],[1.,0.,0.,4.]])
AS = sp.csc_matrix(A)
AS.data        # returns array([ 1.,  3.,  1.,  2.,  4.])
AS.indptr      # returns array([0, 3, 3, 4, 5])
AS.indices     # returns array([0, 2, 3, 0, 3])
AS.nnz         # returns 5
```

Row-based linked list format (LIL)

The linked list sparse format stores the nonzero matrix entries row-wise in a list data such that data[k] is a list of the nonzero entries in row k. If all entries in that row are 0, it contains an empty list.

A second list, rows, contains at position k a list of column indexes of the nonzero elements in row k. Here is an example in row-based **linked list** (LIL) format:

```
import scipy.sparse as sp
A = array([[1,0,2,0],[0,0,0,0], [3.,0.,0.,0.], [1.,0.,0.,4.]])
AS = sp.lil_matrix(A)
AS.data     # returns array([[1.0, 2.0], [], [3.0], [1.0, 4.0]],
dtype=object)
AS.rows     # returns array([[0, 2], [], [0], [0, 3]], dtype=object)
AS.nnz      # returns 5
```

Altering and slicing matrices in LIL format

The LIL format is the one best suited for slicing, that is, extracting submatrices in LIL format, and for changing the sparsity pattern by inserting nonzero elements. Slicing is demonstrated by the next example:

```
BS = AS[1:3,0:2]
BS.data     # returns array([[], [3.0]], dtype=object)
BS.rows     # returns array([[], [0]], dtype=object)
```

The insertion of a new nonzero element automatically updates the attributes:

```
AS[0,1] = 17
AS.data # returns array([[1.0, 17.0, 2.0], [], [3.0], [1.0, 4.0]])
AS.rows              # returns array([[0, 1, 2], [], [0], [0, 3]])
AS.nnz               # returns 6
```

These operations are discouraged in the other sparse matrix formats as they are extremely inefficient.

5.6.2 Generating sparse matrices

The NumPy commands eye, identity, diag, and rand have their sparse counterparts. They take an additional argument; it specifies the sparse matrix format of the resulting matrix.

The following commands generate the identity matrix but in different sparse matrix formats:

```
import scipy.sparse as sp
sp.eye(20,20,format = 'lil')
sp.spdiags(ones((20,)),0,20,20, format = 'csr')
sp.identity(20,format ='csc')
```

The command sp.rand takes an additional argument describing the density of the generated random matrix. A dense matrix has density 1 while a zero matrix has density 0:

```
import scipy.sparse as sp
AS=sp.rand(20,200,density=0.1,format='csr')
AS.nnz # returns 400
```

There is no direct correspondence to the NumPy command zeroes. Matrices completely filled with zeros are generated by instantiating the corresponding type with the shape parameters as constructor parameters:

```
import scipy.sparse as sp
Z=sp.csr_matrix((20,200))
Z.nnz    # returns 0
```

After having studied different sparse matrix formats, we now turn to special methods for a sparse matrix, mainly conversion methods.

5.6.3 Sparse matrix methods

There are methods to convert one sparse type into another or into an array:

```
AS.toarray # converts sparse formats to a numpy array
AS.tocsr
AS.tocsc
AS.tolil
```

The type of a sparse matrix can be inspected by the methods `issparse`, `isspmatrix_lil`, `isspmatrix_csr`, and `isspmatrix_csc`.

Elementwise operations +, *, /, and ** on sparse matrices are defined as for NumPy arrays. Regardless of the sparse matrix format of the operands, the result is always `csr_matrix`. Applying elementwise operating functions to sparse matrices requires first transforming them to either CSR or CSC format and applying the functions to their `data` attribute, as demonstrated by the next example.

The elementwise sine of a sparse matrix can be defined by an operation on its `data` attribute:

```
import scipy.sparse as sp
def sparse_sin(A):
    if not (sp.isspmatrix_csr(A) or sp.isspmatrix_csc(A)):
        A = A.tocsr()
    A.data = sin(A.data)
    return A
```

For matrix-matrix or matrix-vector multiplications, there is a sparse matrix method, `dot`. It returns either a `csr_matrix` or a 1D NumPy `array`:

Consider the following function on which we will demonstrate how to vectorize a function:

```
import scipy.sparse as sp
A = array([[1,0,2,0],[0,0,0,0],[3.,0.,0.,0.],[1.,0.,0.,4.]])
AS = sp.csr_matrix(A)
b = array([1,2,3,4])
c = AS.dot(b)       # returns array([ 7., 0., 3., 17.])
C = AS.dot(AS)      # returns  csr_matrix
d = dot(AS,b)       # does not return the expected result!
```

Avoid using NumPy's command `dot` on sparse matrices, as this might lead to unexpected results. Use the command `dot` from `scipy.sparse` instead.

Other linear algebra operations such as system solving, least squares, eigenvalues, and singular values are provided by the module `scipy.sparse.linalg`.

5.7 Summary

The concept of views is one of the important topics you should have learned from this chapter. Missing this topic will give you a hard time when debugging your code. Boolean arrays occur at various places throughout this book. They are handy and compact tools for avoiding lengthy `if` constructions and loops when working with arrays. In nearly all large computational projects, sparse matrices become an issue. You have seen how they are handled and which related methods are available.

6
Plotting

Plotting in Python can be done with the `pyplot` part of the module Matplotlib. With `matplotlib`, you can create high-quality figures and graphics and also plot and visualize your results. Matplotlib is open source and freely available software. The Matplotlib website also contains excellent documentation with examples, see 35. In this section, we will show you how to use the most common features. The examples in the upcoming sections assume that you have imported the module as:

```
from matplotlib.pyplot import *
```

In case you want to use the plotting commands in IPython, it is recommended that you run the *magic command* `%matplotlib` directly after starting the IPython shell. This prepares IPython for interactive plotting.

6.1 Making plots with basic plotting commands

In this section, we will create plots by means of basic commands. It is the entry point for studying how to make graphical representations of mathematical objects and data using Python.

6.1.1 Using the plot command and some of its variants

The standard plotting function is `plot`. Calling `plot(x,y)` creates a figure window with a plot of y as a function of x. The input arguments are arrays (or lists) of equal length. It is also possible to use `plot(y)`, in which case the values in y will be plotted against their index, that is, `plot(y)` is a short form of `plot(range(len(y)),y)`.

Here is an example that shows how to plot $\sin(x)$ for $x \in [-2\pi, 2\pi]$ using 200 sample points and with markers at every fourth point:

```
# plot sin(x) for some interval
x = linspace(-2*pi,2*pi,200)
plot(x,sin(x))

# plot marker for every 4th point
samples = x[::4]
plot(samples,sin(samples),'r*')

# add title and grid lines
title('Function sin(x) and some points plotted')
grid()
```

The result is shown in the following figure (*Figure 6.1*):

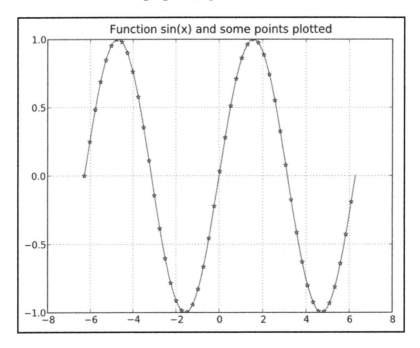

Figure 6.1: A plot of the function sin(x) with grid lines shown

As you can see, the standard plot is a solid blue curve. Each axis gets automatically scaled to fit the values, but can also be set manually. Color and plot options can be given after the first two input arguments. Here, `r*` indicates red star-shaped markers. Formatting is covered in more detail in the next section. The command `title` puts a title text string above the plot area.

Calling `plot` multiple times will overlay the plots in the same window. To get a new clean figure window, use `figure()`. The command `figure` might contain an integer, for example, `figure(2)`, which can be used to switch between figure windows. If there is no figure window with that number, a new one is created, otherwise, the window is activated for plotting and all subsequent plotting commands apply to that window.

Multiple plots can be explained by using the function `legend`, along with adding labels to each plot call. The following example fits polynomials to a set of points using the commands `polyfit` and `polyval`, and plots the result with a legend:

```
# —Polyfit example—
x = range(5)
y = [1,2,1,3,5]
p2 = polyfit(x,y,2) # coefficients of degree 2 polynomial
p4 = polyfit(x,y,4) # coefficients of degree 4 polynomial

# plot the two polynomials and points
xx = linspace(-1,5,200)
plot(xx, polyval(p2, xx), label='fitting polynomial of degree 2')
plot(xx, polyval(p4, xx),
                label='interpolating polynomial of degree 4')
plot(x,y,'*')

# set the axis and legend
axis([-1,5,0,6])
legend(loc='upper left', fontsize='small')
```

Here, you can also see how to manually set the range of the axis using `axis([xmin,xmax,ymin,ymax])`. The command `legend` takes optional arguments on placement and formatting; in this case, the legend is put in the upper-left corner and typeset with a small font size, as shown in the following figure (*Figure 6.2*):

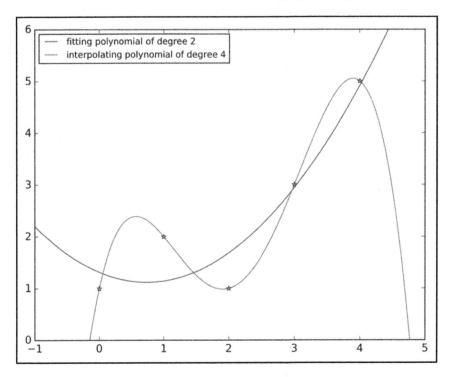

Figure 6.2: Two polynomials fitted to the same points

As final examples for basic plotting, we demonstrate how to do scatter plots and logarithmic plots in two dimensions.

Here is an example of a 2D point scatter plot:

```
# create random 2D points
import numpy
x1 = 2*numpy.random.standard_normal((2,100))
x2 = 0.8*numpy.random.standard_normal((2,100)) + array([[6],[2]])
plot(x1[0],x1[1],'*')
plot(x2[0],x2[1],'r*')
title('2D scatter plot')
```

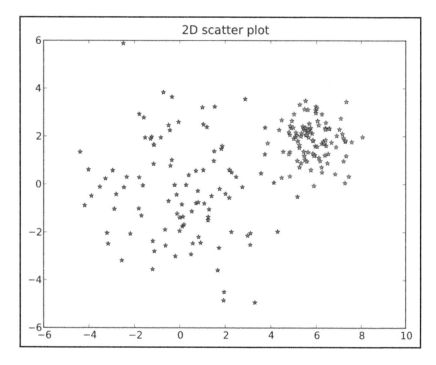

Figure 6.3(a): An example of a scatter plot

The following code is an example of a logarithmic plot using `loglog`:

```
# log both x and y axis
x = linspace(0,10,200)
loglog(x,2*x**2, label = 'quadratic polynomial',
                        linestyle = '-', linewidth = 3)
loglog(x,4*x**4, label = '4th degree polynomial',
                        linestyle = '-.', linewidth = 3)
loglog(x,5*exp(x), label = 'exponential function', linewidth = 3)
title('Logarithmic plots')
legend(loc = 'best')
```

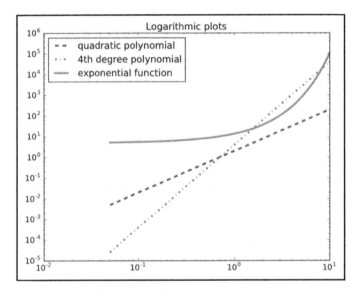

Figure 6.3(b): An example of a plot with logarithmic *x* and *y* axes

The examples shown in the preceding figure (*Figure 6.3(a)* and *Figure 6.3(b)*) used some parameters of `plot` and `loglog`, which allow special formatting. In the next section, we will explain the parameters in more detail.

6.1.2 Formatting

The appearance of figures and plots can be styled and customized to look how you want them to look. Some important variables are `linewidth`, which controls the thickness of plot lines, `xlabel` and `ylabel`, which set the axis labels, `color` for plot colors, and `transparent` for transparency.

This section will tell you how to use some of them. The following is an example with more keywords:

```
k = 0.2
x = [sin(2*n*k) for n in range(20)]
plot(x, color='green', linestyle='dashed', marker='o',
               markerfacecolor='blue', markersize=12, linewidth=6)
```

There are short commands that can be used if you only need basic style changes, for example, setting the color and line style. The following table (*Table 6.1*) shows some examples of these formatting commands. You may use either the short string syntax `plot(..., 'ro-')`, or the more explicit syntax `plot(..., marker='o', color='r', linestyle='-')`.

Line Style linestyle		Marker marker		Color color	
String Argument	Description	String Argument	Description	String Argument	Description
–	solid	.	point	b	blue
– –	dashed	,	pixel	g	green
–.	dashed dotted	o	circle	r	red
:	dotted	v , ^	triangle down up	c	cyan
		< , >	triangle left, right	m	magenta
		s , p	square, pentagon	y	yellow
		*, + , x	star, plus, x	k	black
		d , D	thin diamond, diamond	w	white

Table 6.1: Some common plot formatting arguments

To set the color to green with the marker `'o'`, we write the following:

```
plot(x,'go')
```

To plot histograms instead of regular plots, the command `hist` is used:

```
# random vector with normal distribution
sigma, mu = 2, 10
x = sigma*numpy.random.standard_normal(10000)+mu
hist(x,50,density=True)
z = linspace(0,20,200)
plot(z, (1/sqrt(2*pi*sigma**2))*exp(-(z-mu)**2/(2*sigma**2)),'g')
# title with LaTeX formatting
title(fr'Histogram with $\mu={mu}, \sigma={sigma}')
```

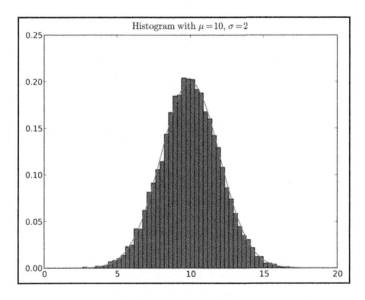

Figure 6.4: Normal distribution with 50 bins and a green curve indicating the true distribution

The resulting plot looks similar to *Figure 6.4*. The title, and any other text, can be formatted using LaTeX to show mathematical formulas. LaTeX formatting is enclosed within a pair of $ signs. Also, note the string formatting done using the method `format`; see `Section 2.4.3`, *String formatting*.

Sometimes, the brackets for the string formatting interfere with LaTeX bracket environments. If this occurs, replace the LaTeX bracket with a double bracket; for example, x_{1} should be replaced with x_{{1}}. The text might contain sequences that overlap with string escape sequences, for example, \tau will be interpreted as the tab character, \t. An easy workaround is to add r before the string, for example, r'\tau'. This makes it a raw string.

Placing several plots in one figure window can be done using the command subplot. Consider the following example, which iteratively averages out the noise on a sine curve.

```
def avg(x):
    """ simple running average """
    return (roll(x,1) + x + roll(x,-1)) / 3
# sine function with noise
x = linspace(-2*pi, 2*pi,200)
y = sin(x) + 0.4*numpy.random.standard_normal(200)

# make successive subplots
for iteration in range(3):
    subplot(3, 1, iteration + 1)
    plot(x,y, label = '{:d} average{}'.format(iteration, 's' if iteration >
1 else ''))
    yticks([])
    legend(loc = 'lower left', frameon = False)
    y = avg(y) #apply running average
subplots_adjust(hspace = 0.7)
```

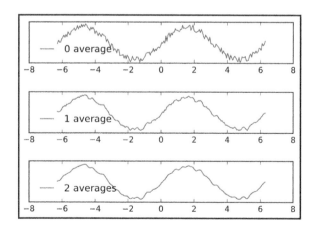

Figure 6.5: An example of plotting several subplots in the same figure window

The function `avg` uses the NumPy function `roll` to shift all values of the array. `subplot` takes three arguments: the number of vertical plots, the number of horizontal plots, and an index indicating which location to plot in (counted row-wise). Note that we used the command `subplots_adjust` to add extra space to adjust the distance between the subplots.

A useful command is `savefig`, which lets you save a figure as an image (this can also be done from the figure window). Many image and file formats are supported by this command; they are specified by the filename's extension as:

```
savefig('test.pdf')   # save to pdf
```

or

```
savefig('test.svg')   # save to svg (editable format)
```

You can place the image against a non-white background, for example, a web page. For this, the parameter `transparent` can be set to make the figure's background transparent:

```
savefig('test.pdf', transparent=True)
```

If you intend to embed a figure into a LaTeX document, it is recommended that you reduce the surrounding white space by setting the figure's bounding box tight around the drawing, as shown here:

```
savefig('test.pdf', bbox_inches='tight')
```

6.1.3 Working with meshgrid and contours

A common task is a graphical representation of a scalar function over a rectangle:

$$f : [a, b] \times [c, d] \to \mathbb{R}$$

For this, first we have to generate a grid on the rectangle $[a, b] \times [c, d]$. This is done using the command `meshgrid`:

```
n = ... # number of discretization points along the x-axis
m = ... # number of discretization points along the x-axis
X,Y = meshgrid(linspace(a,b,n), linspace(c,d,m))
```

X and Y are arrays with an `(n,m)` shape such that `X[i,j]` and `Y[i,j]` contain the coordinates of the grid point P_{ij}, as shown in *Figure 6.6*:

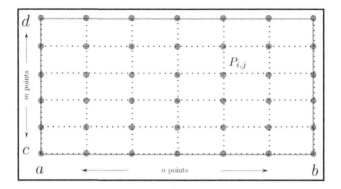

Figure 6.6: A rectangle discretized by meshgrid.

A rectangle discretized by `meshgrid` will be used in the next section to visualize the behavior of an iteration, while we will use it here to plot the level curves of a function. This is done by the command `contour`.

As an example, we choose Rosenbrock's banana function:

$$f(x,y) = (1-x)^2 + 100(y-x^2)^2$$

It is used to challenge optimization methods, see [27]. The function values descend toward a banana-shaped valley, which itself decreases slowly toward the function's global minimum at (1, 1).

First, we display the level curves using `contour`:

```
rosenbrockfunction = lambda x,y: (1-x)**2+100*(y-x**2)**2
X,Y = meshgrid(linspace(-.5,2.,100), linspace(-1.5,4.,100))
Z = rosenbrockfunction(X,Y)
contour(X,Y,Z,logspace(-0.5,3.5,20,base=10),cmap='gray')
title('Rosenbrock Function: ')
xlabel('x')
ylabel('y')
```

This plots the level curve at the levels given by the fourth parameter and uses the colormap `gray`. Furthermore, we used logarithmically spaced steps from $10^{0.5}$ to 10^3 using the function `logscale` to define the levels, see *Figure 6.7*.

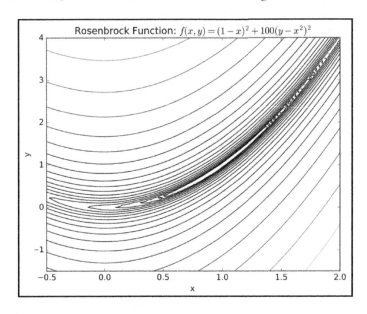

Figure 6.7: A contour plot of the Rosenbrock function

In the preceding example, an anonymous function indicated by the keyword `lambda` is used to keep the code compact. Anonymous functions are explained in `Section 7.7`, *Anonymous Functions* . If levels are not given as arguments to `contour`, the function chooses appropriate levels by itself.

The function `contourf` performs the same task as `contour`, but fills the plot with colors according to different levels. Contour plots are ideal for visualizing the behavior of a numerical method. We illustrate this here by showing the iterations of an optimization method.

We continue the preceding example and depict the steps toward the minimum of the Rosenbrock function generated by Powell's method, which we will apply to find the minimum of the Rosenbrock function:

```
import scipy.optimize as so
rosenbrockfunction = lambda x,y: (1-x)**2+100*(y-x**2)**2
X,Y=meshgrid(linspace(-.5,2.,100),linspace(-1.5,4.,100))
Z=rosenbrockfunction(X,Y)
cs=contour(X,Y,Z,logspace(0,3.5,7,base=10),cmap='gray')
```

```
rosen=lambda x: rosenbrockfunction(x[0],x[1])
solution, iterates = so.fmin_powell(rosen,x0=array([0,-0.7]),retall=True)
x,y=zip(*iterates)
plot(x,y,'ko') # plot black bullets
plot(x,y,'k:',linewidth=1) # plot black dotted lines
title("Steps of Powell's method to compute a minimum")
clabel(cs)
```

The iterative method `fmin_powell` applies Powell's method to find a minimum. It is started by a given start value x_0 and reports all iterates when the option `retall=True` is given. After 16 iterations, the solution $x = 0, y = 0$ was found. . The iterations are depicted as bullets in the contour plot; see *Figure 6.8*.

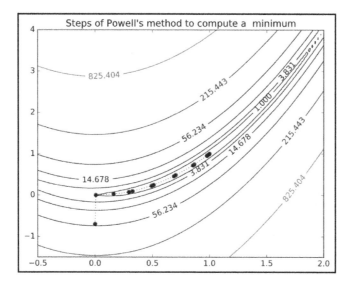

Figure 6.8: A contour plot of the Rosenbrock function with a search path of an optimization method

The function `contour` also creates a contour set object that we assigned to the variable `cs`. This is then used by `clabel` to annotate the levels of the corresponding function values, as shown in the *Figure 6.8*.

6.1.4 Generating images and contours

Let's take a look at some examples of visualizing arrays as images. The following function will create a matrix of color values for the Mandelbrot fractal, see also [20]. Here, we consider a fixed-point iteration, which depends on a complex parameter, c:

$$z_{n+1} = z_n^2 + c \quad \text{with} \quad z_0 = c \in \mathbb{C}.$$

Depending on the choice of this parameter, it may or may not create a bounded sequence of complex values, z_n.

For every value of c, we check whether z_n exceeds a prescribed bound. If it remains below the bound within `maxit` iterations, we assume the sequence to be bounded.

Note how, in the following piece of code, `meshgrid` is used to generate a matrix of complex parameter values, c:

```
def mandelbrot(h,w, maxit=20):
    X,Y = meshgrid(linspace(-2, 0.8, w), linspace(-1.4, 1.4, h))
    c = X + Y*1j
    z = c
    exceeds = zeros(z.shape, dtype=bool)

    for iteration in range(maxit):
        z  = z**2 + c
        exceeded = abs(z) > 4
        exceeds_now = exceeded & (logical_not(exceeds))
        exceeds[exceeds_now] = True
        z[exceeded] = 2   # limit the values to avoid overflow
    return exceeds

imshow(mandelbrot(400,400),cmap='gray')
axis('off')
```

The command `imshow` displays the matrix as an image. The selected color map shows the regions where the sequence appeared unbounded in white and others in black. Here, we used `axis('off')` to turn off the axis as this might not be so useful for images.

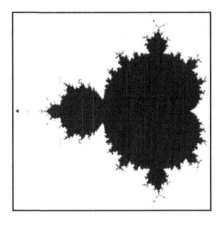

Figure 6.9: An example of using imshow to visualize a matrix as an image

By default, `imshow` uses interpolation to make the images look nicer. This is clearly seen when the matrices are small. The next figure shows the difference between using:

```
imshow(mandelbrot(40,40),cmap='gray')
```

and

```
imshow(mandelbrot(40,40), interpolation='nearest', cmap='gray')
```

In the second example, pixel values are just replicated, see [30].

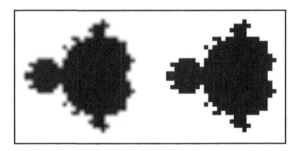

Figure 6.10: The difference between using the linear interpolation of imshow compared to using nearest-neighbor interpolation

For more details on working and plotting with images using Python.

After having seen how to make plots in the "command-way," we will consider a more object-oriented approach in the following sections. Although slightly more complicated, it opens up a vast range of applications.

6.2 Working with Matplotlib objects directly

Till now, we have used the `pyplot` module of matplotlib. This module makes it easy for us to use the most important plot commands directly. Mostly, we are interested in creating a figure and displaying it immediately. Sometimes, though, we want to generate a figure that should be modified later by changing some of its attributes. This requires us to work with graphical objects in an object-oriented way. In this section, we will present some basic steps to modify figures. For a more sophisticated object-oriented approach to plotting in Python, you have to leave `pyplot` and have to dive directly into `matplotlib` with its extensive documentation.

6.2.1 Creating axes objects

When creating a plot that should be modified later, we need references to a figure and an axes object. For this, we have to create a figure first and then define some axes and their location in the figure, and we should not forget to assign these objects to a variable:

```
fig = figure()
ax = subplot(111)
```

A figure can have several axes objects depending on the use of `subplot`. In a second step, plots are associated with a given axes object:

```
fig = figure(1)
ax = subplot(111)
x = linspace(0,2*pi,100) # We set up a function that modulates the
                         # amplitude of the sin function
amod_sin = lambda x: (1.-0.1*sin(25*x))*sin(x)
# and plot both...
ax.plot(x,sin(x),label = 'sin')
ax.plot(x, amod_sin(x), label = 'modsin')
```

Here, we used an anonymous function indicated by the keyword `lambda`. We will explain this construct later in Section 7.7, *Anonymous functions*. In fact, these two plot commands fill the list `ax.lines` with two `Lines2D` objects:

```
ax.lines #[<matplotlib.lines.Line2D at ...>, <matplotlib.lines.Line2D at
...>]
```

It is a good practice to use labels so that we can later identify objects in an easy way:

```
for il,line in enumerate(ax.lines):
    if line.get_label() == 'sin':
        break
```

We have now set things up in a way that allows further modifications. The figure we have obtained thus far is shown in *Figure 6.11, (left)*.

6.2.2 Modifying line properties

We just identified a particular line object by its label. It is an element of the list `ax.lines` with the index `il`. All of its properties are collected in a dictionary:

```
dict_keys(['marker', 'markeredgewidth', 'data', 'clip_box',
'solid_capstyle', 'clip_on', 'rasterized', 'dash_capstyle', 'path',
'ydata', 'markeredgecolor', 'xdata', 'label', 'alpha', 'linestyle',
'antialiased', 'snap', 'transform', 'url',
'transformed_clip_path_and_affine', 'clip_path', 'path_effects',
'animated', 'contains', 'fillstyle', 'sketch_params', 'xydata',
'drawstyle', 'markersize', 'linewidth', 'figure', 'markerfacecolor',
'pickradius', 'agg_filter', 'dash_joinstyle', 'color', 'solid_joinstyle',
'picker', 'markevery', 'axes', 'children', 'gid', 'zorder', 'visible',
'markerfacecoloralt'])
```

This can be obtained by the following command:

```
ax.lines[il].properties()
```

They can be changed by corresponding setter methods. Let's now change the line style of the sine curve:

```
ax.lines[il].set_linestyle('-.')
ax.lines[il].set_linewidth(2)
```

We can even modify the data, as shown:

```
ydata=ax.lines[il].get_ydata()
ydata[-1]=-0.5
ax.lines[il].set_ydata(ydata)
```

The result is shown in *Figure 6.11, (right)*:

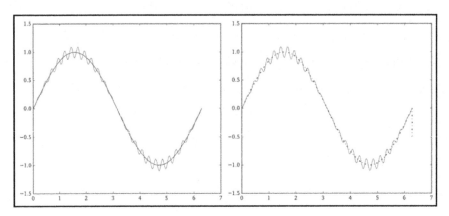

Figure 6.11: The amplitude-modulated sine function (left) and a curve with the last data point corrupted (right)

6.2.3 Making annotations

One useful axes method is `annotate`. It sets an annotation at a given position and points, with an arrow, to another position in the drawing. The arrow can be given properties in a dictionary:

```
annot1=ax.annotate('amplitude modulated\n curve', (2.1,1.0),(3.2,0.5),
        arrowprops={'width':2,'color':'k',
                    'connectionstyle':'arc3,rad=+0.5',
                    'shrink':0.05},
        verticalalignment='bottom', horizontalalignment='left',fontsize=15,
                bbox={'facecolor':'gray', 'alpha':0.1, 'pad':10})
annot2=ax.annotate('corrupted data', (6.3,-0.5),(6.1,-1.1),
        arrowprops={'width':0.5,'color':'k','shrink':0.1},
        horizontalalignment='center', fontsize=12)
```

In the first annotation example above, the arrow points to a point with the coordinates (*2.1, 1.0*), and the left-bottom coordinate of the text is (*3.2, 0.5*). If not otherwise specified, the coordinates are given in the convenient data coordinate system, which refers to the data used to generate the plots.

Furthermore, we demonstrated a couple of arrow properties specified by the dictionary `arrowprop`. You can scale the arrow by the key `shrink`. The setting `'shrink':0.05` reduces the arrow size by 5% to keep a distance to the curve it points to. You can let the arrow take the form of a spline arc or give it other shapes using the key `connectionstyle`.

Text properties, or even a bounding box around the text, can be made by extra keyword arguments to the annotate method, see *Figure 6.12, (left)*.

Experimenting with annotations sometimes requires several attempts and we need to reject some of those. Therefore, we assigned the annotate object to a variable, which allows us to remove the annotation by its `remove` method:

```
annot1.remove()
```

6.2.4 Filling areas between curves

Filling is an ideal tool for highlighting differences between curves, such as noise on top of expected data and approximations versus exact functions.

Filling is done by the axis method, `fill_between`:

```
ax.fill_between(x,y1,y2)
```

For the next figure, we used the following command:

```
axf = ax.fill_between(x, sin(x), amod_sin(x), facecolor='gray')
```

From the last chapter, we already know the NumPy method, `where`. In the context here, `where` is a very convenient parameter that requires a Boolean array to specify the additional filling conditions:

```
axf = ax.fill_between(x, sin(x), amod_sin(x),where=amod_sin(x)-sin(x) > 0,
facecolor='gray')
```

The Boolean array that selects the regions to fill is given by the condition `amod_sin(x)-sin(x) > 0`.

The next figure shows the curve with both variants of filling areas:

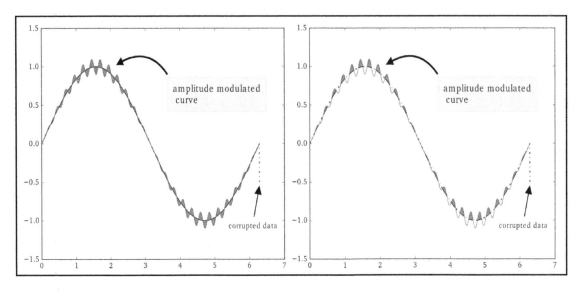

Figure 6.12: The amplitude-modulated sine function with annotations and filled areas (left), and a modified figure with only partially filled areas, by using the where parameter (right)

If you test these commands yourself, do not forget to remove the complete filling before you try out the partial filling, otherwise you will not see any change:

```
axf.remove()
```

Related filling commands are `fill` for filling polygons and `fill_betweenx` for filling the areas in horizontal directions.

6.2.5 Defining ticks and tick labels

Figures in talks, posters, and publications look much nicer if they are not overloaded with unnecessary information. You want to direct the spectator to those parts that contain the message. In our example, we clean up the picture by removing ticks from the x axis and the y axis and by introducing problem-related tick labels:

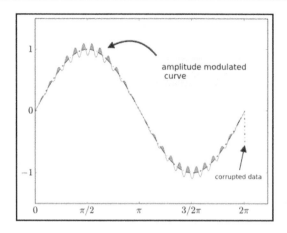

Figure 6.13: The completed example of the amplitude-modulated sine function, with annotations and filled areas and modified ticks and tick labels

The ticks in *Figure 6.13* were set by the following commands. Note the LaTeX-way of setting labels with Greek letters:

```
ax.set_xticks(array([0,pi/2,pi,3/2*pi,2*pi]))
ax.set_xticklabels(('$0$','$\pi/2$','$\pi$','$3/2 \pi$','$2
\pi$'),fontsize=18)
ax.set_yticks(array([-1.,0.,1]))
ax.set_yticklabels(('$-1$','$0$','$1$'),fontsize=18)
```

Note that we used LaTeX formatting in the strings to represent Greek letters, to set formulas correctly, and to use a LaTeX font. It is also a good practice to increase the font size so that the resulting figure can be scaled down into a
text document without affecting the readability of the axes. The final result of this guiding example is shown in *Figure 6.13*.

6.2.6 Setting spines makes your plot more instructive – a comprehensive example

Spines are the lines with ticks and labels displaying the coordinates in a figure. If you do not take a special action, Matplotlib places them as four lines – bottom, right, top, and left, forming a frame defined by the axis parameters.

Often, pictures look better when not framed, and frequently there is a more instructive place to put the spines. In this section, we demonstrate different ways to alter the position of spines.

Let's start with a guiding example, see *Figure* 6.14.

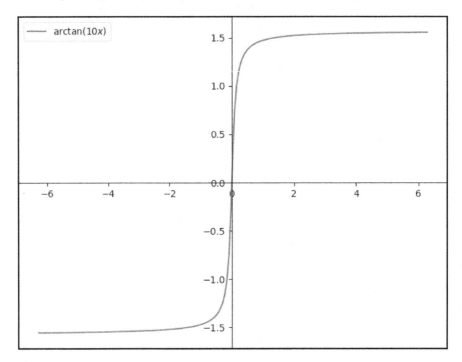

Figure 6.14: A Matplotlib figure with a non-automatic placement of the spines

In this example, we choose to display only two of the four spines.

We deselected the spines at the top and on the right by using the method `set_visible`, and positioned the left and bottom spines in data coordinates by using the method `set_position`:

```
fig = figure(1)
ax = fig.add_axes((0.,0.,1,1))
ax.spines["left"].set_position(('data',0.))
ax.spines["bottom"].set_position(("data",0.))
ax.spines["top"].set_visible(False)
ax.spines["right"].set_visible(False)
x=linspace(-2*pi,2*pi,200)
ax.plot(x,arctan(10*x), label=r'$\arctan(10 x)$')
ax.legend()
```

Spines carry ticks and tick labels. Normally, they are set automatically, but often placing them manually is advantageous.

In the following example, we even exploited the possibility of two sets of ticks, with different placement parameters. Matplotlib refers to these sets as '*minor*' and '*major*'. One of these sets was used for horizontally aligning the tick labels on the left side of the y axis:

```
ax.set_xticks([-2*pi,-pi,pi,2*pi])
ax.set_xticklabels([r"$-2\pi$",r"$-\pi$",r"$\pi$", r"$2\pi$"])
ax.set_yticks([pi/4,pi/2], minor=True)
ax.set_yticklabels([r"$\pi/4$", r"$\pi/2$"], minor=True)
ax.set_yticks([-pi/4,-pi/2], minor=False,)
ax.set_yticklabels([r"$-\pi/4$", r"$-\pi/2$"], minor=False) # major label
set
ax.tick_params(axis='both', which='major', labelsize=12)
ax.tick_params(axis='y', which='major',pad=-35) # move labels to the right
ax.tick_params(axis='both', which='minor', labelsize=12)
```

The result is shown in Figure 6.15.

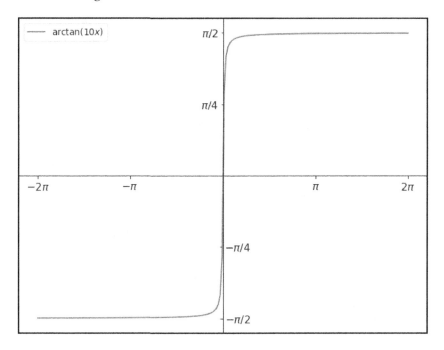

Figure 6.15: Changing the position of ticks and labels

This example can be elaborated much more by adding more axes and annotations. We refer to *Exercise 7* and *Figure 6.20*.

So far, we have considered 2D plots. We turn now in the next section to the visualization of 3D mathematical objects.

6.3 Making 3D plots

There are some useful `matplotlib` toolkits and modules that can be used for a variety of special purposes. In this section, we describe a method for producing 3D plots.

The toolkit `mplot3d` provides the 3D plotting of points, lines, contours, surfaces, and all other basic components, as well as 3D rotation and scaling. A 3D plot is generated by adding the keyword `projection='3d'` to the axes object, as shown in the following example:

```
from mpl_toolkits.mplot3d import axes3d

fig = figure()
ax = fig.gca(projection='3d')
# plot points in 3D
class1 = 0.6 * random.standard_normal((200,3))
ax.plot(class1[:,0],class1[:,1],class1[:,2],'o')
class2 = 1.2 * random.standard_normal((200,3)) + array([5,4,0])
ax.plot(class2[:,0],class2[:,1],class2[:,2],'o')
class3 = 0.3 * random.standard_normal((200,3)) + array([0,3,2])
ax.plot(class3[:,0],class3[:,1],class3[:,2],'o')
```

As you can see, you need to import the type `axes3D` from `mplot3d`. The resulting plot displays the scattered 3D data, which can be seen in *Figure 6.16*.

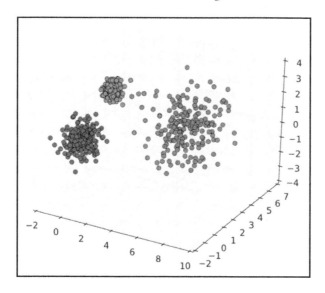

Figure 6.16: Plotting 3D data using the mplot3d toolkit

Plotting surfaces is just as easy. The following example uses the built-in function `get_test_data` to create sample data for plotting a surface. Consider the following example of a surface plot with transparency:

```
X,Y,Z = axes3d.get_test_data(0.05)

fig = figure()
ax = fig.gca(projection='3d')
# surface plot with transparency 0.5
ax.plot_surface(X,Y,Z,alpha=0.5)
```

The *alpha* value sets the transparency. The surface plot is shown *Figure 6.17.*

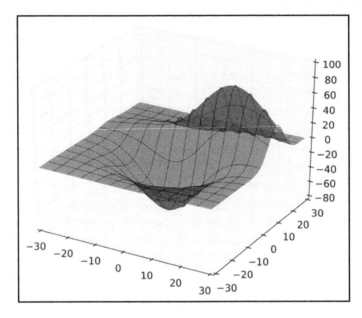

Figure 6.17: Example of plotting a surface mesh

You can also plot contours in any of the coordinate projections, as in the following example:

```
fig = figure()
ax = fig.gca(projection = '3d')
ax.plot_wireframe(X,Y,Z,rstride = 5,cstride = 5)

# plot contour projection on each axis plane
ax.contour(X,Y,Z, zdir='z',offset = -100)
ax.contour(X,Y,Z, zdir='x',offset = -40)
ax.contour(X,Y,Z, zdir='y',offset = 40)

# set axis limits
ax.set_xlim3d(-40,40)
ax.set_ylim3d(-40,40)
ax.set_zlim3d(-100,100)

# set labels
ax.set_xlabel('X axis')
ax.set_ylabel('Y axis')
ax.set_zlabel('Z axis')
```

Note the commands for setting the axis limits. The standard `matplotlib` command for setting the axis limits is `axis([-40, 40, -40, 40])`. This works fine for 2D plots. However, `axis([-40,40,-40,40,-40,40])` does not work. For 3D plots, you need to use the object-oriented version of this command, `ax.set_xlim3d(-40,40)`. The same goes for labeling the axis; note the commands for setting the labels. For 2D plots, you can do `xlabel('X axis')` and `ylabel('Y axis')`, but there is no command `zlabel`. Instead, in 3D plots, you need to use `ax.set_xlabel('X axis')` and likewise for the other labels, as shown in the preceding example.

The resulting figure from this code is the following:

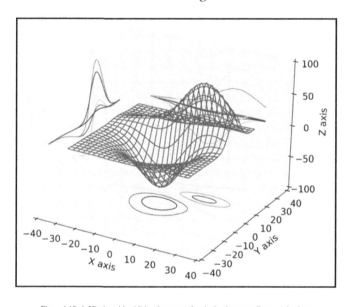

Figure 6.18: A 3D plot with additional contour plots in the three coordinate projections

There are many options for formatting the appearance of the plots, including color and the transparency of surfaces. The `mplot3d` documentation website [23], has the details.

Mathematical objects are sometimes better visualized dynamically by a sequence of pictures or even movies. This is the topic of the next section.

6.4 Making movies from plots

If you have data that evolves, you might want to save it as a movie as well as showing it in a figure window, similar to the command `savefig`. One way to do this is with the module `visvis`, see [37].

Here is a simple example of evolving a circle using an implicit representation. Let the circle be represented by the zero level,

$\{x; f(x) = 0\}$ of a function $f : \mathbb{R}^2 \to \mathbb{R}$.

Alternatively, consider the disk $\{x; f(x) \leq 0\}$ inside the zero set of f. If the value of f decreases at a rate v, then the circle will move outward at the rate $v/\|\nabla f\|$.

This can be implemented as:

```
import visvis.vvmovie as vv

# create initial function values
x = linspace(-255,255,511)
X,Y = meshgrid(x,x)
f = sqrt(X*X+Y*Y) - 40 #radius 40

# evolve and store in a list
imlist = []
for iteration in range(200):
    imlist.append((f>0)*255)
    f -= 1 # move outwards one pixel
vv.images2swf.writeSwf('circle_evolution.swf',imlist)
```

The result is a flash movie (`*.swf` file) of a growing black circle, as shown in *Figure 6.19*.

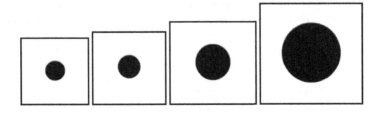

Figure 6.19: An example of evolving a circle

In this example, a list of arrays was used to create the movie. The module `visvis` can also save a GIF animation and, on certain platforms, an AVI animation (`*.gif` and `*.avi` files), and there is also the possibility of capturing movie frames directly from the figure window. These options, however, require some more packages to be installed on your system (for example, `PyOpenGL` and `PIL`, the Python Imaging Library). See the documentation on the `visvis` web page for more details.

Another option is to use `savefig` to create images, one for each frame. The following code example creates a sequence of 200 picture files, which can then be combined into a video:

```python
# create initial function values
x = linspace(-255,255,511)
X,Y = meshgrid(x,x)
f = sqrt(X*X+Y*Y) - 40 #radius 40
for iteration in range(200):
    imshow((f>0)*255, aspect='auto')
    gray()
    axis('off')
    savefig('circle_evolution_{:d}.png'.format(iteration))
    f -= 1
```

These images can then be combined using standard video editing software, for example, Mencoder or ImageMagick. This approach has the advantage that you can make high-resolution videos by saving high-resolution images.

6.5 Summary

A graphical representation is the most compact form in which to present mathematical results or the behavior of an algorithm. This chapter provided you with the basic tools for plotting and introduced you to a more sophisticated way to work with graphical objects, such as figures, axes, and lines in an object-oriented way.

In this chapter, you learned how to make plots, not only classical *x/y* plots, but also 3D plots and histograms. We gave you an appetizer on making films. You also saw how to modify plots, considering them to be graphical objects with related methods and attributes that can be set, deleted, or modified.

6.6 Exercises

Ex. 1: Write a function that plots an ellipse given its center coordinates (x,y), the half axis a, and b rotation angle θ.

Ex. 2: Write a short program that takes a 2D array, for example, the preceding Mandelbrot contour image, and iteratively replace each value by the average of its neighbors. Update a contour plot of the array in a figure window to animate the evolution of the contours. Explain the behavior.

Ex. 3: Consider an $N \times N$ matrix or image with integer values. The mapping

$$I : (x, y) \mapsto (2x + y, x + y) \bmod N$$

is an example of a mapping of a toroidal square grid of points onto itself. This has the interesting property that it distorts the image by shearing and then moving the pieces outside the image back using the modulo function, mod. Applied iteratively, this results in randomizing the image in a way that eventually returns the original. Implement the following sequence,

$$I^{(m+1)}(x, y) = I^{(m)}(2x + y \bmod N, x + y \bmod N),$$

and save out the first N steps to files or plot them in a figure window.

As an example image, you can use the classic 512×512 Lena test image from `scipy.misc`:

```
from scipy.misc import lena
I = lena()
```

The result should look like this:

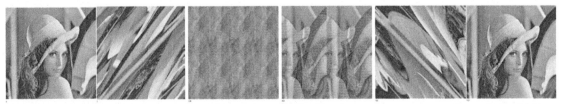

Compute the x and y mappings and use array indexing (see `Section 5.3`: *Array indexing*) to copy the pixel values.

Ex. 4: Reading and plotting on images. SciPy comes with the function `imread` (in the `scipy.misc` module) for reading images (see `Section 14.6`: *Reading and Writing Images*). Write a short program that reads an image from file and plots the image contour at a given gray-level value overlaid on the original image. You can get a grey-level version of the image by averaging the color channels like this: `mean(im, axis=2)`

Ex. 5: Image edges. The zero crossings of the 2D Laplacian are a good indication of image edges. Modify the program in the previous exercise to use the `gaussian_laplace` or `laplace` function from the `scipy.ndimage` module to compute the 2D Laplacian and overlay the edges on top of the image.

Ex. 6: Reformulate the Mandelbrod fractal example `Section 6.1.4`: *Generating images and contours* by using `orgid` instead of `meshgrid`. See also the explanation of `ogrid` in `Section 5.5.3`, *Typical examples*. What is the difference between `orgid`, `mgrid`, and `meshgrid`?

Ex. 7: In *Figure 6.20*, the use of the arctan function for approximating a jump (Heaviside function) is studied. A section of this curve is zoomed in to visualize the quality of the approximation. Reproduce this picture by means of your own code.

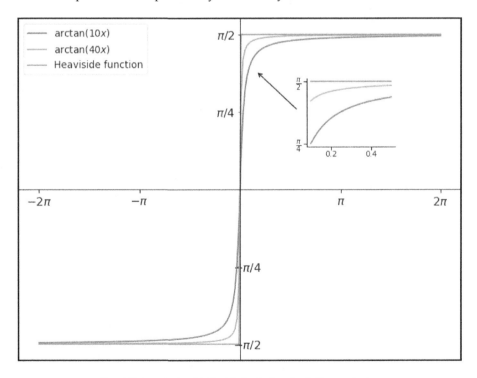

Figure 6.20: Approximation of the Heaviside function (jump function) by arctan functions

7
Functions

This chapter introduces functions, a fundamental building block in programming. We show how to define them, how to handle input and output, how to properly use them, and how to treat them as objects.

The following topics are covered in this chapter:

- Functions in mathematics and functions in Python
- Parameters and arguments
- Return values
- Recursive functions
- Function documentation
- Functions are objects
- Anonymous functions – the keyword `lambda`
- Functions as decorators

7.1 Functions in mathematics and functions in Python

In mathematics, a function is written as a map that uniquely assigns to every element x from the domain D a corresponding element y from the range R.

This is expressed by $f : D \to R$.

Alternatively, when considering particular elements x and y, you write $f : x \mapsto y$.

Here, f is called the name of the function and $f(x)$ is its value when applied to x. Here, x is sometimes called the argument of f. Let's first look at an example before considering functions in Python.

For example, $D = \mathbb{R} \times \mathbb{R}$ and $y = f(x_1, x_2) = x_1 - x_2$. This function maps two real numbers to their difference.

In mathematics, functions can have numbers, vectors, matrices, and even other functions as arguments. Here is an example of a function with mixed arguments:

$$I(f, a, b) = \int_a^b f(x)\mathrm{d}x$$

In this case, a real number is returned. When working with functions, we have to distinguish between two different steps:

- The definition of the function
- The evaluation of the function, that is, the computation of $f(x)$ for a given value of x

The first step is done once, while the second can be performed many times for various arguments.

Functions in programming languages follow mainly the same concept and apply it to a wide range of types of input arguments, for example, strings, lists, floats, or simply any object. We demonstrate a definition of a function by considering the given example again:

```
def subtract(x1, x2):
    return x1 - x2
```

The keyword `def` indicates that we are going to define a function. `subtract` is the function's name and `x1` and `x2` are its parameters. The colon indicates that we are using a block command. The value that is returned by the function follows the keyword `return`.

Now, we can evaluate this function. The function is called with its parameters replaced by input arguments:

```
r = subtract(5.0, 4.3)
```

The result `0.7` is computed and assigned to the variable `r`.

7.2 Parameters and arguments

When defining a function, its input variables are called the *parameters* of the function. The input used when executing the function is called its *argument*.

7.2.1 Passing arguments – by position and by keyword

We will consider the previous example again, where the function takes two parameters, namely x1 and x2.

Their names serve to distinguish the two numbers, which in this case cannot be interchanged without altering the result. The first parameter defines the number from which the second parameter is subtracted. When subtract is called, every parameter is replaced by an argument. Only the order of the arguments matters; the arguments can be any object. For instance, we may call the following:

```
z = 3
e = subtract(5,z)
```

Besides this standard way of calling a function, which is bypassing the arguments by position, it might sometimes be convenient to pass arguments using keywords. The names of the parameters are the keywords; consider the following instance:

```
z = 3
e = subtract(x2 = z, x1 = 5)
```

Here, the arguments are assigned to the parameters by name and not by position in the call. Both ways of calling a function can be combined so that the arguments given by position come first and the arguments given by keyword follow last. We show this by using the function plot, which was described in Section 6.1: *Basic plotting*:

```
plot(xp, yp, linewidth = 2, label = 'y-values')
```

7.2.2 Changing arguments

The purpose of parameters is to provide the function with the necessary input data. Changing the value of the parameter inside the function normally has no effect on its value outside the function:

```
def subtract(x1, x2):
    z = x1 - x2
    x2 = 50.
    return z
a = 20.
b = subtract(10, a)    # returns -10
a     # still has the value 20
```

This applies to all immutable arguments, such as strings, numbers, and tuples. The situation is different if mutable arguments, such as lists or dictionaries, are changed.

For example, passing mutable input arguments to a function and changing them inside the function can change them outside the function too:

```
def subtract(x):
    z = x[0] - x[1]
    x[1] = 50.
    return z
a = [10,20]
b = subtract(a)    # returns -10
a    # is now [10, 50.0]
```

Such a function misuses its arguments to return results. We strongly dissuade you from such constructions and recommend that you do not change input arguments inside the function (for more information, see Section 7.2.4: *Default arguments*).

7.2.3 Access to variables defined outside the local namespace

Python allows functions to access variables defined in any of its enclosing program units. These are called global variables, in contrast to local variables. The latter is only accessible within the function. For example, consider the following code:

```
import numpy as np # here the variable np is defined
def sqrt(x):
    return np.sqrt(x) # we use np inside the function
```

This feature should not be abused. The following code is an example of what not to do:

```
a = 3
def multiply(x):
    return a * x # bad style: access to the variable a defined outside
```

When changing the variable a, the function `multiply` tacitly changes its behavior:

```
a=3
multiply(4)   # returns 12
a=4
multiply(4)   # returns 16
```

It is much better, in that case, to provide the variable as a parameter through the argument list:

```
def multiply(x, a):
    return a * x
```

Global variables can be useful when working with closures; see also the related example in `Section 7.7`: *Anonymous functions – the keyword lambda.*

7.2.4 Default arguments

Some functions can have many parameters, and among them, some might only be of interest in nonstandard situations. It would be practical if arguments could automatically be set to standard (default) values.

We demonstrate the use of default arguments by looking at the command `norm` in the module `scipy.linalg`. It computes various norms of matrices and vectors. More on matrix norms can be found in [10 , §2.3].

The following calls for computing the Frobenius **norm** of the 3×3 identity matrix are equivalent:

```
import scipy.linalg as sl
sl.norm(identity(3))
sl.norm(identity(3), ord = 'fro')
sl.norm(identity(3), 'fro')
```

Note that in the first call, no information about the keyword `ord` is given. How does Python know that it should compute the Frobenius norm and not another norm, for example, the Euclidean 2-norm?

The answer to the previous question is the use of default values. A default value is a value already given by the function definition. If the function is called without providing this argument, Python uses the value that the programmer provided when the function was defined.

Suppose we call the function `subtract` and provide it with only one argument; we would get an error message:

```
TypeError: subtract() takes exactly 2 arguments (1 given)
```

To allow the omission of the argument $x2$, the definition of the function has to provide a *default value*, for example:

```
def subtract(x1, x2 = 0):
    return x1 - x2
```

Default arguments are given in the definition of the function by assigning a value to one of the parameters.

To summarize, arguments can be given as positional arguments and keyword arguments. All positional arguments have to be given first. You do not need to provide all keyword arguments as long as those omitted arguments have default values in the function definition.

Beware of mutable default arguments

The default arguments are set upon function definition. Changing mutable arguments inside a function has a side effect when working with default values, for example:

```
def my_list(x1, x2 = []):
    x2.append(x1)
    return x2
my_list(1)  # returns [1]
my_list(2)  # returns [1,2]
```

Recall, lists are mutable objects.

7.2.5 Variable number of arguments

Lists and dictionaries may be used to define or call functions with a variable number of arguments. Let's define a list and a dictionary as follows:

```
data = [[1,2],[3,4]]
style = dict({'linewidth':3,'marker':'o','color':'green'})
```

Then we can call the `plot` function using starred (*) arguments:

```
plot(*data,**style)
```

A variable name prefixed by *, such as *data in the preceding example, means that a list that gets unpacked to provide the function with its arguments. In this way, a list generates positional arguments. Similarly, a variable name prefixed by **, such as **style in the example, unpacks a dictionary to keyword arguments; see *Figure 7.1*:

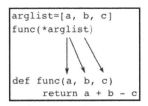

Figure 7.1: Starred arguments in function calls

You might also want to use the reverse process, where all given positional arguments are packed into a list and all keyword arguments are packed into a dictionary when passed to a function. In the function definition, this is indicated by parameters prefixed by * and **, respectively. You will often find the parameters *args and **kwargs in code documentation; see *Figure 7.2*.

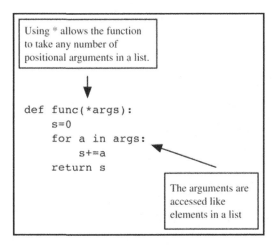

Figure 7.2: Starred arguments in function definitions

7.3 Return values

A function in Python always returns a single object. If a function has to return more than one object, these are packed and returned as a single tuple object.

For instance, the following function takes a complex number z and returns its polar coordinate representation as magnitude r and angle φ:

```
def complex_to_polar(z):
    r = sqrt(z.real ** 2 + z.imag ** 2)
    phi = arctan2(z.imag, z.real)
    return (r,phi)  # here the return object is formedcite
```

(See also Euler's formula, $z = re^{i\varphi}$.)

Here, we used the NumPy function `sqrt(x)` for the square root of a number `x` and `arctan2(x,y)` for the expression $\tan^{-1}(x/y)$.

Let's try our function:

```
z = 3 + 5j  # here we define a complex number
a = complex_to_polar(z)
r = a[0]
phi = a[1]
```

The last three statements can be written more elegantly in a single line:

```
r,phi = complex_to_polar(z)
```

We can test our function by calling `polar_to_comp` defined in *Exercise 1* in the *Exercises* section.

If a function has no `return` statement, it returns the value `None`. There are many cases where a function does not need to return any value. This could be because the variables passed to a function may be subject to modification. Consider, for instance, the following function:

```
def append_to_list(L, x):
    L.append(x)
```

The preceding function does not return anything because it modifies one of the objects that is given as a mutable argument. There are many methods that behave in the same way. To mention the list methods only, the methods `append`, `extend`, `reverse`, and `sort` do not return anything (that is, they return `None`). When an object is modified by a method in this way, the modification is called *in place*. It is difficult to know whether a method changes an object, except by looking at the code or the documentation.

Another reason for a function, or a method, not to return anything is when it prints out a message or writes to a file.

The execution stops at the first occurring `return` statement. Lines after that statement are dead code that will never be executed:

```
def function_with_dead_code(x):
    return 2 * x
    y = x ** 2 # these two lines ...
    return y   # ... are never executed!
```

7.4 Recursive functions

In mathematics, many functions are defined recursively. In this section, we will show how this concept can be used even when programming a function. This makes the relation of the program to its mathematical counterpart very clear, which may ease the readability of the program.

Nevertheless, we recommend using this programming technique with care, especially within scientific computing. In most applications, the more straightforward iterative approach is more efficient. This will become immediately clear from the following example.

Chebyshev polynomials are defined by a three-term recursion:

$$T_n(x) = 2xT_{n-1}(x) - T_{n-2}(x)$$

Such a recursion needs to be initialized, that is, $T_0(x) = 1, \ T_1(x) = x$.

In Python, this *three-term recursion* can be realized by the following function definition:

```
def chebyshev(n, x):
    if n == 0:
        return 1.
    elif n == 1:
        return x
```

```
        else:
            return 2. * x * chebyshev(n - 1, x) \
                             - chebyshev(n - 2 ,x)
```

To compute $T_5(0.52)$, the function is then called like this:

```
chebyshev(5, 0.52) # returns 0.39616645119999994
```

This example also illustrates the risk of dramatically wasting computation time. The number of function evaluations increases exponentially with the recursion level and most of these evaluations are just duplicates of previous computations. While it might be tempting to use recursive programs for demonstrating the strong relation between code and mathematical definition, production code will avoid this programming technique (see also *Exercise 6* in the *Exercises* section). We also refer to a technique called memoization that combines recursive programming with a caching technique to save replicated function evaluations, see [22].

A recursive function usually has a level parameter. In the previous example, it is n. It is used to control the function's two main parts:

- The base case; here, the first two if branches
- The recursive body, in which the function itself is called once or several times with smaller-level parameters

The number of levels passed by the execution of a recursive function is called the recursion depth. This quantity should not be too large; otherwise, the computation might no longer be efficient and, in the ultimate case, the following error will be raised:

```
RuntimeError: maximum recursion depth exceeded
```

The maximal recursion depth depends on the memory of the computer you use. This error also occurs when the initialization step is missing in the function definition. We encourage the use of recursive programs for very small recursion depths only (for more information, see Section 9.7.2: *Recursion*).

7.5 Function documentation

You should document your functions using a string at the beginning. This string is called a *docstring*:

```
def newton(f, x0):
    """
    Newton's method for computing a zero of a function
```

```
on input:
f   (function) given function f(x)
x0 (float) initial guess
on return:
y   (float) the approximated zero of f
"""

...
```

When calling `help(newton)`, you get this docstring displayed together with the call of this function:

```
Help on function newton in module __main__:

newton(f, x0)
    Newton's method for computing a zero of a function
    on input:
    f   (function) given function f(x)
    x0 (float) initial guess
    on return:
    y   (float) the approximated zero of f
```

The docstring is internally saved as an attribute, `__doc__`, of the given function. In the example, it is `newton.__doc__`. The minimal information you should provide in a docstring is the purpose of the function and the description of the input and output objects. There are tools to automatically generate full code documentation by collecting all docstrings in your program (for more information, see the documentation of Sphinx, [32]).

7.6 Functions are objects

Functions are objects, like everything else in Python. You may pass functions as arguments, change their names, or delete them. For example:

```
def square(x):
    """
    Return the square of x
    """
    return x ** 2
square(4) # 16
sq = square # now sq is the same as square
sq(4) # 16
del square # square doesn't exist anymore
print(newton(sq, .2)) # passing as argument
```

Passing functions as arguments is very common when applying algorithms in scientific computing. The function `fsolve` in `scipy.optimize` for computing a zero of a given function or `quad` in `scipy.integrate` for computing integrals are typical examples.

A function itself can have a different number of arguments with differing types. So, when passing your function `f` to another function `g` as an argument, make sure that `f` has exactly the form described in the docstring of `g`.

The docstring of `fsolve` gives information about its parameter `func`:

```
fun c -- A Python function or method which takes at least one
              (possibly vector) argument.
```

7.6.1 Partial application

Let's start with an example of a function with two variables.

The function $(\omega, t) \mapsto f(\omega, t) = \sin(2\pi\omega t)$ can be viewed as a function in two variables. Often you consider ω not as a free variable but as a fixed parameter of a family of functions f_ω:

$$t \mapsto f_\omega(t) = \sin(2\pi\omega t)$$

This interpretation reduces a function in two variables to a function in one variable t given a fixed parameter value ω. The process of defining a new function by fixing (freezing) one or several parameters of a function is called partial application.

Partial applications are easily created using the Python module `functools`, which provides a function called `partial` for precisely this purpose. We illustrate this by constructing a function that returns a sine for a given frequency:

```
import functools
def sin_omega(t, freq):
    return sin(2 * pi * freq * t)

def make_sine(frequency):
    return functools.partial(sin_omega, freq = frequency)

fomega=make_sine(0.25)
fomega(3) # returns -1.0
```

In the last line, the newly created function is evaluated at $t = 3$.

7.6.2 Using closures

Using the view that functions are objects, partial applications can be realized by writing a function, which itself returns a new function, with a reduced number of input arguments. For instance, the function `make_sine` could be defined as follows:

```
def make_sine(freq):
    "Make a sine function with frequency freq"
    def mysine(t):
        return sin_omega(t, freq)
    return mysine
```

In this example, the inner function `mysine` has access to the variable `freq`; it is neither a local variable of this function nor is it passed to it via the argument list. Python allows such a construction, see `Section` 13.1, *Namespaces*.

7.7 Anonymous functions – the keyword lambda

The keyword `lambda` is used in Python to define anonymous functions, that is, functions without a name and described by a single expression. You might just want to perform an operation on a function that can be expressed by a simple expression without naming this function and without defining this function by a lengthy `def` block.

The name *lambda* originates from a special branch of calculus and mathematical logic, the λ-calculus.

We demonstrate the use of `lambda`-functions by numerically evaluating the following integral:

$$\int_0^1 x^2 + 5 \, dx$$

We use SciPy's function `quad`, which requires as its first argument the function to be integrated and the integration bounds as the next two arguments. Here, the function to be integrated is just a simple one-liner and we use the keyword `lambda` to define it:

```
import scipy.integrate as si
si.quad(lambda x: x ** 2 + 5, 0, 1)
```

The syntax is as follows:

```
lambda parameter_list: expression
```

The definition of the function `lambda` can only consist of a single expression and, in particular, cannot contain loops. `lambda` functions are, just like other functions, objects and can be assigned to variables:

```
parabola = lambda x: x ** 2 + 5
parabola(3) # gives 14
```

7.7.1 The lambda construction is always replaceable

It is important to note that the `lambda` construction is only syntactic sugar in Python. Any `lambda` construction may be replaced by an explicit function definition:

```
parabola = lambda x: x**2+5
# the following code is equivalent
def parabola(x):
    return x ** 2 + 5
```

The main reason to use this construction is for very simple functions when a full function definition would be too cumbersome.

`lambda` functions provide a third way to make closures as we demonstrate by continuing with the previous example, $f(x, \omega) = \sin(wt)$.

We use the function `sin_omega` from `Section 7.6.1`, *Partial Application,* to compute the integral of the sine function for various frequencies:

```
import scipy.integrate as si
for iteration in range(3):
    print(si.quad(lambda x: sin_omega(x, iteration*pi), 0, pi/2.) )
```

7.8 Functions as decorators

In `Section 7.6.1`: *Partial application,* we saw how a function can be used to modify another function. A *decorator* is a syntax element in Python that conveniently allows us to alter the behavior of a function without changing the definition of the function itself. Let's start with the following situation.

Assume that we have a function that determines tcitehe degree of sparsity of a matrix:

```
def how_sparse(A):
    return len(A.reshape(-1).nonzero()[0])
```

This function returns an error if it is not called with an array object as input. More precisely, it will not work with an object that does not implement the method `reshape`. For instance, the function `how_sparse` will not work with a list, because lists have no method `reshape`. The following helper function modifies any function with one input parameter so that it tries to make a type conversion to an array:

```
def cast2array(f):
    def new_function(obj):
        fA = f(array(obj))
        return fA
    return new_function
```

Thus, the modified function `how_sparse = cast2array(how_sparse)` can be applied to any object that can be cast to an array. The same functionality is achieved if the definition of `how_sparse` is decorated with this type conversion function:

```
@cast2array def how_sparse(A): return len(A.reshape(-1).nonzero()[0])
```

To define a decorator, you need a callable object such as a function that modifies the definition of the function to be decorated. The main purposes are:

- To increase code readability by separating parts from a function that do not directly serve its functionality (for example, memoizing)
- To put common preamble and epilogue parts of a family of similar functions in a common place (for example, type checking)
- To be able to easily switch off and on additional functionalities of a function (for example, test prints or tracing)

It is recommended also to consider `functools.wraps`, see also [8].

7.9 Summary

Functions are not only the ideal tools for making your program modular, but they also reflect mathematical thinking. You learned the syntax of function definitions and how to distinguish between defining and calling a function.

We considered functions as objects that can be modified by other functions. When working with functions, it is important to be familiar with the notion of the scope of a variable and how information is passed into a function by parameters.

Sometimes, it is convenient to define functions on the fly with so-called anonymous functions. For this, we introduced the keyword `lambda`.

7.10 Exercises

Ex 1: Write a function `polar_to_comp`, which takes two arguments r and φ and returns the complex number $z = re^{i\varphi}$. Use the NumPy function `exp` for the exponential function.

Ex 2: In the description of the Python module `functools`, [8], you find the following Python function:

```
def partial(func, *args, **keywords):
    def newfunc(*fargs, **fkeywords):
        newkeywords = keywords.copy()
        newkeywords.update(fkeywords)
        return func(*(args + fargs), **newkeywords)
    newfunc.func = func
    newfunc.args = args
    newfunc.keywords = keywords
    return newfunc
```

Explain and test this function.

Ex 3: Write a decorator for the function `how_sparse`, which cleans the input matrix A by setting the elements that are less than `1.e-16` to zero (consider the example in `Section 7.8`: *Functions as decorators*).

Ex 4: A continuous function f with $f(a)f(b) < 0$ changes its sign in the interval $[a, b]$ and has at least one root (zero) in this interval. Such a root can be found with the *bisection method*. This method starts from the given interval. Then it investigates the sign changes in the subintervals

$$[a, \frac{a+b}{2}] \text{ and } [\frac{a+b}{2}, b].$$

If the sign changes in the first subinterval, b is redefined to be:

$$b := \frac{a+b}{2}$$

Otherwise, it is redefined in the same manner to:

$$a := \frac{a+b}{2}$$

The process is repeated until the length of the interval, $b - a$, is less than a given tolerance.

- Implement this method as a function that takes as arguments:
  - The function f
  - The initial interval $[a, b]$
  - The tolerance
- This function `bisec` should return the final interval and its midpoint.
- Test the method with the function `arctan` and also with the polynomial $f(x) = 3x^2 - 5$ in the interval $[1.1, 1.4]$, and alternatively in $[1.3, 1.4]$.

Ex. 5: The greatest common divisor of two integers can be computed with *Euclid's algorithm* described by the following recursion:

$$gcd(a, b) = \begin{cases} a & \text{if} \quad b = 0 \\ gcd(b, a \bmod b) & \text{otherwise} \end{cases}$$

Write a function that computes the greatest common divisor of two integers. Write another function that computes the least common multiple of these numbers using the relation:

$$lcm(a, b) = \frac{|ab|}{gcd(a, b)}$$

Ex. 6: Study the recursive implementation of Chebyshev polynomials. Consider the example in `Section 7.4`: *Recursive functions*. Rewrite the program in a non-recursive way and study computation time versus polynomial degree (see also the module `timeit`).

8
Classes

In mathematics, when we write $\sin$, we refer to a mathematical object for which we know many methods from elementary calculus. For example:

- We might want to evaluate $\sin(x)$ at $x = 0.5$, that is, compute $\sin(0.5)$, which returns a real number.
- We might want to compute its derivative, which gives us another mathematical object, **cos**.
- We might want to compute the first three coefficients of its Taylor polynomial.

These methods may be applied not only to **sin** but also to other sufficiently smooth functions. There are, however, other mathematical objects, for example, the number 5, for which these methods would make no sense.

Objects that have the same methods are grouped together in abstract classes, for example, functions. Every statement and every method that can be applied to functions in general applies in particular to **sin** or **cos**.

Other examples for such classes might be a rational number, for which a denominator and numerator method exist; an interval, which has a left and right boundary method; an infinite sequence, for which we can ask whether it has a limit, and so on.

In this case, $\sin$ is called an *instance* of the class. The mathematical phrase *Let g be a function...* is, in this context, called **instantiation**. Here, g is the name of the function, one of many *attributes* that can be assigned to it. Another attribute might be its domain.

The mathematical object $p(x) = 2x^2 - 5$ is just like the sine function. Every function method applies to p, but we can also define special methods for p. We might, for instance, ask for p's coefficients. These methods can be used to define the class of polynomials. As polynomials are functions, they additionally *inherit* all methods of the function class.

In mathematics, we often use the same operator symbol for completely different operations. For instance, in $5 + 4$ and $\sin + \cos$, the operator symbol + has different meanings. By using the same symbol, similarities to corresponding mathematical operations are emphasized. We have introduced these terms from object-oriented programming by applying them to mathematical examples, such as classes, instance and instantiation, inheritance, methods, attributes, and operator overloading.

Specifically, in this chapter, we are going to cover the following topics:

- Introduction to classes
- Bound and unbound methods
- Class attributes and class methods
- Subclasses and inheritance
- Encapsulation
- Classes as decorators

In this chapter, we will show how these concepts are used in Python and start with some fundamentals.

8.1 Introduction to classes

This section introduces the most common terms of classes and their realization in Python.

First, we set up a guiding example.

8.1.1 A guiding example: Rational numbers

We will illustrate the concept of classes with the example of rational numbers, that is, numbers of the form $q = q_N / q_D$, where q_N and q_D are integers.

The following figure gives an example of a class declaration:

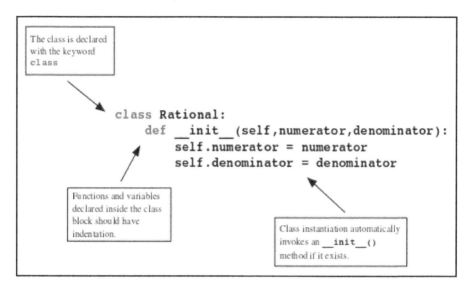

Figure 8.1: Example of a class declaration

We use rational numbers here only as an example of the class concept. For future work in Python with rational numbers, use the Python module `fractions`.

8.1.2 Defining a class and making an instance

The definition of a class is made by a block command with the keyword `class`, the name of the class, and some statements in the block (see *Figure 8.1*):

```
class RationalNumber:
    pass
```

An instance of this class (or in other words, an object of the type `RationalNumber`) is created by `r = RationalNumber()` and the query `type(r)` returns the answer, `<class'__main__.RationalNumber'>`. If we want to investigate whether an object is an instance of this class, we can use the following lines:

```
if isinstance(r, RationalNumber):
    print('Indeed, it belongs to the class RationalNumber')
```

So far, we have generated an object of the type `RationalNumber` that has no data yet. Furthermore, there are no methods defined to perform operations with these objects. This is the subject of the next sections.

8.1.3 The __init__ method

Now we provide our example class with some attributes, that is, we give it defining data. In our case, this data will be the values of the denominator and the numerator. To this end, we have to define a method, __init__, used to initialize the class with these values:

```
class RationalNumber:
    def __init__(self, numerator, denominator):
        self.numerator = numerator
        self.denominator = denominator
```

Before we explain the special function __init__, which we added to the class, we demonstrate the instantiation of a `RationalNumber` object:

```
q = RationalNumber(10, 20)      # Defines a new object
q.numerator                     # returns 10
q.denominator                   # returns 20
```

A new object of type `RationalNumber` is created by using the class name as if it were a function. This statement does two things:

1. It first creates an empty object, q.
2. Then it applies the __init__ function to it; that is, q.__init__(10, 20) is executed.

The first parameter of __init__ refers to the new object itself. On a function call, this first parameter is replaced by the object's instance. This applies to all methods of the class and not just to the special method __init__. The special role of this first parameter is reflected by the convention to name it `self`.

In the previous example, the function __init__ defines two attributes of the new object, `numerator` and `denominator`.

8.1.4 Attributes and methods

One of the main reasons for working with classes is that objects can be grouped together and bound to a common object. We saw this already when looking at rational numbers; `denominator` and `numerator` are two objects that we bound to an instance of the class `RationalNumber`. They are called **attributes of the instance**. The fact that an object is an attribute of a class instance becomes apparent from the way they are referenced, which we have used tacitly before:

```
_<object>.attribute
```

Here are some examples of instantiation and attribute reference:

```
q = RationalNumber(3, 5)  # instantiation
q.numerator               # attribute access
q.denominator

a = array([1, 2])         # instantiation
a.shape

z = 5 + 4j                # instantiationstepz.imag
```

Once an instance is defined, we can set, change, or delete attributes of that particular instance. The syntax is the same as for regular variables:

```
q = RationalNumber(3, 5)
r = RationalNumber(7, 3)
q.numerator = 17
del r.denominator
```

Changing or deleting an attribute may have undesired side effects, which might even render the object useless. We will be learning more about this in Section 8.2: *Attributes that depend on each other*. As functions are objects too, we can also use functions as attributes; they are called methods of the instance:

```
<object>.method(<arguments...>)
```

For example, let's add a method to the class `RationalNumber` that converts the number to a float:

```
class RationalNumber:
    ...
    def convert2float(self):
        return float(self.numerator) / float(self.denominator)
```

Again, this method takes as its first (and only) argument `self`, the reference to the object itself. We use this method with a regular function call:

```
q = RationalNumber(10, 20)    # Defines a new object
q.convert2float() # returns 0.5
```

This is equivalent to the following call:

```
RationalNumber.convert2float(q)
```

Note again that the object instance is inserted as the first argument of the function. This use of the first argument explains the error message that would occur if this particular method were used with additional arguments. The call `q.convert2float(15)` provokes this error message:

```
TypeError: convert2float() takes exactly 1 argument (2 given)
```

The reason this does not work is that `q.convert2float(15)` is precisely equivalent to `RationalNumber.comvert2float(q,15)`, which fails because `RationalNumber.convert2float` takes only one argument.

8.1.5 Special methods

The special method `__repr__` gives us the ability to define the way the object is represented in a Python interpreter. For rational numbers, a possible definition of this method could be as follows:

```
class RationalNumber:
    ...
    def __repr__(self):
        return f'{self.numerator} / {self.denominator}'
```

With this method defined, just typing `q` returns `10 / 20`.

We would like to have a method that performs the addition of two rational numbers. A first attempt could result in a method like this:

```
class RationalNumber:
    ...
    def add(self, other):
        p1, q1 = self.numerator, self.denominator
        if isinstance(other, int):
            p2, q2 = other, 1
        else:
            p2, q2 = other.numerator, other.denominator
        return RationalNumber(p1 * q2 + p2 * q1, q1 * q2)
```

A call to this method takes the following form:

```
q = RationalNumber(1, 2)
p = RationalNumber(1, 3)
q.add(p)    # returns the RationalNumber for 5/6
```

It would be much nicer if we could write q + p instead. But so far, the plus sign is not defined for the type RationalNumber. This is done by using the special method __add__. So, just renaming add to __add__ allows using the plus sign for rational numbers:

```
q = RationalNumber(1, 2)
p = RationalNumber(1, 3)
q + p # RationalNumber(5, 6)
```

The expression q + p is, in fact, an alias for the expression q.__add__(p). In *Table 8.1*, you find special methods for binary operators such as +, −, or *:

Operator	Method	Operator	Method
+	__add__	+=	__iadd__
*	__mul__	*=	__imul__
−	__sub__	−=	__isub__
/	__truediv__	/=	__itruediv__
//	__floordiv__	//=	__ifloordiv__
**	__pow__		
==	__eq__	!=	__ne__
<=	__le__	<	__lt__
>=	__ge__	>	__gt__
()	__call__	[]	__getitem__

Table 8.1: Some Python operators and corresponding class methods

The implementation of those operators for a new class is called **operator overloading**. Another example of operator overloading is a method for examining whether two rational numbers are the same:

```
class RationalNumber:
    ...
    def __eq__(self, other):
        return self.denominator * other.numerator == \
            self.numerator * other.denominator
```

It is used like this:

```
p = RationalNumber(1, 2) # instantiation
q = RationalNumber(2, 4) # instantiation
p == q # True
```

Operations between objects belonging to different classes need special care:

```
p = RationalNumber(1, 2) # instantiation
p + 5   # corresponds to p.__add__(5)
5 + p   # returns an error
```

By default, the operator + invokes the left operand's method, __add__. We programmed it so that it allows both objects of type int and objects of type RationalNumber. In the statement 5+p, the operands are commuted and the method __add__ of the built-in type int is invoked. This method returns an error as it cannot know how to handle rational numbers. This case can be handled by the method __radd__, with which we now will equip the class RationalNumber. The method __radd__ is called **reverse addition**.

Reverse operations

If operations such as + are applied to two operands of different types, the corresponding method (in this case, __add__) of the left operand is invoked first. If this raises an exception, the reverse method (here, __radd__) of the right operand is called. If this method does not exist, a TypeError exception is raised.

In order to enable the operation $5 + p$, where p is an instance of RationalNumber, we define __radd__ as:

```
class RationalNumber:
    ....
    def __radd__(self, other):
        return self + other
```

Note that __radd__ interchanges the order of the arguments; self is the object of type RationalNumber while other is the object that has to be converted.

Methods mimicking function calls and iterables

Using a class instance together with parentheses or brackets, () or [], invokes a call to one of the special methods __call__ or __getitem__, giving the instance the behavior of a function or of an iterable; see also *Table 8.1*.

```
class Polynomial:
    ...
    def __call__(self, x):
        return self.eval(x)
```

Which now may be used as follows:

```
p = Polynomial(...)     # Creating a polynomial object
p(3.) # value of p at 3.
```

The special method __getitem__ makes sense if the class provides an iterator (it is recommended that you review Section 9.2.1: *Generators* before you consider the following example).

The recursion $u_{i+1} = a_1 u_i + a_0 u_{i-1}$ is called a **three-term recursion**. It plays an important role in applied mathematics, in particular in the construction of orthogonal polynomials. We can set up a three-term recursion as a class in the following way:

```
import itertools

class  Recursion3Term:
    def __init__(self, a0, a1, u0, u1):
        self.coeff = [a1, a0]
        self.initial = [u1, u0]
    def __iter__(self):
        u1, u0 = self.initial
        yield u0  # (see also Iterators section in Chapter 9)
        yield u1
        a1, a0 = self.coeff
        while True :
            u1, u0 = a1 * u1 + a0 * u0, u1
            yield u1
    def __getitem__(self, k):
        return list(itertools.islice(self, k, k + 1))[0]
```

Here, the method __iter__ defines a generator object, which allows us to use an instance of the class as an iterator:

```
r3 = Recursion3Term(-0.35, 1.2, 1, 1)
for i, r in enumerate(r3):
    if i == 7:
        print(r)   # returns 0.194167
        break
```

The method __getitem__ enables us to directly access the iterations as if r3 were a list:

```
r3[7] # returns 0.194167
```

Note that we used itertools.islice when coding __getitem__ (see Section 9.3.2: *Iterator tools* for more information).

8.2 Attributes that depend on each other

Attributes of an instance can be changed (or created) by simply assigning them a value. However, if other attributes depend on the one just changed, it is desirable to change them simultaneously.

To demonstrate this, we consider an example: let's define a class that defines an object for planar triangles from three given points. A first attempt to set up such a class could be as follows:

```
class Triangle:
    def __init__(self,  A, B, C):
        self.A = array(A)
        self.B = array(B)
        self.C = array(C)
        self.a = self.C - self.B
        self.b = self.C - self.A
        self.c = self.B - self.A
    def area(self):
        return abs(cross(self.b, self.c)) / 2
```

An instance of this triangle is created by this:

```
tr = Triangle([0., 0.], [1., 0.], [0., 1.])
```

Then its area is computed by calling the corresponding method:

```
tr.area() # returns 0.5
```

If we change an attribute, say point *B*, the corresponding edges *a* and *c* are not automatically updated and the computed area is wrong:

```
tr.B = [12., 0.]
tr.area() # still returns 0.5, should be 6 instead.
```

A remedy is to define a method that is executed when an attribute is changed; such a method is called a **setter method**. Correspondingly, you might ask for a method that is executed when a value of an attribute is requested; such a method is called a **getter method**. We explain now how these two methods are defined.

8.2.1 The function property

The special function `property` links an attribute to such a getter, setter, and deleter method. It might also be used to assign a documentation string to an attribute:

```
attribute = property(fget = get_attr, fset = set_attr,
                     fdel = del_attr, doc = string)
```

We continue with the previous example with a setter method and consider the class `Triangle` again. If the following statement is included in the definition of this class, the command `tr.B = <something>` invokes the setter method `set_B`:

```
B = property(fget = get_B, fset = set_B, fdel = del_B,
             doc = 'The point B of a triangle')
```

Let's modify the `Triangle` class accordingly:

```
class Triangle:
    def __init__(self, A, B, C):
        self._A = array(A)
        self._B = array(B)
        self._C = array(C)
        self._a = self._C - self._B
        self._b = self._C - self._A
        self._c = self._B - self._A
    def area(self):
        return abs(cross(self._c, self._b)) / 2.
    def set_B(self, B):
        self._B = B
        self._a = self._C - self._B
        self._c = self._B - self._A
    def get_B(self):
        return self._B
    def del_Pt(self):
```

```
        raise Exception('A triangle point cannot be deleted')
    B = property(fget = get_B, fset = set_B, fdel = del_Pt)
```

If the attribute B is changed, then the set_B method stores the new value in the internal attribute _B and changes all depending attributes:

```
tr.B = [12., 0.]
tr.area() # returns 6.0
```

The way the deleter method is used here is to prevent the deletion of attributes:

```
del tr.B # raises an exception
```

The use of an underscore as a prefix of attribute names is a convention used to indicate attributes that are not designed to be accessed directly. They are intended to hold data for attributes handled by setters and getters. These attributes are not private in the sense of other programming languages; they are just not intended to be accessed directly.

8.3 Bound and unbound methods

We will now take a closer look at attributes that are methods. Let's consider an example:

```
class A:
    def func(self,arg):
        pass
```

A little inspection shows us how the nature of func changes after creating an instance:

```
A.func   # <unbound method A.func>
instA = A()   # we create an instance
instA.func   #  <bound method A.func of ... >
```

Calling, for example, A.func(3) would result in an error message such as this:

```
TypeError: func() missing 1 required positional argument: 'arg'
```

instA.func(3) is executed as expected. Upon creation of an instance, the method func is bound to the instance. The argument self gets the instance assigned as its value. Binding a method to an instance makes the method applicable as a function. Before that, it is of no use. Class methods, which we will consider in Section 8.4.2: *Class methods*, are different in this aspect.

8.4 Class attributes and class methods

So far, we have seen attributes and methods that are bound to an instance of a class. In this section, we introduce class attributes and class methods. They allow access to methods and data before an instance is created.

8.4.1 Class attributes

Attributes specified in the class declaration are called **class attributes**. Consider the following example:

```
class Newton:
    tol = 1e-8 # this is a class attribute
    def __init__(self,f):
        self.f = f # this is not a class attribute
    ...
```

Class attributes are useful for simulating default values and can be used if values have to be reset:

```
N1 = Newton(f)
N2 = Newton(g)
```

Both instances have an attribute, `tol`, with the value initialized in the class definition:

```
N1.tol # 1e-8
N2.tol # 1e-8
```

Altering the class attribute automatically affects all the corresponding attributes of all instances:

```
Newton.tol = 1e-10
N1.tol # 1e-10
N2.tol # 1e-10
```

Altering `tol` for one instance does not affect the other instance:

```
N2.tol = 1.e-4
N1.tol  # still 1.e-10
```

But now, `N2.tol` is detached from the class attribute. Changing `Newton.tol` no longer has any effect on `N2.tol`:

```
Newton.tol = 1e-5
# now all instances of the Newton classes have tol=1e-5
```

```
N1.tol # 1.e-5
N2.tol # 1.e-4
# N2.tol is now detached and therefore not altered
```

8.4.2 Class methods

We saw in `Section 8.3`: *Bound and unbound methods* how methods are either bound to an instance of a class or remain in a state as unbound methods. Class methods are different. They are always bound methods. They are bound to the class itself.

We will first describe the syntactic details and then give some examples to show what these methods can be used for.

To indicate that a method is a class method, the decorator line precedes the method definition:

```
@classmethod
```

While standard methods make a reference to an instance by the use of their first argument, the first argument of a class method refers to the class itself. By convention, the first argument is called `self` for standard methods and `cls` for class methods.

The following is an example of the standard case:

```
class A:
    def func(self,*args):
        <...>
```

This is contrasted by an example of the `classmethod` case:

```
class B:
    @classmethod
    def func(cls,*args):
        <...>
```

In practice, class methods may be useful for executing commands before an instance is created, for instance, in a preprocessing step. See the following example.

In this example, we show how class methods can be used to prepare data before creating an instance:

```
class Polynomial:
    def __init__(self, coeff):
        self.coeff = array(coeff)
    @classmethod
```

```
    def by_points(cls, x, y):
        degree = x.shape[0] - 1
        coeff = polyfit(x, y, degree)
        return cls(coeff)
    def __eq__(self, other):
        return allclose(self.coeff, other.coeff)
```

The class is designed so that a polynomial object is created by specifying its coefficients. Alternatively, the class method `by_points` allows us to define a polynomial by interpolation points.

We can transform the interpolation data to the polynomial coefficients even when no instance of `Polynomial` is available:

```
p1 = Polynomial.by_points(array([0., 1.]), array([0., 1.]))
p2 = Polynomial([1., 0.])

print(p1 == p2)   # prints True
```

Another example of a class method is presented in Section 8.7: *Classes as decorators*. There, a class method is used to access information related to several (or all) instances from this class.

8.5 Subclasses and inheritance

In this section, we introduce some central concepts from object-oriented programming: **abstract classes**, **subclasses**, and **inheritance**. To guide you through these concepts, we consider another mathematical example: one-step methods for solving a differential equation.

The generic form of an ordinary initial value problem is as follows:

$$x'(t) = f(x(t), t) \qquad x(0) = x_0 \qquad t \in [t_0, t_e].$$

The data is the right-hand side function f, the initial value x_0, and the interval of interest $[t_0, t_e]$.

The solution to this problem is a function $x : [t_0, t_e] \rightarrow \mathbb{R}$. A numerical algorithm gives this solution as a vector u of discrete values u_i being approximations to $x(t_i)$. Here, $t_i \in [t_0, t_e]$ and $t_i = t_{i-1} + h$ are discretized values of the independent variable t, which in physical models often represents time.

A one-step method constructs the solution values u_i by the recursion steps:

$$u_{i+1} = u_i + h\Phi(f, u_i, t_i, h)$$

Here, Φ is a step function that characterizes the individual methods, see also [28]:

- Explicit Euler: $\Phi(f, u_i, t_i, h) = f(u_i, t_i)$

- Midpoint rule: $\Phi(f, u_i, t_i, h) = f(u_i + \frac{h}{2}f(u_i), t_i + \frac{h}{2})$

- Runge–Kutta 4: $\Phi(f, u_i, t_i, h) = \frac{1}{6}(s_1 + 2s_2 + 2s_3 + s_4)$ with
  $s_1 = f(u_i, t_i), s_2 = f(u_i + \frac{h}{2}s_1, t_i + \frac{h}{2}), s_3 = f(u_i + \frac{h}{2}s_2, t_i + \frac{h}{2}), s_4 = f(u_i + s_3, t_i + h)$

What we did here is the typical way of describing a mathematical algorithm. We first described a method by its idea, giving its steps in an abstract way. To actually use it, we have to fill in the parameters of a concrete method, in this example, the function Φ. This is also the way things are explained in object-oriented programming. First, we set up a class with the abstract description of the method:

```python
class OneStepMethod:
    def __init__(self, f, x0, interval, N):
        self.f = f
        self.x0 = x0
        self.interval = [t0, te] = interval
        self.grid = linspace(t0, te, N)
        self.h = (te - t0) / N

    def generate(self):
        ti, ui = self.grid[0], self.x0
        yield ti, ui
        for t in self.grid[1:]:
            ui = ui + self.h * self.step(self.f, ui, ti)
            ti = t
            yield ti, ui

    def solve(self):
```

```
            self.solution = array(list(self.generate()))

    def plot(self):
        plot(self.solution[:, 0], self.solution[:, 1])

    def step(self, f, u, t):
        raise NotImplementedError()
```

This abstract class, with its methods, is used as a template for the individual methods:

```
class ExplicitEuler(OneStepMethod):
    def step(self, f, u, t):
        return f(u, t)

class MidPointRule(OneStepMethod):
    def step(self, f, u, t):
        return f(u + self.h / 2 * f(u, t), t + self.h / 2)
```

Note that in the class definitions, the name of the abstract class that we used as a template, OneStepMethod, is given as an extra argument:

```
class ExplicitEuler(OneStepMethod)
```

That class is called the **parent class**. All methods and attributes of the parent class are inherited by the subclasses as long as they are not overridden. They are overridden if they are redefined in the subclass. The method step is redefined in the subclasses, while the method generate is generic for the entire family and therefore inherited from the parent.

Before considering further details, we will demonstrate how these three classes can be used:

```
def f(x, t):
    return -0.5 * x

euler = ExplicitEuler(f, 15., [0., 10.], 20)
euler.solve()
euler.plot()
hold(True)
midpoint = MidPointRule(f, 15., [0., 10.], 20)

midpoint.solve()
midpoint.plot()
```

You can avoid the repetition of common parameter lists by using the star operator (see Section 7.2.5: *Variable number of arguments* for more details):

```
...
argument_list = [f, 15., [0., 10.], 20]
euler = ExplicitEuler(*argument_list)
```

```
...
midpoint = MidPointRule(*argument_list)
...
```

Note that the abstract class has never been used to create an instance. As the method `step` was not completely defined, calling it raises an exception of type `NotImplementedError`.

Sometimes you have to access the methods or attributes of a parent class. This is done using the command `super`. This is useful when the child class uses its own __init__ method in order to extend the parent's __init__ method.

For example, let's assume that we want to give every solver class a string variable with the solver's name. To this end, we provide the solver with an __init__ method as it overrides the parent's __init__ method. In the case that both methods should be used, we have to refer to the parent's method by the command `super`:

```
class ExplicitEuler(OneStepMethod):
    def __init__(self,*args, **kwargs):
        self.name='Explicit Euler Method'
        super(ExplicitEuler, self).__init__(*args,**kwargs)
    def step(self, f, u, t):
        return f(u, t)
```

Note, you could have used the name of the parent class explicitly. The use of `super` instead allows us to change the name of the parent class without having to change all the references to the parent class.

8.6 Encapsulation

Sometimes the use of inheritance is impractical or even impossible. This motivates the use of encapsulation.

We will explain the concept of encapsulation by considering Python functions, that is, objects of the Python type `function`, which we encapsulate in a new class, `Function`, and provide with some relevant methods:

```
class Function:
    def __init__(self, f):
        self.f = f
    def __call__(self, x):
        return self.f(x)
    def __add__(self, g):
        def sum(x):
            return self(x) + g(x)
```

```
        return type(self)(sum)
    def __mul__(self, g):
        def prod(x):
            return self.f(x) * g(x)
        return type(self)(prod)
    def __radd__(self, g):
        return self + g
    def __rmul__(self, g):
        return self * g
```

Note that the operations __add__ and __mul__ should return an instance of the same class. This is achieved by the statement `return type(self)(sum)`, which in this case is a more general form of writing `return Function(sum)`. We can now derive subclasses by inheritance.

Consider as an example Chebyshev polynomials. They can be computed in the interval $[-1, 1]$ by:

$$T_i(x) = \cos(i \arccos(x))$$

We construct a Chebyshev polynomial as an instance of the class `Function`:

```
T5 = Function(lambda x: cos(5 * arccos(x)))
T6 = Function(lambda x: cos(6 * arccos(x)))
```

Chebyshev polynomials are orthogonal in the sense:

$$\int_{-1}^{1} \frac{1}{\sqrt{1 - x^2}} T_i(x) T_j(x) \, dx = 0 \text{ for } i \neq j$$

This can easily be checked using this construction:

```
import scipy.integrate as sci

weight = Function(lambda x: 1 / sqrt((1 - x ** 2)))
[integral, errorestimate] = \
        sci.quad(weight * T5 * T6, -1, 1)
# (6.510878470473995e-17, 1.3237018925525037e-14)
```

Without encapsulation, multiplying functions as simply as writing `weight * T5 * T6` would not have been possible.

8.7 Classes as decorators

In Section 7.8: *Function as decorators,* we saw how functions can be modified by applying another function as a decorator. In Section 8.1.5: *Special methods,* we saw how classes can be made to behave as functions as long as they are provided with the method __call__. We will use this here to show how classes can be used as decorators.

Let's assume that we want to change the behavior of some functions in such a way that before the function is invoked, all input parameters are printed. This could be useful for debugging purposes. We take this situation as an example to explain the use of a decorator class:

```
class echo:
    text = 'Input parameters of {name}\n'+\
        'Positional parameters {args}\n'+\
        'Keyword parameters {kwargs}\n'
    def __init__(self, f):
        self.f = f
    def __call__(self, *args, **kwargs):
        print(self.text.format(name = self.f.__name__,
            args = args, kwargs = kwargs))
        return self.f(*args, **kwargs)
```

We use this class to decorate function definitions:

```
@echo
def line(m, b, x):
    return m * x + b
```

Then, call the function as usual:

```
line(2., 5., 3.)
line(2., 5., x=3.)
```

On the second call, we obtain the following output:

```
Input parameters of line
Positional parameters (2.0, 5.0)
Keyword parameters {'x': 3.0}

11.0
```

This example shows that both classes and functions can be used as decorators. Classes allow more possibilities, as they can be used to collect data as well.

Indeed, we observe that:

- Every decorated function creates a new instance of the decorator class.
- Data collected by one instance can be saved and made accessible to another instance by class attributes; see Section 8.4: *Class attributes and class methods*.

The last point emphasizes the difference between function decorators. We show this now with a decorator that counts function calls and stores the result in a dictionary with the function as the key.

In order to analyze the performance of algorithms, it might be useful to count the calls of particular functions. We can get counter information without changing the function definition:

```python
class CountCalls:
    """
    Decorator that keeps track of the number of times
    a function is called.
    """
    instances = {}
    def __init__(self, f):
        self.f = f
        self.numcalls = 0
        self.instances[f] = self
    def __call__(self, *args, **kwargs):
        self.numcalls += 1
        return self.f(*args, **kwargs)
    @classmethod
    def counts(cls):
        """
        Return a dict of {function: # of calls} for all
        registered functions.
        """
        return dict([(f.__name__, cls.instances[f].numcalls)
                            for f in cls.instances])
```

Here, we use the class attribute `CountCalls.instances` to store the counters for each individual instance.

Let's see how this decorator works:

```python
@CountCalls
def line(m, b, x):
    return m * x + b
@CountCalls
def parabola(a, b, c, x):
    return a * x ** 2 + b * x + c
```

```
line(3., -1., 1.)
parabola(4., 5., -1., 2.)

CountCalls.counts()  # returns {'line': 1, 'parabola': 1}
parabola.numcalls  # returns 1
```

8.8 Summary

One of the most important programming concepts in modern computer science is object-oriented programming. We learned in this chapter how to define objects as instances of classes, which we provide with methods and attributes. The first parameter of methods, usually denoted by `self`, plays an important and special role. You saw methods that can be used to define basic operations for your own classes such as + and *.

While in other programming languages attributes and methods can be protected against unintended use, Python allows a technique to hide attributes and access these hidden attributes through special getter and setter methods. To this end, you met an important function, `property`.

8.9 Exercises

1. Write a method simplify to the class `RationalNumber`. This method should return the simplified version of the fraction as a tuple.

2. To provide results with confidence intervals, a special calculus, so-called interval arithmetic, is introduced in numerical mathematics. Define a class called `Interval` and provide it with methods for addition, subtraction, division, multiplication, and power (with positive integers only). These operations obey the following rules:

$$[a,b] + [c,d] = [a+c, b+d]$$
$$[a,b] \cdot [c,d] = [\min(a \cdot c, a \cdot d, b \cdot c, b \cdot d), \max(a \cdot c, a \cdot d, b \cdot c, b \cdot d)]$$
$$[a,b]/[c,d] = [\min(\frac{a}{c}, \frac{a}{d}, \frac{b}{c}, \frac{b}{d}), \max(\frac{a}{c}, \frac{a}{d}, \frac{b}{c}, \frac{b}{d})] \quad 0 \notin [c,d]$$
$$[a,b]^n = [a^n, b^n]$$

Provide this class with methods that allow operations of the type `a + I`, `a I`, `I + a`, `I a`, where `I` is an interval and `a` is an integer or float. Convert an integer or float into an interval `[a,a]` first. (Hint: you may want to use function decorators for this; see `Section` 7.8: *Function as decorators*.) Furthermore, implement the method `__contains__`, which enables you to check whether a given number belongs to the interval using the syntax `x in I` for an object `I` of type `Interval`. Test your class by applying a polynomial `f=lambda x:` `25*x**2-4*x+1` to an interval.

3. Consider the example in `Section 8.7`: *Classes as decorators*. Extend this example to obtain a *function decorator* that counts how often a certain function is called; see also `Section` 7.8: *Functions as decorators*.

4. Compare the two ways to implement a method for reverse addition `__radd__` in the class `RationalNumber`: the one given in the example in `Section 8.1.5`: *Special methods* and the one given here:

```
class RationalNumber:
    ....
    def __radd__(self, other):
        return other + self
```

Do you expect an error in this version? What is the error and how do you explain it? Test your answer by executing:

```
q = RationalNumber(10, 15)
5 + q
```

5. Consider the decorator class `CountCalls` as in the example in `Section 8.7`: *Classes as decorators*. Provide this class with a method, `reset`, that sets the counters of all functions in the dictionary `CountCalls.instances` to 0. What would happen if the dictionary were replaced by an empty dictionary instead?

9
Iterating

In this chapter, we will present iterations using loops and iterators. We will show examples of how this can be used with lists and generators. Iteration is one of the fundamental operations a computer is useful for. Traditionally, iteration is achieved with a `for` loop. A `for` loop is a repetition of a block of instructions a certain number of times. Inside the loop, you have access to a loop variable, in which the iteration number is stored.

A `for` loop in Python is primarily designed to exhaust a list, that is, to repeat the same sequence of commands for each element of that list. The effect is similar to the repetition effect just described if you use a list containing the first n integers.

A `for` loop only needs one element of the list at a time. It is therefore desirable to use a `for` loop with objects that are able to create those elements on demand, one at a time, instead of providing a complete list. This is what iterators achieve in Python.

The following topics are covered in this chapter:

- The for statement
- Controlling the flow inside the loop
- Iterable objects
- List-filling patterns
- When iterators behave as lists
- Iterator objects
- Infinite iterations

9.1 The for statement

The primary aim of the `for` statement is to traverse a list, that is, to apply the same sequence of commands to each element of a given list:

```
for s in ['a', 'b', 'c']:
    print(s) # a b c
```

In this example, the loop variable, `s`, is successively assigned to one element of the list. Notice that the loop variable is available after the loop has terminated. This may sometimes be useful; see, for instance, the example in `Section 9.2`: *Controlling the flow inside the loop.*

One of the most frequent uses of a `for` loop is to repeat, that is, to apply the same sequence of commands to each element of a given list: a given task a defined number of times, using the function `range`, see `Section 1.3.1`: *Lists.*

```
for iteration in range(n): # repeat the following code n times
    ...
```

If the purpose of a loop is to go through a list, many languages (including Python) offer the following pattern:

```
for k in range(...):
    ...
    element = my_list[k]
```

If the purpose of that code were to go through the list `my_list`, the preceding code would not make it very clear. For this reason, a better way to express this is as follows:

```
for element in my_list:
    ...
```

It is now clear at first glance that the preceding piece of code goes through the list `my_list`. Note that if you really need the index variable k, you may replace the preceding code with this (see also `Section 9.3.3`: *Iterator tools*):

```
for k, element in enumerate(my_list):
    ...
```

The intent of this piece of code is to go through `my_list` while keeping the index variable k available. A similar construction for arrays is the command `ndenumerate`:

```
a=ones((3,5))
for k,el in ndenumerate(a):
    print(k,el)
# prints something like this:   (1, 3) 1.0
```

9.2 Controlling the flow inside the loop

Sometimes it is necessary to jump out of the loop or to go directly to the next loop iteration. These two operations are performed by the commands `break` and `continue`.

The keyword `break` is used to terminate the loop before it is completely executed—it breaks the loop.

Two situations can occur in loops with a `break` statement:

- The loop is completely executed.

- The loop is left when reaching `break` before it was completely executed.

For the first case, special actions can be defined in an `else` block, which is executed if the whole list is traversed. This is useful in general if the purpose of the `for` loop is to find something and stop. Examples might be searching for one element satisfying a certain property inside a list. If such an element is not found, the `else` block is executed.

Here is a common usage in scientific computing: Quite often, we use an iterating algorithm that is not guaranteed to succeed. In that case, it is preferable to use a (big) finite loop so that the program does not get caught in an infinite loop. The `for/else` construct allows such an implementation:

```
maxIteration = 10000
for iteration in range(maxIteration):
    residual = compute() # some computation
    if residual < tolerance:
        break
else: # only executed if the for loop is not broken
    raise Exception("The algorithm did not converge")
print(f"The algorithm converged in {iteration + 1} steps")
```

9.3 Iterable objects

A `for` loop is primarily used to traverse a list, but it picks the elements of the list one at a time. In particular, there is no need to store the whole list in memory for the loop to work properly. The mechanism that allows `for` loops to work without lists is that of iterators.

An iterable object produces objects to be passed to a loop. Such an object may be used inside a loop as if it were a list:

```
for element in obj:
    ...
```

The notion of iterable objects thus generalizes the idea of lists.

The simplest example of an iterable object is given by lists. The produced objects are simply the objects stored in the list:

```
L = ['A', 'B', 'C']
for element in L:
    print(element)
```

An iterable object need not produce existing objects. The objects may, instead, be produced on the fly.

A typical iterable is the object returned by the function `range`. This function works as if it would generate a list of integers, but instead, the successive integers are produced on the fly when they are needed:

```
for iteration in range(100000000):
    # Note: the 100000000 integers are not created at once
    if iteration > 10:
        break
```

If you really need a list with all integers between 0 and 100,000,000, then it has to be formed explicitly:

```
l=list(range(100000000))
```

Iterable objects have a method called __iter__. That's how you can check whether a given object in Python is iterable.

So far, we have met the following datatypes, which are iterable objects:

- lists
- tuples
- strings
- range objects
- dictionaries
- arrays
- enumerate and ndenumerate objects

By executing the method __iter__ on an iterable object, an iterator is created. This is tacitly done when a `for` loop is invoked. An iterator has a __next__ method, which returns the next element of a sequence:

```
l=[1,2]
li=l.__iter__()
li.__next__() # returns 1
li.__next__() # returns 2
li.__next__() # raises StopIteration exception
```

9.3.1 Generators

You can create your own iterator by using the keyword `yield`. For example, a generator for odd numbers smaller than n can be defined by:

```
def odd_numbers(n):
    "generator for odd numbers less than n"
    for k in range(n):
        if k % 2 == 1:
            yield k
```

Then you can use it as follows:

```
g = odd_numbers(10)
for k in g:
    ...    # do something with k
```

Or even like this:

```
for k in odd_numbers(10):
    ... # do something with k
```

9.3.2 Iterators are disposable

One salient feature of iterators is that they may be used only once. In order to use the iterator again, you will have to create a new iterator object. Note that an iterable object is able to create new iterators as many times as necessary. Let's examine the case of a list:

```
L = ['a', 'b', 'c']
iterator = iter(L)
list(iterator) # ['a', 'b', 'c']
list(iterator) # [] empty list, because the iterator is exhausted
```

```
new_iterator = iter(L) # new iterator, ready to be used
list(new_iterator) # ['a', 'b', 'c']
```

Each time a generator object is called, it creates a new iterator. Hence, when that iterator is exhausted, you have to call the generator again to obtain a new iterator:

```
g = odd_numbers(10)
for k in g:
    ... # do something with k

# now the iterator is exhausted:
for k in g: # nothing will happen!!
    ...

# to loop through it again, create a new one:
g = odd_numbers(10)
for k in g:
    ...
```

9.3.3 Iterator tools

Now, we will introduce a couple of iterator tools that often come in very handy:

- enumerate is used to enumerate another iterator. It produces a new iterator that yields pairs (iteration, element), where iteration stores the index of the iteration:

```
A = ['a', 'b', 'c']
for iteration, x in enumerate(A):
    print(iteration, x)      # result: (0, 'a') (1, 'b') (2, 'c')
```

- reversed creates an iterator from a list by going through that list backward. Notice that this is different from creating a reversed list:

```
A = [0, 1, 2]
for elt in reversed(A):
    print(elt)      # result: 2 1 0
```

- itertools.count is a possibly infinite iterator of integers:

```
for iteration in itertools.count():
    if iteration > 100:
        break # without this, the loop goes on forever
        print(f'integer: {iteration}')
        # prints the 100 first integer
```

- `intertools.islice` truncates an iterator using the familiar `slicing` syntax; see `Section 3.1.1`: *Slicing.* One application is creating a finite iterator from an infinite one:

```
from itertools import count, islice
for iteration in islice(count(), 10):
    # same effect as range(10)
        ...
```

For example, let's find some odd numbers by combining `islice` with an infinite generator. First, we modify the generator for odd numbers so that it becomes an infinite generator:

```
def odd_numbers():
    k=-1
    while True:  # this makes it an infinite generator
        k+=1
        if k%2==1:
            yield k
```

Then, we use it with `islice` to get a list of some odd numbers:

```
list(itertools.islice(odd_numbers(),10,30,8))
# returns [21, 37, 53]
```

This command takes from an assumed list of all odd numbers, the one with index 10 to index 29 in steps of 8.

9.3.4 Generators of recursive sequences

Assume that a sequence is given by an induction formula. For instance, consider the Fibonacci sequence, defined by the recurrence formula:

$$u_n = u_{n-1} + u_{n-2}.$$

This sequence depends on two initial values, namely u_0 and u_1, although for the standard Fibonacci sequence those numbers are taken as 0 and 1 respectively. A nifty way of programming the generation of such a sequence is by using generators, as follows:

```
def fibonacci(u0, u1):
    """
    Infinite generator of the Fibonacci sequence.
    """
    yield u0
    yield u1
    while True:
```

```
        u0, u1 = u1, u1 + u0
        # we shifted the elements and compute the new one
        yield u1
```

This may then be used, for instance, like this:

```
# sequence of the 100 first Fibonacci numbers:
list(itertools.islice(fibonacci(0, 1), 100))
```

9.3.5 Examples for iterators in mathematics

Arithmetic geometric mean

A more elaborate example for a generator is its use for an iteration based
on iteratively computing arithmetic and geometric means – the so-called **AGM iteration,**
see [1]:

$$a_{i+1} = \frac{a_i + b_i}{2},$$
$$b_{i+1} = \sqrt{a_i b_i}$$

We demonstrate this iteration here in the context of computing elliptic integrals for
determining the period of a mathematical pendulum.

When started with the values $a_0 = 1$ and $b_0 = \sqrt{1-k^2}$, the AGM iteration generates a sequence
of numbers with the following (astonishing) property:

$$\frac{\pi}{2} \lim_{i \to \infty} \frac{1}{a_i} = \int_0^{\frac{\pi}{2}} \frac{1}{\sqrt{1 - k^2 \sin^2(\theta)}} d\theta =: F(k, \pi/2)$$

The integral on the right-hand side is called a complete elliptic integral of the first kind.
We'll now proceed to compute this elliptic integral. We use a generator to describe the
iteration:

```
def arithmetic_geometric_mean(a, b):
    """
    Generator for the arithmetic and geometric mean
    a, b initial values
    """
    while True:    # infinite loop
        a, b = (a+b)/2, sqrt(a*b)
        yield a, b
```

As the sequences $\{a_i\}$ and $\{b_i\}$ converge to the same value, the sequence $\{c_i\}$ defined by $c_i = a_i - b_i$ converges to zero—a fact that will be used to terminate the iteration in the program to compute the elliptic integral:

```
def elliptic_integral(k, tolerance=1.e-5):
    """
    Compute an elliptic integral of the first kind.
    """
    a_0, b_0 = 1., sqrt(1-k**2)
    for a, b in arithmetic_geometric_mean(a_0, b_0):
        if abs(a-b) < tolerance:
            return pi/(2*a)
```

We have to make sure that the algorithm stops. Note that this code fully relies on the mathematical statement that the arithmetic-geometric mean iteration converges (fast). In practical computing, we have to be careful while applying theoretical results, as they might no longer be valid in limited-precision arithmetic. The right way to make the preceding code safe is to use `itertools.islice`. The safe code is as follows:

```
from itertools import islice
def elliptic_integral(k, tolerance=1e-5, maxiter=100):
    """
    Compute an elliptic integral of the first kind.
    """
    a_0, b_0 = 1., sqrt(1-k**2)
    for a, b in islice(arithmetic_geometric_mean(a_0, b_0), maxiter):
        if abs(a-b) < tolerance:
            return pi/(2*a)
    else:
        raise Exception("Algorithm did not converge")
```

As an application, elliptic integrals may be used to compute the period T of a pendulum of length L starting at an angle θ using:

$$T = 4\sqrt{\frac{L}{g}}\mathrm{F}\left(\sin\frac{\theta}{2}, \frac{\pi}{2}\right)$$

Using this formula, the period of the pendulum is easily obtained, see [18]:

```
def pendulum_period(L, theta, g=9.81):
    return 4*sqrt(L/g)*elliptic_integral(sin(theta/2))
```

Convergence acceleration

We'll give an example of the application of generators for convergence acceleration. This presentation closely follows the example given in [9].

Note that a generator may take another generator as an input parameter. For instance, suppose that we have defined a generator that generates the elements of a converging sequence. It is then possible to improve the convergence by an acceleration technique due to *Euler* and *Aitken*, often called Aitken's Δ^2-method, see [33]. It transforms a sequence s_i into another by defining

$$s_i' := s_i - \frac{(s_{i+1} - s_i)^2}{s_{i+2} - 2s_{i+1} + s_i}.$$

Both sequences have the same limit, but the sequence s_i' converges significantly faster. One possible implementation is as follows:

```
def Euler_accelerate(sequence):
    """
    Accelerate the iterator in the variable `sequence`.
    """
    s0 = sequence.__next__()  # Si
    s1 = sequence.__next__()  # Si+1
    s2 = sequence.__next__()  # Si+2
    while True:
        yield s0 - ((s1 - s0)**2)/(s2 - 2*s1 + s0)
        s0, s1, s2 = s1, s2, sequence.__next__()
```

As an example, we use the series $S_N = \sum_{n=0}^{N} \frac{(-1)^n}{2n + 1}$, which converges to $\pi/4$.

We implement this series as a generator in the following code:

```
def pi_series():
    sum = 0.
    j = 1
    for i in itertools.cycle([1, -1]):
        yield sum
        sum += i/j
        j += 2
```

We may now use the accelerated version of that sequence using this:

```
Euler_accelerate(pi_series())
```

Accordingly, the first N elements of that accelerated sequence are obtained with:

```
list(itertools.islice(Euler_accelerate(pi_series()), N))
```

Note, here we stacked three generators: `pi_series`, `Euler_accelerate`, and `itertools.islice`.

Figure 9.1 shows the convergence rate of the log of the error for the standard version of the sequence defined by the preceding formula and its accelerated version:

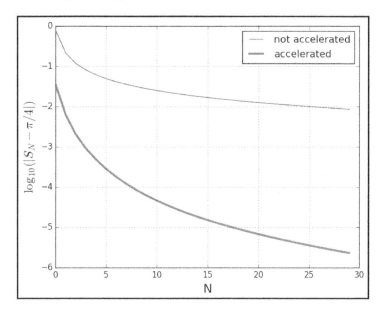

Figure 9.1: Comparison between the sequence and its accelerated version

9.4 List-filling patterns

In this section, we will compare different ways to fill lists. They are different in computational efficiency and also in code readability.

9.4.1 List filling with the append method

A ubiquitous programming pattern is to compute elements and store them in a list:

```
L = []
for k in range(n):
    # call various functions here
    # that compute "result"
    L.append(result)
```

This approach has a number of disadvantages:

- The number of iterations is decided in advance. If there is a break instruction, then the preceding code takes care of both generating values and deciding when to stop. This is not desirable and lacks flexibility.
- It makes the assumption that the user wants the whole history of the computation, for all the iterations. Suppose we are only interested in the sum of all the computed values. If there are many computed values, it does not make sense to store them, as it is much more efficient to add them one at a time.

9.4.2 List from iterators

Iterators provide us with an elegant solution to problems discussed previously:

```
def result_iterator():
    for k in itertools.count(): # infinite iterator
        # call various functions here
        # that t lists compute "result"
        ...
        yield result
```

With iterators, we separate the task of generating the computed values without bothering about the stopping condition or about the storage.

- If the user of that code wants to store the n first values, it is easily done using the list constructor:

  ```
  L = list(itertools.islice(result_iterator(), n)) # no append
  needed!
  ```

- If the user wants the sum of the first *n* generated values, this construction is recommended:

  ```
  # make sure that you do not use numpy.sum here
  s = sum(itertools.islice(result_iterator(), n))
  ```

- If the user wants to generate all elements until a certain condition is fulfilled, the function `itertools.takewhile` comes in handy:

```
L=list(itertools.takewhile(lambda x: abs(x) > 1.e-8,
result_iterator()))
```

The function `takewhile` takes as a first argument a function that returns a Boolean. Its second argument is a generator. The generator is iterated as long as the function evaluates to `True`.

What we did here was separate the generation of elements on one hand, and store those elements on the other.

- If the purpose is really to build a list, and when the result at each step does not depend on previously computed elements, you may use the list comprehension syntax (see `Section 3.1.6`: *List Comprehension*):

```
L = [some_function(k) for k in range(n)]
```

When iteratively computing values that depend on the previously computed values, list comprehensions cannot help.

9.4.3 Storing generated values

Using iterators to fill out lists will work nicely most of the time, but there are complications to this pattern when the algorithm computing the new values is liable to throw an exception; if the iterator raises an exception along the way, the list will not be available! The following example illustrates this problem.

Suppose we generate the sequence defined recursively by $u_{n+1} = u_n^2$. This sequence quickly diverges to infinity if the initial data u_0 is greater than one. Let's generate it with a generator:

```
import itertools
def power_sequence(u0):
    u = u0
    while True:
        yield u
        u = u**2
```

If you try to obtain the first *20* elements of the sequence (initialized by $u_0 = 2$) by executing:

```
list(itertools.islice(power_sequence(2.), 20))
```

An `OverflowError` exception will be raised and no list will be available, not even the list of elements before the exception was raised. There is currently no way to obtain a partially filled list from a possibly faulty generator. The only way around this is to use the method `append` wrapped in an exception-catching block (see `Section 12.1:` *What are exceptions?*, for more details):

```
generator = power_sequence(2.)
L = []
for iteration in range(20):
    try:
        L.append(next(generator))
    except Exception:
        break
```

9.5 When iterators behave as lists

Some list operations also work on iterators. We will now examine the equivalents of *list comprehensions* and *list zipping* (see `Section 3.1.6:` *List Comprehension,* and `Section 3.1.5:` *Merging Lists*).

9.5.1 Generator expressions

There is an equivalent of list comprehension for generators. Such a construction is called a generator expression:

```
g = (n for n in range(1000) if not n % 100)
# generator for  100, 200, ... , 900
```

This is useful in particular for computing sums or products because those operations are incremental; they only need one element at a time:

```
sum(n for n in range(1000) if not n % 100)
# returns 4500 (sum is here the built-in function)
```

In that code, you notice that the `sum` function is given one argument, which is a generator expression. Note that Python syntax allows us to omit the enclosing parentheses of generators when a generator is used as the *only* argument of a function.

Let's compute the Riemann zeta function ζ, whose expression is

$$\zeta(s) := \sum_{n=1}^{\infty} \frac{1}{n^s}.$$

With a generator expression, we may compute a partial sum of this series in one line:

```
sum(1/n**s for n in itertools.islice(itertools.count(1), N))
```

Note that we could also have defined a generator of the sequence $1/n^s$ as follows:

```
def generate_zeta(s):
    for n in itertools.count(1):
        yield 1/n**s
```

Then we simply obtain the sum of the first N terms using:

```
def zeta(N, s):
    # make sure that you do not use the scipy.sum here
    return sum(itertools.islice(generate_zeta(s), N))
```

We point out that we used this way of computing the zeta (ζ) function as a demonstration of the use of generators in an elegant way. It is certainly not the most accurate and computationally efficient way to evaluate this function.

9.5.2 Zipping iterators

We saw in `Section 3.1.5`: *Merging Lists* that it is possible to create a list out of two or more lists by zipping them together. The same operation exists for iterators:

```
xg = x_iterator()  # some iterator
yg = y_iterator()  # another iterator

for x, y in zip(xg, yg):
    print(x, y)
```

The zipped iterator stops as soon as one of the iterators is exhausted. This is the same behavior as the operation zip on lists.

9.6 Iterator objects

As we mentioned earlier, a `for` loop only needs an iterable object. Lists, in particular, are iterable objects. This means that a list is able to create an iterator from its contents. In fact, this is true for any object (not only lists): any object may be made iterable.

This is achieved via the method __iter__, which should return an iterator. Here we give an example where the method __iter__ is a generator:

```
class OdeStore:
    """
    Class to store results of ode computations
    """
    def __init__(self, data):
        "data is a list of the form [[t0, u0], [t1, u1],...]"
        self.data = data
    def __iter__(self):
        "By default, we iterate on the values u0, u1,..."
        for t, u in self.data:
            yield u

store = OdeStore([[0, 1], [0.1, 1.1], [0.2, 1.3]])
for u in store:
    print(u)
# result: 1, 1.1, 1.3
list(store) # [1, 1.1, 1.3]
```

If you try to use the features of an iterator with an object that is not iterable, an exception will be raised:

```
>>> list(3)
TypeError: 'int' object is not iterable
```

In this example, the function list tries to iterate through object 3 by calling the method __iter__. But this method is not implemented for integers and thus the exception is raised. The same would happen if we tried to cycle through a non-iterable object:

```
>>> for iteration in 3: pass
TypeError: 'int' object is not iterable
```

9.7 Infinite iterations

Infinite iterations are obtained either with an infinite iterator, with a `while` loop, or by recursion. Obviously, in practical cases, some condition stops the iteration. The difference with finite iterations is that it is impossible to say from a cursory examination of the code whether the iteration will stop or not.

9.7.1 The while loop

The `while` loop may be used to repeat a code block until a condition is fulfilled:

```
while condition:
    <code>
```

A `while` loop is equivalent to the following code:

```
for iteration in itertools.count():
    if not condition:
        break
    <code>
```

So a `while` loop used to repeat a code block until a condition is fulfilled is equivalent to an infinite iterator, which might be stopped if a condition is fulfilled. The danger of such a construction is obvious: the code may be trapped in an infinite loop if the condition is never fulfilled.

The problem in scientific computing is that you are not always sure that an algorithm will converge. Newton iteration, for instance, might not converge at all. If that algorithm were implemented inside a `while` loop, the corresponding code would be trapped in an infinite loop for some choices of initial conditions.

We, therefore, advise that finite iterators are often better suited for such a task. The following construction replaces, often advantageously, the use of a `while` loop:

```
maxit = 100
for nb_iterations in range(maxit):
    ...
else:
    raise Exception(f"No convergence in {maxit} iterations")
```

The first advantage is that the code is guaranteed to execute in a finite time no matter what happens. The second advantage is that the variable `nb_iterations` contains the number of iterations that were necessary for the algorithm to converge.

9.7.2 Recursion

Recursion occurs when a function calls itself (see `Section 7.4`: *Recursive functions*).

When doing recursions, it is the recursion depth, which is the number of iterations, that brings your computer to its limits. We demonstrate this here by considering a simple recursion, which actually contains no computations at all. It assigns to the iterates only the value zero:

```
def f(N):
    if N == 0:
        return 0
    return f(N-1)
```

Depending on your system, this program may choke for $N \geq 10000$ (too much memory is used). The result is that the Python interpreter crashes without further exception. Python provides a mechanism to raise an exception when a too high recursion depth is detected. This maximum recursion depth may be changed by executing:

```
import sys
sys.setrecursionlimit(1000)
```

Be aware though, that choosing too high a number may imperil the stability of your code since Python might crash before that maximum depth is reached. It is therefore often wise to leave the recursion limit as it is. The actual value of the recursion limit can be obtained with `sys.getrecursionlimit()`.

By comparison, the following, non-recursive, program runs ten of millions of iterations without any problem:

```
for iteration in range(10000000):
    pass
```

We advocate that, if possible, recursion should be avoided in Python. This applies obviously only if there is an appropriate alternative iterative algorithm available. The first reason is that a recursion of depth N involves N function calls at the same time, which might result in significant overhead. The second reason is that it is an infinite iteration, that is, it is difficult to give an upper bound to the number of steps necessary before the recursion is over.

Note that in some very special cases (tree traversal) recursion is unavoidable. Besides, in some cases (with small recursion depths), recursive programs might be preferred due to readability.

9.8 Summary

In this chapter, we studied iterators, a programming construct very near to a mathematical description of iterative methods. You saw the keyword `yield` and met finite and infinite iterators.

We showed that an iterator can be exhausted. More special aspects such as iterator comprehension and recursive iterators were introduced and demonstrated with the help of examples.

9.9 Exercises

Ex. 1: Compute the value of the sum:

$$\sum_{i=1}^{200} \frac{1}{\sqrt{i}}$$

Ex. 2: Create a generator that computes the sequence defined by the relation:

$$u_n = 2u_{n-1}$$

Ex. 3: Generate all the even numbers.

Ex. 4: Let $s_n := (1 + \frac{1}{n})^{2n}$. In calculus, it is shown that $\lim_{n \to \infty} s_n = e^2$. Determine experimentally the smallest number n such that $|s_n - e^2| < 10^{-5}$. Use a generator for this task.

Ex. 5: Generate all prime numbers less than a given integer. Use the algorithm called *Sieve of Eratosthenes*.

Ex. 6: Solving the differential equation $u' = -\sin u$ by applying the explicit Euler method results in the recursion:

$$u_{n+1} = u_n - h \sin u_n$$

Write a generator that computes the solution values u_n for a given initial value u_0 and for a given value of the time step h.

Ex. 7: Compute π using the formula:

$$\pi = \int_0^1 \frac{4}{1+x^2}\,\mathrm{d}x$$

The integral can be approximated using the composite trapezoidal rule, that is, with this formula:

$$\int_a^b f(x)\mathrm{d}x \approx \frac{h}{2}\left(f(a) + f(b)\right) + h\sum_{i=1}^{n-1} f(x_i)$$

where $x_i = a + ih$, $h = \dfrac{b-a}{n}$.

Program a *generator* for the values $y_i = f(x_i)$ and evaluate the formula by summing one term after the other. Compare your results with the `quad` function of SciPy.

Ex. 8: Let x = `[1, 2, 3]` and y = `[-1, -2, -3]`. What is the effect of the code `zip(*zip(x, y))`? Explain how it works.

Ex. 9: Complete elliptic integrals can be computed by the function `scipy.special.ellipk`. Write a function that counts the number of iterations needed with the AGM iteration until the result coincides up to a given tolerance (note that the input parameter m in `ellipk` corresponds to k^2 in the definition in `Section 9.3.5: Examples for iterators in mathematics`).

Ex. 10: Consider the sequence $\{E_n\}_{n=1}^{\infty}$ defined by:

$$E_n := \int_0^1 x^n e^{x-1}\,\mathrm{d}x$$

It converges monotonically to zero: $E_1 > E_2 > \cdots > 0$. By integration by parts, we can show that the sequence E_n fulfills the following recursion:

$$E_n = 1 - nE_{n-1} \quad \text{with} \quad E_1 = 1 - \int_0^1 e^{x-1}\,\mathrm{d}x = e^{-1}$$

Compute the first 20 terms of the recursion by using an appropriate generator and compare the results with those obtained by numerical integration with `scipy.integrate.quad`. Do the same by reversing the recursion:

$$E_{n-1} := \frac{1}{n}(1 - E_n) \qquad \text{with} \quad E_{20} = 0$$

Use the function `exp` to evaluate the exponential function. What do you observe? Do you have an explanation? See also [29].

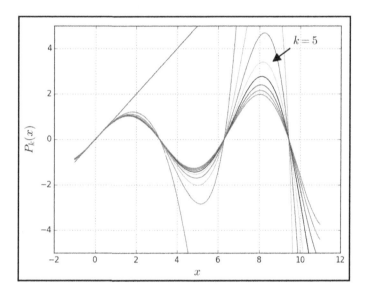

Figure 9.2: A convergence study of functions approximating $\sin(x)$

Ex. 11: The sine-function can be expressed due to Euler as:

$$\sin x = x \prod_{k=1}^{\infty}\left(1 - \frac{x^2}{k^2\pi^2}\right) = \underbrace{x\left(1 - \frac{x^2}{\pi^2}\right)\left(1 - \frac{x^2}{4\pi^2}\right)\left(1 - \frac{x^2}{9\pi^2}\right)}_{=:P_3(x)}\cdots$$

Write a generator that generates the function values $P_k(x)$.
Set `x=linspace(-1,3.5*pi,200)` and demonstrate graphically how
well $P_k(x)$ approximates **sin** for increasing k. In *Figure 9.2*, the possible result is shown.
Consult also Theorem 5.2, p. 65 in [11].

10

Series and Dataframes - Working with Pandas

In this chapter, we give a brief introduction to pandas—the central tool in Python for data analysis and data handling. You will learn how to work with various time series in Python, the concept of dataframes, and how to access and visualize data. You will also find examples that demonstrate how smoothly pandas interacts with the other central modules in this book, namely NumPy and Matplotlib.

But please note, this chapter can, within the scope of this book, only serve as an *appetizer*. Its purpose is to equip you with the basic concepts. The full range of visualization, data analysis, and data conversion tools in pandas is impressive.

pandas offers many ways of importing data. Some of them will be presented together with guiding examples throughout this chapter.

The following topics will be covered in this chapter:

- A guiding example: Solar cells
- NumPy arrays and pandas DataFrames
- Creating and modifying dataframes
- Working with dataframes

10. 1 A guiding example: Solar cells

To describe pandas in the best way, we need data. Thus, in this chapter, we will use production data from solar cell panels on the roof of a private house in the south of Sweden.

In the file `solarWatts.dat` there is data about the electricity production in watts per minute. A semicolon is used as a data separator and the first line in the file is a header line, explaining the content of the data columns:

```
Date;Watt
            :
2019-10-20 08:22:00 ; 44.0
2019-10-20 08:23:00 ; 61.0
2019-10-20 08:24:00 ; 42.0
            :
```

In another file, `price.dat`, we find the hourly electricity production price in Swedish crowns. The file is otherwise organized as before:

```
Date;SEK
2019-10-20 01:00 ; 0.32
2019-10-20 02:00 ; 0.28
2019-10-20 03:00 ; 0.29
        :
```

Finally, in a third file, `rates.dat`, we find the daily conversion rates from Swedish crowns to Euros (€):

```
Date;Euro_SEK
2019-10-21 ; 10.7311
2019-10-22 ; 10.7303
2019-10-23 ; 10.7385
        :
```

We want to extract from this data information about the maximal and minimal production per day, the number of hours of sun per month, the sunniest day so far, information about sunrise and sunset, and some economic information. We also aim to graphically present data.

Note, the data is not collected at the same time points and there might be missing data.

Each file contains a so-called time-series, that is, data depending on time or a discrete sampling of a time-depending function.

We now introduce the concept of dataframes in pandas and compare it to NumPy arrays.

10.2 NumPy arrays and pandas dataframes

Let's start by just looking at an example of a 2×3 NumPy array:

```
A=array( [[ 1., 2., 3.],
          [4., 5., 6.]])
```

It is displayed as:

```
[[1. 2. 3.]
 [4. 5. 6.]]
```

And its elements are accessed by using indexes generated simply by counting rows and columns, for example, `A[0,1]`.

This matrix can be converted to the pandas datatype `DataFrame` by keeping the same data and order but representing and accessing it in a different way:

```
import pandas as pd
A=array( [[ 1., 2., 3.],
          [ 4., 5., 6.]] )
AF = pd.DataFrame(A)
```

This `DataFrame` object, which we will explain in more detail in this chapter, is displayed as

```
     0   1   2
0   1.0 2.0 3.0
1   4.0 5.0 6.0
```

We see that a pandas dataframe has extra labels for the rows and columns called *index* and *columns*. These are the metadata of a dataframe.

Here, they coincide with NumPy's indexing, but that is not always so. The index and columns metadata allows the pandas dataframe to label the data in a way that's known from classical table design:

```
AF.columns = ['C1','C2','C3']
AF.index = ['R1', 'R2']
```

This gives us the following output:

```
    C1 C2 C3
R1 1.0 2.0 3.0
R2 4.0 5.0 6.0
```

We will see now how to work with these labels to address a subframe or just a value in the dataframe.

10.2.1 Indexing rules

Similar to the way dictionaries use keys to address a value, pandas dataframes use row labels—the dataframe index—and column labels to access individual values:

```
AF.loc['R1', 'C2']        # this returns 2.0
```

Or to generate a subframe:

```
AF.loc[['R1','R2'],['C1','C2']]
```

Resulting in:

```
     C1    C2
R1   1    2.0
R2   4    5.0
```

You can also address a complete row by using the index label:

```
AF.loc['R1']
```

This returns a pandas `Series` object:

```
C1     1.0
C2     2.0
C3     3.0
Name: R1, dtype: float64
```

If `loc` or `iloc` are called with list arguments or slices, the result is a dataframe.

In that way, an individual dataframe element can also be addressed as follows:

```
AF.loc['R1'].loc['C1']     # returns 1.0
```

An entire column is addressed directly as follows:

```
AF['C1']
```

This again returns a pandas `Series` object:

```
R1     1.0
R2     4.0
Name: C1, dtype: float64
```

Alternatively, the column label can be used as an attribute, AF.C1.

A single column is an instance of the pandas datatype, `Series`.

```
type(AF.C1) == pd.Series # True
```

Note, a pandas series has no column label. It is just a single column corresponding to a single type of measured data.

Still, you can use classical indexing by applying the dataframe method `iloc`:

```
AF.iloc[[0],[1]]
```

This returns:

```
    C2
R1 2.0
```

If `loc` or `iloc` are called with list arguments or slices, the result is a dataframe:

```
AF.loc['R1':,'C2':]
```

Or equivalently:

```
AF.loc[['R1','R2'], ['C2','C2']]
```

While calling with a pair of single labels just gives an element of the dataframe:

```
AF.loc['R1','C2'] # returns 2.0
```

This is in full agreement with the way NumPy handles the indexing of arrays. Recall that indexing with slices returns an array, while indexing with single integers returns a single element of the indexed array.

It is important to note that `loc` and `iloc` are not dataframe methods. Rather, they are attributes that have __getitem__ method; see also `Section 8.1.5`: *Special methods*. That explains the use of brackets instead of parentheses.

10.3 Creating and modifying dataframes

We return now to the solar cell data and explain how to create a dataframe from a data file. The format of the file with the given data is CSV. Each line in the file contains one data record with a comma or another character string as a data separator. Here, we used a semicolon as a separator because in many countries the comma is used instead of a decimal separator.

10.3.1 Creating a dataframe from imported data

We want to organize the dataframe in such a way that the dates are used as the index of the dataframe. To be better prepared for operating with dates, we also want that the data import process automatically converts date strings to a pandas `Timestamp` object. Finally, you might have noted that the way the date is written in the data files is in the ISO-format `YY-MM-DD` format and not in the American `MM-DD-YY` or the European `DD-MM-YY` format. We can put on our wishlist that pandas automatically recognizes the date format and performs the correct conversion:

```
solarWatts = pd.read_csv("solarWatts.dat",
                         sep=';',
                         index_col='Date',
                         parse_dates=[0], infer_datetime_format=True)
```

The pandas command `read_csv` is the central tool. It has many more parameters than we used here and carefully studying their functionalities saves a lot of programming effort.

We now have a pandas dataframe, `solarWatts`, with more than 200,000 data records. Let's directly check the first one:

```
solarWatts.iloc[0]
```

This returns the following output:

```
Watt      7893.0
Name: 2019-10-06 13:23:00, dtype: float64
```

We can also ask for the last date. To this end, we use the attribute `index` of the dataframe:

```
solarWatts.index[-1]   # asking for the last index
```

This returns a pandas `Timestamp` object `Timestamp('2020-06-27 17:54:00')`. This object or its string representation can be used for indexing.

`Timestamp` objects make it easy to perform calculations with dates, define time ranges, and compare dates. We can check how much time passed between the measurements:

```
# returns: Timedelta('0 days 00:01:00')
solarWatts.index[1]-solarWatts.index[0]
```

The resulting object `Timedelta` tells us that the time elapsed between the first and second records is one minute.

But is all data collected every minute? As pandas is compatible with NumPy, we can apply Numpy's command `diff`, which returns an array with the datatype `timedelta64[ns]`, that is, the differences are given in nanoseconds. We convert the result directly to minutes and ask for the maximal difference:

```
max(numpy.diff(solarWatts.index).astype('timedelta64[m]'))
```

With `numpy.argmax`, we find the corresponding date:

```
solarWatts.iloc[np.argmax(np.diff(solarWatts.index))]
```

In this piece of code, we first form an array with the time differences (`timedelta`). We use this as an index to locate the data record in the pandas dataframe.

10.3.2 Setting the index

The default index of a dataframe is the row numbers. These are generated automatically when a dataframe is created and no index is specified. Here is an example.

We create a dataframe from a list of lists:

```
towns=[['Stockholm', 'Sweden', 188,975904],
       ['Malmö', 'Sweden', 322, 316588],
       ['Oslo', 'Norway', 481, 693491],
       ['Bergen', 'Norway', 464, 28392]]
town=pd.DataFrame(towns, columns=['City','Country','area','population'])
```

This produces a dataframe with rows labeled by their row numbers:

```
        City  Country   area  population
0  Stockholm   Sweden    188      975904
1      Malmö   Sweden    322      316588
2       Oslo   Norway    481      693491
3     Bergen   Norway    464       28392
```

We can change this by choosing a column to be the index. The column can be duplicated—one serving as the index and the other belonging to the data section of the dataframe—or it can be moved to replace the default index column:

```
town.set_index('City', drop=False)      # duplicating
# droping the column and making an index out of it
town.set_index('City', drop=True)
```

A *new* dataframe is generated, which looks like this when the drop parameter was set to True (default):

```
          Country   area   population
City
Stockholm   Sweden   188      975904
Malmö       Sweden   322      316588
Oslo        Norway   481      693491
Bergen      Norway   464      283929
Trondheim   Norway   322      199039
```

The additional parameter inplace enables to change the dataframe directly, that is, *in place*, without generating a new object.

pandas is not restricted to one index only; indeed, several columns can be chosen as an index. Such a multi-index opens for **hierarchical indexing**, a feature of pandas which we will meet again in Section 10.4.3: *Grouping data*.

Several indexes are specified by a list of columns:

```
town.set_index(['Country','City'], inplace=True)
```

This gives us the following output:

```
                  area   population
Country City
Sweden  Stockholm   188      975904
        Malmö       322      316588
Norway  Oslo        481      693491
```

Note how the dataframe is displayed now: the first index, Country, is taken as the one with higher hierarchy level than the second index, City.

We can address all Swedish towns in the frame as shown here:

```
town.loc['Sweden']
```

We can even address a particular one:

```
town.loc[('Sweden','Malmö')]
```

10.3.3 Deleting entries

Entries in a dataframe are deleted by the method `drop`.

Again, we use the dataframe from the previous section:

```
town=pd.DataFrame(towns, columns=['City','Country','area','population'])
town.set_index('City', inplace=True)
```

An entire row is deleted by:

```
town.drop('Bergen', axis=0)
```

The parameter `axis` specifies here that we look for a row. Deleting a row requires the column label and the correct parameter `axis`:

```
town.drop('area', axis=1)
```

10.3.4 Merging dataframes

From the three datafiles we provided for this chapter we used the first one, `solarwatts.dat`, to set up a dataframe `solarWatts`; see Section 10.3.1, *Creating a dataframe from imported data*. In a similar way, we can create dataframes `price` and `rates` from the other two files.

We show now how to merge these three dataframes into one and to treat rows with missing data in the resulting dataframe.

First, we merge `solarWatts` with `price`. For this, we use the pandas command `merge`:

```
solar_all=pd.merge(solarWatts, price, how='outer', sort=True, on='Date')
solar_all=pd.merge(solar_all, rates, how='outer', sort=True, on='Date')
```

It sets the column `Date`, which exists in both dataframes as the index of the new frame. The parameter `how` defines how to set up the new index column. By specifying `outer` we decided to choose the union of both index columns. Finally, we want to sort the index.

As `solarWatts` has data for every minute and the price changes on an hourly basis, we obtain in the new dataframe lines like the following:

```
                     Watt   SEK   Euro_SEK
Date
2019-10-06 15:03:00  4145.0  NaN       NaN
2019-10-06 15:04:00  5784.0  NaN       NaN
```

The missing data is automatically filled with NaN (which means *not a number*; see Section 2.2: *Numeric types*).

We will study now how to treat missing data.

10.3.5 Missing data in a dataframe

We saw in the last section that missing data is often indicated by NaN. The way missing data is indicated depends on the datatype of the column. Missing timestamps are indicated by the pandas object NaT, while missing data with another non-numeric datatype is indicated by None.

The dataframe method isnull returns a Boolean dataframe with the entry True at all places with missing data.

We will study various methods for treating missing data before returning to the solar cell data example.

Let's demonstrate these methods on a small dataframe:

```
frame = pd.DataFrame(array([[1., -5.,   3., NaN],
                            [3.,   4., NaN, 17.],
                            [6.,   8., 11.,  7.]]),
                     columns=['a','b','c','d'])
```

This dataframe is displayed as:

```
     a     b     c     d
0  1.0  -5.0   3.0   NaN
1  3.0   4.0   NaN  17.0
2  6.0   8.0  11.0   7.0
```

Dataframes with missing data can be handled in different ways:

- Drop all rows containing missing data, frame.dropna(axis=0):

```
     a    b     c    d
2  6.0  8.0  11.0  7.0
```

- Drop all columns containing missing data, frame.dropna(axis=1):

```
     a     b
0  1.0  -5.0
1  3.0   4.0
2  6.0   8.0
```

- Replace the missing data by padding data from previous the
  row, `frame.fillna(method='pad',axis=0)`:

```
       a     b      c      d
0    1.0  -5.0    3.0    NaN
1    3.0   4.0    3.0   17.0
2    6.0   8.0   11.0    7.0
```

In this case, if there is no data to pad with, `NaN` remains.

- Interpolate numeric data column-wise, `frame.interpolate(axis=0,`
  `method='linear')`:

```
       a     b      c
0    1.0  -5.0    3.0    NaN
1    3.0   4.0    7.0   17.0
2    6.0   8.0   11.0    7.0
```

Again, values that cannot be computed by interpolation remain as `NaN`.

The way we used the method interpolate assumes that data is collected on an equidistant grid. If the index is numeric or a datetime object it can be used as the x-axis. This is achieved, for example, by using the parameter value `method='polynomial'`.

To use different methods on different columns is possible by using the parameter inplace:

```
frame['c'].fillna(method='pad', inplace=True)
frame['d'].fillna(method='bfill',inplace=True)
```

We return now to the solar cell example. Electricity prices change on an hourly basis, valuta exchange rates on a daily basis, and the energy production by the solar panels is recorded every minute during daylight times. This is the reason why the dataframe merging step introduced many NaN (see `Section 10.3.4`, Merging dataframes).

We replace these missing values by padding:

```
solar_all['SEK'].fillna(method='pad', axis=0, inplace=True)
solar_all['Euro_SEK'].fillna(method='pad', axis=0, inplace=True)
```

There are still `NaN` values in the table. The solar cells produce only energy during the daytime with sufficient light. Outside these periods, the column Watt contains the value `NaN`.

In the next section, we visualize the data with pandas' dataframe plot functionality and we will see that `NaN` values are simply ignored in the plot.

10.4 Working with dataframes

So far, we have seen how to create and modify a dataframe. Now, we turn to data interpretation. We will look at examples of visualization, show how to make simple calculations, and see how to group data. These are all stepping stones into the world of pandas. The strength of this module is in its large range of statistical tools. We leave the presentation of these tools to textbooks on practical statistics, while we focus here on the basic principles of pandas programming. We do not aim for completeness. Again, let's serve an appetizer.

10.4.1 Plotting from dataframes

To demonstrate the plotting functionality, we plot the energy price changes on May 16, 2020. For this, we construct a subframe of the data from that day:

```
solar_all.loc['2020-05-16'].plot(y='SEK')
```

You can see that we indexed here with the full day. This is a short form of slicing:

```
solar_all.loc['2020-05-16 00:00':'2020-05-16 23:59']
```

The resulting plot, Figure 10.1, shows the hourly variation of electricity prices in Swedish crowns on a typical day of the year.

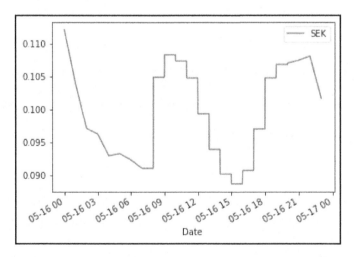

Figure 10.1: Plotting one column of a dataframe: the hourly price in Swedish crowns (SEK) per kWh on May 16, 2020

pandas' plot command is built upon plot from the module matplotlib.pyplot, which we met in `Chapter 6`, Plotting.

It accepts the same parameters, for example, linestyle or marker.

The data for the x axis is taken from the dataframe index if not otherwise specified. Alternatively, you can plot one dataframe column versus another.

Line plots leave gaps where data is missing. You see this in the next figure that displays the solar cell's power in the first week of June 2020. As there is no solar cell data outside daylight time, the plot has gaps. See Figure 10.2.

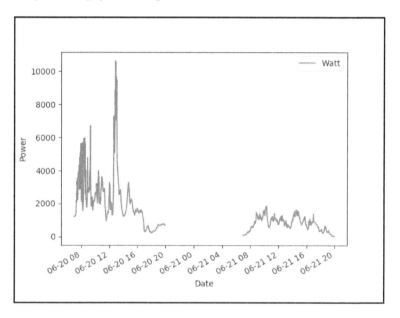

Figure 10.2: A plot of a data series with missing data (NaN): the power in Watts of the solar cells in the first week of June 2020. You can clearly see the periods where no energy was produced

The command we used for this plot is as follows:

```
ax1=solar_all.loc['2020-06-20':'2020-06-21'].plot(None,'Watt')
ax1.set_ylabel('Power')
```

Here, you can see the advantage of working with an axis object, ax1 in this case. This allows us to modify the axis labels or the legend, for example, ax1.legend(['Power [W]']).

We give more plot examples in the next sections, when we see how to do some calculations within dataframes and how to group data.

10.4.2 Calculations within dataframes

We can do simple calculations on dataframe columns by applying functions on every element of the column, that is, elementwise application of functions. These functions can be built-in Python functions, NumPy functions, or user-defined functions, such as lambda functions (see `Section 7.7`, Anonymous functions).

The simplest way is to operate on the columns directly. In the following example, we convert watts into kilowatts and Swedish crowns (SEK) into Euros by using the conversion rate, which was the actual rate on the day of the measurement:

```
solar_converted=pd.DataFrame()
solar_converted['kW']=solar_all['Watt']/1000
solar_converted['Euro']=solar_all['SEK']/solar_all['Euro_SEK']
```

Tacitly, we also adjusted the column labels to the converted units.

The command `solar_converted.loc['2020-07-01 7:00':'2020-07-01 7:04']` then returns the converted data for July, 1st 2020:

```
                      kW       Euro
Date
2020-07-01 07:00:00  2.254    0.037147
2020-07-01 07:01:00  1.420    0.037147
2020-07-01 07:02:00  2.364    0.037147
2020-07-01 07:03:00  0.762    0.037147
2020-07-01 07:04:00  2.568    0.037147
```

We can also apply NumPy's (universal) functions to entire rows or columns. The following example computes the maximal power supplied by the solar cells:

```
import numpy as np
np.max(solar_all['Watt']) # returns 12574
```

To print the corresponding date, we use the function argmax :

```
print(solar_all.index[np.argmax(solar_all['Watt'])])
```

The printed date is then:

```
2020-05-16 10:54:00
```

From the preceding examples, one can see that missing data marked by NaN is treated really as missing data, that is, as if it was not there. As not all computational methods have this property, it might be safer to replace NaN with 0 in these cases:

```
solar_all['Watt'].fillna(value=0., inplace=True)
```

For the application of general user-defined functions, there is a dataframe method apply. It performs row- or column-wise operations on the entire dataframe.

10.4.3 Grouping data

The ability to group data is one of the essential features for pandas' dataframes. In the solar cell example, you saw that we had a data frequency of one measurement per minute. What if you want to report on an hourly or daily basis instead? We just form groups and aggregate the data in a prescribed way.

The following example forms a new dataframe with the two columns labeled Watt and SEK reporting the peak solar cell power per day and the average price in SEK:

```
solar_day=solar_all.groupby(solar_all.index.date).agg({'Watt':'max',
                                                        'SEK':'mean'})
```

Again, we can visualize the results by using the dataframe method plot:

```
solar_day.index=pd.to_datetime(solar_day.index,format='%Y-%m-%d')
ax=solar_day.loc['2020-06-01':'2020-06-30'].plot.bar('Watt')
```

Note, we created an axis object, ax, in order to change the tick labels on the x-axis:

```
ax.set_xticklabels([tf.strftime("%m-%d")
                    for tf in
solarday.loc['2020-06-01':'2020-06-30'].index])
```

This results in Figure 10.3:

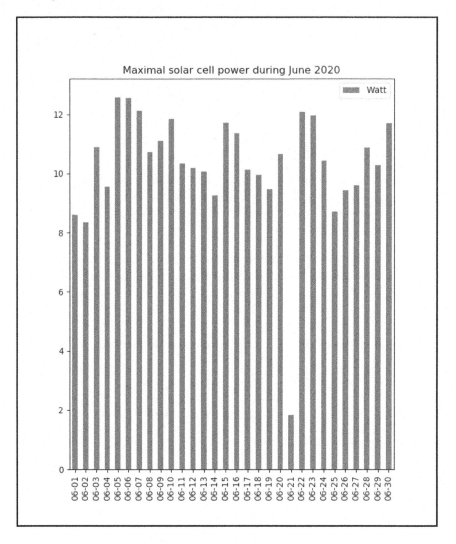

Figure 10.3: Peak solar cell power per day in June 2020

Here, we grouped all days within a month.

We can also jump hierarchies when grouping: In the preceding example we grouped days within a month but we can also group by hours within a month or even from the entire set. For example, to see if the price for electrical energy normally has two peaks per day, we can group the data by hour and form the mean:

```
solar_hour=solar_all.groupby(solar_all.index.hour).agg({'SEK':mean})
ax=solar_hour.plot()
ax=solar_hour.plot(marker='*')
ax.set_title('The average energy price change on a day')
ax.set_xlabel('hour of day')
ax.set_ylabel('SEK/kWh')
```

These commands result in Figure 10.4:

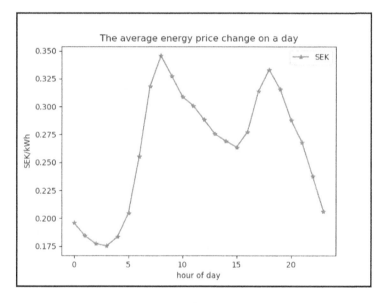

Figure 10.4: The result of data grouping hour-wise

Grouping data is often a starting point for getting answers to special questions that require computational steps on grouped data. For instance, in our example, we have the minute-wise power (in Watts) of the solar cells, but what is the hourly energy output in kWh of this system? To answer this question, we have to:

- Group the data hour-wise in a hierarchical way.
- Form the discrete integral of the data on 60 minute intervals.
- Store this in a new dataframe or series object.

For the first task, we make use of pandas' ability to make a hierarchical indexer. We group hierarchically by year, month, day, and hour:

```
grouping_list=[solar_all.index.year, solar_all.index.month,
                solar_all.index.day, solar_all.index.hour]
solar_hour=solar_all.groupby(grouping_list)
```

Integration can be done in this case, as we started with the per-minute data, just by summing the data:

```
# integrating by summing up the data
solar_hour=solar_hour.agg({'Watt':sum})

solar_hour=solar_hour/(1000*60) # Conversion from Wmin to kWh
```

Then we visualize the result in the usual way:

```
ax=solar_hour['Watt'].loc[(2020,6,19)].plot.bar()
ax.set_title('Energy production on June, 19 2020')
ax.set_xlabel('Hour')
ax.set_ylabel('Energy [kWh]')
```

This gives us Figure 10.5:

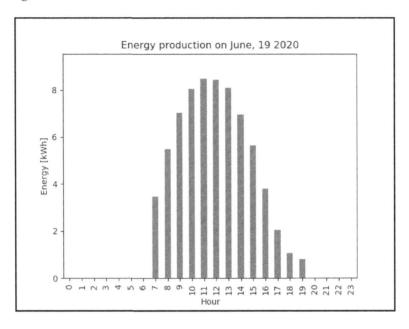

Figure 10.5: An example plot of a dataframe produced by hierarchical grouping

Alternatively, we could have used the command scipy.integrate.simps for the integration of discrete data as a parameter of the aggregate method, agg. As this function does not treat missing data, the remark at the end of Section 10.4.2, Calculations within dataframes, applies, and we would have to replace all NaN values with 0 before we start.

10.5 Summary

In this chapter, you got a brief introduction to pandas and saw how the concept of NumPy arrays is extended to dataframes. Instead of a never-complete explanation of the possibilities of dataframes, we guided you using an example of solar cell energy data through the first steps with pandas: setting up a dataframe from a file, merging frames, grouping data, and making calculations.

11

Communication by a Graphical User Interface

Graphical user interfaces (GUIs) are convenient tools to input user data to your Python program. In all likelihood, you have used tools such as *selection lists, radio buttons,* or *sliders* to communicate with an application. In this chapter, we show how to add some of these tools to your program. We base this chapter on tools provided by the module **Matplotlib**, which we already met in Section 6.2: *Working with Matplotlib objects directly*.

Although there are alternatives such as the module **Tkinter** for a more sophisticated design of GUIs, Matplotlib appears as an ideal entry point with a low threshold to add this comfortable way of communicating with your code.

The purpose of this chapter is to demonstrate the basic principles of GUI programming within Matplotlib. The role of events, slider movements, or mouse clicks and their interaction with so-called call-back functions is explained, along with a couple of examples.

Clearly, we do not aim for completeness. Having understood the basic principles, the Matplotlib documentation is a reservoir of detailed information on various widgets and their parameters.

We'll cover the following main topics in this chapter:

- A guiding example to widgets
- The button widget and mouse events

11.1 A guiding example to widgets

In this section, we present the basic components11.1 A guiding example to widgets of a **widget** and their counterparts in **Python**. We do this by using the guiding example displayed in the following figure:

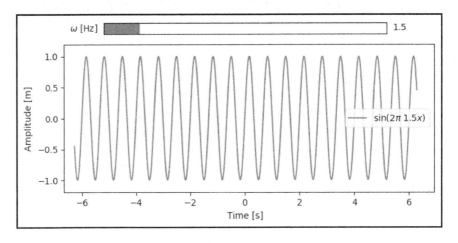

Figure 11.1: A widget to display $\sin(2\pi\omega x)$ for user-given frequencies ω

In this figure, we see a slider bar at the top. With the use of a computer mouse, the blue bar can be moved from left to right and the value for ω, ranging between 1 and 5, is displayed on the right of the bar.

Correspondingly, the frequency of the sine wave displayed in the plot window changes.

This widget consists of three parts:

- A figure object with an axes object and the plot
- An axes object containing a slider object
- A call-back function for updating the plot as soon as the slider value changes

We discussed how to program the first part, in Section 6.2: *Working with Matplotlib objects directly.*

In the following code snippet, we first create a figure with a given size and then a sufficiently large axes object that is placed into the figure such that its lower-left corner point is placed at the pair of figure coordinates $(0.1, 0.15)$. Then, the user is asked to input a floating-point number between 1 and 5 for the frequency ω:

```
from matplotlib.pyplot import *
fig = figure(figsize = (4,2))
ax = axes([0.1, 0.15, 0.8, 0.7]) # axes for the plot
omega=float(input('Give a value for $\omega$ between 1 and 5:\n'))
x = linspace(-2*pi, 2*pi, 800)
ax.set_ylim(-1.2, 1.2)
lines, = ax.plot(x, sin(2.*pi*omega*x))
```

Now, in the next step, we add a second axes object and put it into it a slider:

```
from matplotlib.widgets import Slider
sld_ax = axes([0.2, 0.9, 0.6, 0.05]) # axes for slider
sld = Slider(sld_ax, '$\omega$ [Hz]', 1., 5., valinit=1.)
omega=sld.val
```

The axes object for the slider, sld_ax, is defined by giving its dimensions and the location of the left lower point in the figure's coordinate system.

The new construction element is the Slider object. Its constructor uses the slider axes, a label, and maximum and minimum values displayed on the left and right sides of the slider. The slider object has an attribute val, which contains the value given by the slider position.

Initially, the slider position is set to valinit.

The last part is the core part of the program, the call-back function, and the update of the plot, whenever the slider value changes:

```
def update_frequency(omega):
  lines.set_ydata(np.sin(2.*pi*omega*x))

sld.on_changed(update_frequency)
```

A call-back function is a function called when the slider (or another widget object) is changed. In our case, it is the function update_frequency. The slider method on_changed defines the action to be performed whenever the slider value changes. Here, the function update_frequency is called with the slider value val as its single argument.

We will conclude this introductory section by putting the parts together. Note that there is no longer any need for the input function used in the beginning as we now use the much more elegant GUI method to input values. We also provided the plot with a legend to display the use of the slider value. Note how string formatting and LaTeX commands were combined:

```
from matplotlib.pyplot import *
from matplotlib.widgets import Slider

fig = figure(figsize = (4,2))
sld_ax = axes([0.2, 0.9, 0.6, 0.05]) # axes for slider
ax = axes([0.1, 0.15, 0.8, 0.7]) # axes for the plot
ax.xaxis.set_label_text('Time [s]')
ax.yaxis.set_label_text('Amplitude [m]')
sld = Slider(sld_ax, '$\omega$ [Hz]', 1., 5., valinit=1.5)
omega=sld.val
x = linspace(-2*pi, 2*pi, 800)
ax.set_ylim(-1.2, 1.2)
# Plot of the initial curve
# Note, how LaTeX commands and string formatting is combined in the
# next command
lines, = ax.plot(x, sin(2.*pi*omega*x), label=f'$\sin(2\pi\; {omega} x)$ ')
ax.legend()

def update_frequency(omega):
  lines.set_ydata(np.sin(2.*pi*omega*x))
  # A legend is updated by p text box widget set_varroviding tuples
  # with line objects and tuples with labels
  ax.legend((lines,),(f'$\sin(2\pi\; {omega} x)$',))


sld.on_changed(update_frequency)
```

In this section, we demonstrated the use of a widget for user input. It is a user-friendly way to ask for parameters and to display related results.

11.1.1 Changing a value with a slider bar

In the last section, we covered the use of a slider. The most important attribute of a slider is its value, `val`. This is communicated to the call-back function.

Other attributes are the limits of the value given by the slider, `valmin`, and `valmax`, and a stepping functionality, `valstep`, to make the change to the value discrete. A formatting attribute, `valfmt`, allows us to specify how `valmin` and `valmax` are displayed.

In the next example, we modify the slider definition from above and provide it with these more specific attributes:

```
sld = Slider(sld_ax, label='$\omega$ [Hz]', valmin=1., valmax=5.,
             valinit=1.5, valfmt='%1.1f', valstep=0.1)
```

The formatting argument, %1.1f, in this example says that the value should be displayed as a floating-point number, with one digit to the left of the decimal point and one digit to the right of it.

An example with two sliders

We extend the preceding example by providing two sliders, one for the amplitude and another for the frequency, and we put the sliders in vertical mode.

First, we define the two slider axes:

```
sldo_ax = axes([0.95, 0.15, 0.01, 0.6]) # axes for frequency slider
slda_ax = axes([0.85, 0.15, 0.01, 0.6]) # axes for amplitude slider
```

Then, we define the two sliders with different minimum and maximum values and an orientation parameter:

```
sld_omega = Slider(sldo_ax, label='$\omega$ [Hz]', valmin=1.,
                   valmax=5., valinit=1.5, valfmt='%1.1f',
                   valstep=0.1, orientation='vertical')
sld_amp = Slider(slda_ax, label='$a$ [m]', valmin=0.5,
                 valmax=2.5, valinit=1.0, valfmt='%1.1f',
                 valstep=0.1, orientation='vertical')
```

Both sliders have different call-back functions. They use the value of the related slider as an argument and the value of the other slider as a global variable:

```
def update_frequency(omega):
    lines.set_ydata(sld_amp.val*sin(2.*pi*omega*x))
    ax.legend((lines,),(f'${sld_amp.val} \sin(2\pi\; {omega} x)$',))

def update_amplitude(amp):
    lines.set_ydata(amp*sin(2.*pi*sld_omega.val*x))
    ax.legend((lines,),(f'${amp} \sin(2\pi\; {sld_omega.val} x)$',))
    ax.set_ylim(-(amp+0.2), amp+0.2)

sld_omega.on_changed(update_frequency)
sld_amp.on_changed(update_amplitude)
```

In the following figure, the GUI is displayed:

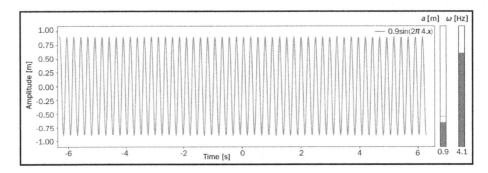

Figure 11.2: A curve with two parameters given by two vertical sliders

Some actions require that the user has to wait until the result of a change is seen. Often, it is more convenient and user-friendly to first collect the changes and then do the update. This can be made by a special button widget, which will be introduced in the next section.

11.2 The button widget and mouse events

The button widget is a simple little tool with a big variety of useful applications. We introduce it here by continuing the previous example and adding an update button to the GUI. Then we use a button to extract data from a curve.

11.2.1 Updating curve parameters with a button

So far, we have updated the curve when the slider value changed and used the method `on_changed` for this. A complicated graphical output might take some computing time to update. In such a case, you would like to design the GUI in such a way that first, the curve parameters are set by sliders, and then a button is pressed to initiate the updating of the curve.

This can be achieved by the `Button` widget:

```
from matplotlib.widgets import Button
button_ax = axes([0.85, 0.01, 0.05, 0.05]) # axes for update button
btn = Button(button_ax, 'Update', hovercolor='red')
```

The coordinates in this example are set in such a way that the button is located under the two sliders. It is labeled by **Update** and its color turns to red when the mouse is placed over the button.

This widget has a method, `on_clicked`, that is used instead of the slider method `on_changed`:

```
def update(event):
    lines.set_ydata(sld_amp.val*sin(2.*pi*sld_omega.val*x))
    ax.legend((lines,),
              (f'${sld_amp.val:1.1f} \sin(2\pi\; \
              {sld_omega.val:1.1f} x)$',))
btn.on_clicked(update)
```

The call-back function has a single parameter, `event`. It is not used in this example. It could be used to assign different actions to the button depending on how the mouse was clicked – by a single click, double click, right-button click, or left-button click. We will look at events in more detail in the next section.

11.2.2 Mouse events and textboxes

In the last example, we encountered mouse events in the context of a button widget. We can also catch a mouse event without using a button. To this end, we need to connect a general button click to a call-back function.

To demonstrate this, we consider again the previously generated plot of the sine wave and pick by mouse clicks points and display their coordinates in a textbox to the plot. If clicked with the right mouse button, we also display the point picked by means of a red circle in the plot.

First, we prepare a textbox widget. We already know that we first have to position the widget by defining an axes object and then providing the widget with the desired properties:

```
from matplotlib.widgets import TextBox
textbox_ax=axes([0.85,0.6,0.1,0.15])
txtbx=TextBox(textbox_ax, label='', initial='Clicked on:\nx=--\ny=--')
```

We provided the box with no label but some initial text. The textbox has the attribute `val` containing the text. We will change this attribute now depending on the position of a mouse click:

```
points, = ax.plot([], [], 'ro')

def onclick(event):
    if event.inaxes == ax:
        txtbx.set_val(
            f'clicked on:\nx={event.xdata:1.1f}\ny={event.ydata:1.1f}')
        if event.button==3:  # Mouse button right
            points.set_xdata([event.xdata])
            points.set_ydata([event.ydata])
    else:
            txtbx.set_val(f'clicked on:\noutside axes\n area')
    fig.canvas.draw_idle()
cid = fig.canvas.mpl_connect('button_press_event', onclick)
```

As there is no widget like a button widget used, we have to couple an event to a call-back function. This is done by the canvas method, `mpl_connect`. The call-back function `onclick` reacts to the position of the mouse click. We know from the event attribute `inaxes` in which axes object the mouse click occurred. Through this, we can even access information about the button pressed, and the exact coordinates of the mouse click are also available. The call-back function makes use of a `Line2D` object, `points`, which is initialized with empty data lists before the call-back function is used for the first time. This initialization defines the plot style, red circles in this case:

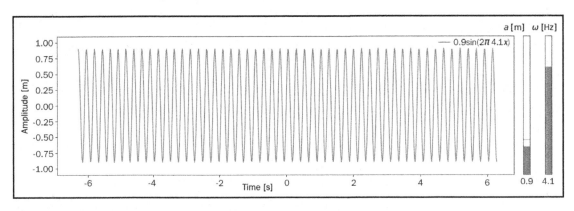

Figure 11.3: Displaying a value on the curve by using a mouse click

11.3 Summary

In this chapter, we learned the basic principles of GUI programming within Matplotlib. We also considered an example that helped us to learn more about widgets. In the next chapter, we are going to learn about error and exception handling.

12
Error and Exception Handling

In this chapter, we will cover errors and exceptions and how to find and fix them. Handling exceptions is an important part of writing reliable and usable code. We will introduce basic built-in exceptions and show how to use and treat exceptions. We'll introduce debugging and show you how to use the built-in Python debugger.

In this chapter, we cover the following topics:

- What are exceptions?
- Finding errors: debugging

12.1 What are exceptions?

The first error that programmers (even experienced ones) are confronted with is when the code has incorrect syntax, meaning that the code instructions are not correctly formatted.

Consider this example of a syntax error:

```
>>> for i in range(10)
  File "<stdin>", line 1
    for i in range(10)
                     ^
SyntaxError: invalid syntax
```

The error occurs because of a missing colon at the end of the `for` declaration. This is an example of an exception being raised. In the case of `SyntaxError`, it tells the programmer that the code has incorrect syntax and also prints the line where the error occurred, with an arrow pointing to where in that line the problem is.

Exceptions in Python are derived (inherited) from a base class called `Exception`. Python comes with a number of built-in exceptions. Some common exception types are listed in *Table 12.1*.

Here are two common examples of exceptions. As you might expect, ZeroDivisionError is raised when you try to divide by zero:

```
def f(x):
    return 1/x

>>> f(2.5)
0.4
>>> f(0)

Traceback (most recent call last):
  File "<stdin>", line 1, in <module>
  File "exception_tests.py", line 3, in f
    return 1/x
ZeroDivisionError: integer division or modulo by zero
```

Exception	Description
IndexError	Index is out of bounds, for example, v[10] when v only has five elements.
KeyError	A reference to an undefined dictionary key.
NameError	A name not found, for example, an undefined variable.
LinAlgError	Errors in the linalg module, for example, when solving a system with a singular matrix.
ValueError	Incompatible data value, for example, when using dot with incompatible arrays.
IOError	I/O operation fails, for example, file not found.
ImportError	A module or name is not found on import.

Table 12.1: Some frequently used built-in exceptions and their meaning

A division by zero raises ZeroDivisionError and prints out the file name, the line, and the function name where the error occurred.

As we have seen before, arrays can only contain elements of the same datatype. If you try to assign a value of an incompatible type, ValueError is raised. An example of a value error is:

```
>>> a = arange(8.0)
>>> a
array([ 0., 1., 2., 3., 4., 5., 6., 7.])
>>> a[3] = 'string'
Traceback (most recent call last):
  File "<stdin>", line 1, in <module>
ValueError: could not convert string to float: string
```

Here, `ValueError` is raised because the array contains floats and an element cannot be assigned a string value.

12.1.1 Basic principles

Let's look at the basic principles on how to use exceptions by raising them with `raise` and catching them with `try` statements.

Raising exceptions

Creating an error is referred to as raising an exception. You saw some examples of exceptions in the previous section. You can also define your own exceptions of a predefined type or use an exception of an unspecified type. Raising an exception is done with a command like this:

```
raise Exception("Something went wrong")
```

Here an exception of an unspecified type was raised.

It might be tempting to print out error messages when something goes wrong, for example, like this:

```
print("The algorithm did not converge.")
```

This is not recommended for a number of reasons. Firstly, printouts are easy to miss, especially if the message is buried in many other messages being printed to your console. Secondly, and more importantly, it renders your code unusable by other code. The calling code will not *read* what you printed and will not have a way of knowing that an error occurred and therefore has no way of taking care of it.

For these reasons, it is always better to raise an exception instead. Exceptions should always contain a descriptive message, for example:

```
raise Exception("The algorithm did not converge.")
```

This message will stand out clearly to the user. It also gives the opportunity for the calling code to know that an error occurred, and to possibly find a remedy.

Here is a typical example of checking the input inside a function to make sure it is usable before continuing. A simple check for negative values and the correct datatype ensures the intended input of a function to compute factorials:

```
def factorial(n):
    if not (isinstance(n, (int, int32, int64))):
        raise TypeError("An integer is expected")
    if not (n >=0):
        raise ValueError("A positive number is expected")
```

The user of the function will immediately know what the error is, if an incorrect input is given, and it is the user's responsibility to handle the exception. Note the use of the exception name when raising a predefined exception type, in this case, ValueError followed by the message. By specifying the type of the exception, the calling code can decide to handle errors differently depending on what type of error is raised.

Summing up, it is always better to raise exceptions than to print error messages.

Catching exceptions

Dealing with an exception is referred to as *catching an exception*. Checking for exceptions is done with the commands try and except.

An exception stops the program execution flow and looks for the closest try enclosing block. If the exception is not caught, the program unit is left and it continues searching for the next enclosing try block in a program unit higher up in the calling stack. If no block is found and the exception is not handled, execution stops entirely and the standard traceback information is displayed.

Let's look at the factorial example from previously and use it with the try statement:

```
n=-3
try:
    print(factorial(n))
except ValueError:
    print(factorial(-n))    # Here we catch the error
```

In this case, if the code inside the try block raises an error of type ValueError, the exception will be caught and the action in the except block is taken. If no exception occurs inside the try block, the except block is skipped entirely and execution continues.

The `except` statement can catch multiple exceptions. This is done by simply grouping them in a tuple, like this:

```
except (RuntimeError, ValueError, IOError):
```

The `try` block can also have multiple `except` statements. This makes it possible to handle exceptions differently depending on the type. Let's see another example of multiple exception types:

```
try:
    f = open('data.txt', 'r')
    data = f.readline()
    value = float(data)
except FileNotFoundError as FnF:
    print(f'{FnF.strerror}: {FnF.filename}')
except ValueError:
    print("Could not convert data to float.")
```

Here, `FileNotFoundError` will be caught if, for example, the file does not exist; and `ValueError` will be caught if, for example, the data in the first line of the file is not compatible with the float data type.

In this example, we assigned `FileNotFoundError` to a variable `FnF` by the keyword `as`. This allows access to more details when handling this exception. Here we printed the error string `FnF.strerror` and the name of the related file `FnF.filename`. Each error type can have its own set of attributes depending on the type. If the file with the name `data.txt` does not exist, in the preceding example, the message is:

```
No such file or directory: data.txt
```

This is a useful way to format the output when catching exceptions.

The `try-except` combination can be extended with optional `else` and `finally` blocks.

An example of using `else` can be seen in `Section 15.2.1`: *Testing the bisection algorithm*. Combining `try` with `finally` gives a useful construction when cleanup work needs to happen at the end. This is illustrated by an example for making sure a file is closed properly is:

```
try:
    f = open('data.txt', 'r')
    # some function that does something with the file
    process_file_data(f)
except:
    ...
```

```
finally:
    f.close()
```

This will make sure that the file is closed at the end no matter what exceptions are thrown while processing the file data. Exceptions that are not handled inside the try statement are saved and raised after the finally block. This combination is used in the with statement; see Section 12.1.3: *Context managers – the with statement.*

12.1.2 User-defined exceptions

Besides the built-in Python exceptions, it is also possible to define your own exceptions. Such user-defined exceptions should inherit from the base class Exception. This can be useful when you define your own classes such as the polynomial class in Section 19.1.

Take a look at this small example of a simple user-defined exception:

```
class MyError(Exception):
    def __init__(self, expr):
        self.expr = expr
    def __str__(self):
        return str(self.expr)

try:
    x = random.rand()
    if x < 0.5:
        raise MyError(x)
except MyError as e:
    print("Random number too small", e.expr)
else:
    print(x)
```

A random number is generated. If the number is below 0.5, an exception is thrown and a message that the value is too small is printed. If no exception is raised, the number is printed.

In this example, you also saw a case of using else in a try statement. The block under else will be executed if no exception occurs.

It is recommended that you define your exceptions with names that end in Error, like the naming of the standard built-in exceptions.

12.1.3 Context managers – the with statement

There is a very useful construction in Python for simplifying exception handling when working with contexts such as files or databases. The statement encapsulates the structure try ... finally in one simple command. Here is an example of using with to read a file:

```
with open('data.txt', 'w') as f:
    process_file_data(f)
```

This will try to open the file, run the specified operations on the file (for example, reading), and close the file. If anything goes wrong during the execution of process_file_data, the file is closed properly and then the exception is raised. This is equivalent to:

```
f = open('data.txt', 'w')
try:
    # some function that does something with the file
    process_file_data(f)
except:
    ...
finally:
    f.close()
```

We will use this option in Section 14.1: *File handling*, when reading and writing files.

The preceding file-reading example is an example of using context managers. Context managers are Python objects with two special methods, __enter__ and __exit__. Any object of a class that implements these two methods can be used as a context manager. In this example, the file object f is a context manager as there are the methods f.__enter__ and f.__exit__.

The method __enter__ should implement the initialization instructions, for example, opening a file or a database connection. If this method has a return statement, the returned object is accessed using the construct as. Otherwise, the keyword as is omitted. The method __exit__ contains the cleanup instructions, for example, closing a file or committing transactions and closing a database connection. For more explanations and an example of a self-written context manager, see Section 15.3.3: *Timing with a context manager.*

There are NumPy functions that can be used as context managers. For example, the function load supports the context manager for some file formats. NumPy's function errstate can be used as a context manager to specify floating-point error handling behavior within a block of code.

Here is an example of working with `errstate` and a context manager:

```
import numpy as np      # note, sqrt in NumPy and SciPy
                        # behave differently in that example
with errstate(invalid='ignore'):
    print(np.sqrt(-1)) # prints 'nan'

with errstate(invalid='warn'):
    print(np.sqrt(-1)) # prints 'nan' and
                 # 'RuntimeWarning: invalid value encountered in sqrt'

with errstate(invalid='raise'):
    print(np.sqrt(-1)) # prints nothing and raises FloatingPointError
```

See `Section 2.2.2:` *Floating-point numbers* for more details on this example and `Section 15.3.3:` *Timing with a context manager* for another example.

12.2 Finding errors: debugging

Errors in software code are sometimes referred to as bugs. Debugging is the process of finding and fixing bugs in code. This process can be performed at varying degrees of sophistication. The most efficient way is to use a tool called a debugger. Having unit tests in place is a good way to identify errors early; see `Section 15.2.2:` *Using the unittest package.* When it is not obvious where or what the problem is, a debugger is very useful.

12.2.1 Bugs

There are typically two kinds of bugs:

- An exception is raised and not caught.
- The code does not function properly.

The first case is usually easier to fix. The second can be more difficult as the problem can be a faulty idea or solution, a faulty implementation, or a combination of the two.

We are only concerned with the first case in what follows, but the same tools can be used to help find why the code does not do what it is supposed to.

12.2.2 The stack

When an exception is raised, you see the call stack. The call stack contains the trace of all the functions that called the code where the exception was raised.

A simple stack example is:

```
def f():
    g()
def g():
    h()
def h():
    1//0

f()
```

The stack, in this case, is f, g, and h. The output generated by running this piece of code looks like this:

```
Traceback (most recent call last):
  File "stack_example.py", line 11, in <module>
    f()
  File "stack_example.py", line 3, in f
    g()
  File "stack_example.py", line 6, in g
    h() File "stack_example.py", line 9, in h
    1//0
ZeroDivisionError: integer division or modulo by zero
```

The error is printed. The sequence of functions leading up to the error is shown. The function f on line 11 was called, which in turn called g and then h. This caused ZeroDivisionError.

A stack trace reports on the active stack at a certain point in the execution of a program. A stack trace lets you track the sequence of functions called up to a given point. Often this is after an uncaught exception has been raised. This is sometimes called post-mortem analysis, and the stack tracepoint is then the place where the exception occurred. Another option is to invoke a stack trace manually to analyze a piece of code where you suspect there is an error, perhaps before the exception occurs.

In the following example, an exception is raised to provoke the generation of a stack trace:

```
def f(a):
    g(a)
def g(a):
    h(a)
```

```
def h(a):
    raise Exception(f'An exception just to provoke a strack trace and a
value a={a}')

f(23)
```

This returns the following output:

```
Traceback (most recent call last):

  File ".../Python_experiments/manual_trace.py", line 17, in <module>
    f(23)

  File "../Python_experiments/manual_trace.py", line 11, in f
    g(a)

  File "../Python_experiments/manual_trace.py", line 13, in g
    h(a)

  File "/home/claus/Python_experiments/manual_trace.py", line 15, in h
    raise Exception(f'An exception just to provoke a strack trace and a
value a={a}')

Exception: An exception just to provoke a strack trace and a value a=23
```

12.2.3 The Python debugger

Python comes with its own built-in debugger called pdb. Some development environments come with the debugger integrated. The following process still holds in most of these cases.

The easiest way to use the debugger is to enable stack tracing at the point in your code that you want to investigate. Here is a simple example of triggering the debugger based on the example mentioned in Section 7.3: *Return values*:

```
import pdb

def complex_to_polar(z):
    pdb.set_trace()
    r = sqrt(z.real ** 2 + z.imag ** 2)
    phi = arctan2(z.imag, z.real)
    return (r,phi)
z = 3 + 5j
r,phi = complex_to_polar(z)

print(r,phi)
```

The command `pdb.set_trace()` starts the debugger and enables the tracing of subsequent commands. The preceding code will show this:

```
> debugging_example.py(7)complex_to_polar()
-> r = sqrt(z.real ** 2 + z.imag ** 2)
(Pdb)
```

The debugger prompt is indicated with `(Pdb)`. The debugger stops the program execution and gives you a prompt that lets you inspect variables, modify variables, step through commands, and so on.

The current line is printed at each step, so you can follow where you are and what will happen next. Stepping through commands is done with the command n (next), like this:

```
> debugging_example.py(7)complex_to_polar()
-> r = sqrt(z.real ** 2 + z.imag ** 2)
(Pdb) n
> debugging_example.py(8)complex_to_polar()
-> phi = arctan2(z.imag, z.real)
(Pdb) n
> debugging_example.py(9)complex_to_polar()
-> return (r,phi)
(Pdb)
...
```

The command n (next) will continue to the next line and print the line. If you need to see more than one line at a time, the command l (list) shows the current line with the surrounding code:

```
> debugging_example.py(7)complex_to_polar()
-> r = sqrt(z.real ** 2 + z.imag ** 2)
(Pdb) l
  2
  3 import pdb
  4
  5 def complex_to_polar(z):
  6 pdb.set_trace()
  7 -> r = sqrt(z.real ** 2 + z.imag ** 2)
  8 phi = arctan2(z.imag, z.real)
  9 return (r,phi)
 10
 11 z = 3 + 5j
 12 r,phi = complex_to_polar(z)
(Pdb)
```

The inspection of variables can be done by printing their values to the console using the command p (print) followed by the variable name. An example of printing variables is:

```
> debugging_example.py(7)complex_to_polar()
-> r = sqrt(z.real ** 2 + z.imag ** 2)
(Pdb) p z
(3+5j)
(Pdb) n
> debugging_example.py(8)complex_to_polar()
-> phi = arctan2(z.imag, z.real)
(Pdb) p r
5.8309518948453007
(Pdb) c
(5.8309518948453007, 1.0303768265243125)
```

The command p (print) will print the variable; the command c (continue) continues execution.

Changing a variable mid-execution is useful. Simply assign the new value at the debugger prompt and step or continue the execution:

```
> debugging_example.py(7)complex_to_polar()
-> r = sqrt(z.real ** 2 + z.imag ** 2)
(Pdb) z = 2j
(Pdb) z
2j
(Pdb) c
(2.0, 1.5707963267948966)
```

Here the variable z is assigned a new value to be used throughout the remaining code. Note that the final printout has changed.

12.2.4 Overview – debug commands

In *Table 12.2*, the most common debug commands are shown. For a full listing and description of commands, see the documentation for more information [24]. Note that any Python command also works, for example, assigning values to variables.

If you want to inspect a variable with a name that coincides with any of the debugger's short commands, for example, h, you must use !h to display the variable.

Command	Action
h	Help (without arguments, it prints available commands)
l	Lists the code around the current line

q	Quit (exits the debugger and the execution stops)
c	Continues execution
r	Continues execution until the current function returns
n	Continues execution until the next line
p <expression>	Evaluates and prints the expression in the current context

Table 12.2: The most common debug commands for the debugger

12.2.5 Debugging in IPython

IPython comes with a version of the debugger called ipdb. At the time of writing this book, the differences to pdb are very minor but this may change.

There is a command in IPython, %pdb, that automatically turns on the debugger in case of an exception. This is very useful when experimenting with new ideas or code. An example of how to automatically turn on the debugger in IPython is:

```
In [1]: %pdb # this is a so - called IPython magic command
Automatic pdb calling has been turned ON

In [2]: a = 10

In [3]: b = 0

In [4]: c = a/b
```

```
ZeroDivisionError                     Traceback (most recent call last)
<ipython-input-4-72278c42f391> in <module>()
---> 1 c = a/b

ZeroDivisionError: integer division or modulo by zero
> <ipython-input-4-72278c42f391>(1)<module>()
      -1 c = a/b
ipdb>
```

The IPython magic command %pdb at the IPython prompt automatically enables the debugger when exceptions are raised. Here the debugger prompt shows ipdb instead to indicate that the debugger is running.

12.3 Summary

The key concepts in this chapter were exceptions and errors. We showed how an exception is raised to be caught later in another program unit. You can define your own exceptions and equip them with messages and current values of given variables.

The code may return unexpected results without throwing an exception. The technique to localize the source of the erroneous result is called debugging. We introduced debugging methods and hopefully encouraged you to train them so that you have them readily available when needed. The need for serious debugging comes sooner than you might expect.

13

Namespaces, Scopes, and Modules

In this chapter, we'll cover Python modules. Modules are files containing functions and class definitions. The concept of a namespace and the scope of variables across functions and modules are also explained in this chapter.

The following topics will be covered in this chapter:

- Namespaces
- The scope of a variable
- Modules

13.1 Namespaces

Names of Python objects, such as the names of variables, classes, functions, and modules, are collected in namespaces. Modules and classes have their own named namespaces with the same name as these objects. These namespaces are created when a module is imported or a class is instantiated. The lifetime of a namespace of a module is as long as the current Python session. The lifetime of a namespace of a class instance is until the instance is deleted.

Functions create a local namespace when they are executed (invoked). It is deleted when the function stops the execution with a regular return or an exception. Local namespaces are unnamed.

The concept of namespaces puts a variable name in its context. For example, there are several functions with the name `sin` and they are distinguished by the namespace they belong to, as shown in the following code:

```
import math
```

```
import numpy
math.sin
numpy.sin
```

They are indeed different, as `numpy.sin` is a universal function accepting lists or arrays as input, while `math.sin` takes only floats. A list with all the names in a particular namespace can be obtained with the command `dir(<name of the namespace>)`. It contains two special names, `__name__` and `__doc__`. The former refers to the name of the module and the latter to its docstring:

```
math.__name__ # returns math
math.__doc__ # returns 'This module provides access to .....'
```

There is a special namespace, `__builtin__`, which contains names that are available in Python without any `import`. It is a named namespace but its name needs not be given when referring to a built-in object:

```
'float' in dir(__builtin__) # returns True
float is __builtin__.float # returns True
```

Let's learn about the scope of a variable in the next section.

13.2 The scope of a variable

A variable defined in one part of a program does not need to be known in other parts. All program units to which a certain variable is known are called the *scope* of that variable. We'll first give an example. Let's consider the two nested functions:

```
e = 3
def my_function(in1):
    a = 2 * e
    b = 3
    in1 = 5
    def other_function():
        c = a
        d = e
        return dir()
    print(f"""
          my_function's namespace: {dir()}
          other_function's namespace: {other_function()}
          """)
    return a
```

The execution of `my_function(3)` results in:

```
my_function's namespace: ['a', 'b', 'in1', 'other_function']
other_function's namespace: ['a', 'c', 'd']
```

The variable e is in the namespace of the program unit that encloses
the function my_function. The variable a is in the namespace of this function, which itself
encloses the innermost function other_function. For the two functions, e is a global
variable, that is, it is not in the local namespace and not listed by dir() but its value is
available.

It is a good practice to pass information to a function only by its parameter list and not use
the construction from the preceding example. An exception can be found in Section 7.7:
Anonymous functions, where global variables are used for closures.

By assigning it a value, a variable automatically becomes a local variable:

```
e = 3
def my_function():
    e = 4
    a = 2
    print(f"my_function's namespace: {dir()}")
```

This can be seen when executing the following code block:

```
e = 3
my_function()
e # has the value 3
```

The output of the preceding code gives shows us the local variables of my_function:

```
my_function's namespace: ['a', 'e']
```

Now, e became a local variable. In fact, this piece of code now has two
variables e belonging to different namespaces.

By using the global declaration statement, a variable defined in a function can be made
global, that is, its value will be accessible even outside this function. The use of
a global declaration is demonstrated as follows:

```
def fun():
    def fun1():
        global a
        a = 3
    def fun2():
        global b
        b = 2
        print(a)
    fun1()
```

```
fun2() # prints a
print(b)
```

It would be advisable to avoid using this construct and the use of `global`. Code using `global` is hard to debug and maintain. The use of classes makes the use of `global` mainly obsolete.

13.3 Modules

In Python, a module is simply a file containing classes and functions. By importing the file in your session or script, the functions and classes become usable.

13.3.1 Introduction

Python comes with many different libraries by default. You may also want to install more of those for specific purposes, such as optimization, plotting, reading/writing file formats, image handling, and so on. NumPy and SciPy are two important examples of such libraries, Matplotlib for plotting is another one. At the end of this chapter, we will list some useful libraries.

To use a library, you may either

- load only certain objects from a library, for example, from NumPy:

    ```
    from numpy import array, vander
    ```

- load the entire library:

    ```
    from numpy import *
    ```

- or give access to an entire library by creating a namespace with the library name:

    ```
    import numpy
    ...
    numpy.array(...)
    ```

    Prefixing a function from the library with the namespace gives access to this function and distinguishes this function from other objects with the same name.

Furthermore, the name of a namespace can be specified together with the `import` command:

```
import numpy as np
```

```
...
np.array(...)
```

Which of these alternatives you use affects the readability of your code as well as the possibilities for mistakes. A common mistake is shadowing:

```
from scipy.linalg import eig
A = array([[1,2],[3,4]])
(eig, eigvec) = eig(A)
...
(c, d) = eig(B) # raises an error
```

A way to avoid this unintended effect is to use `import` instead of `from` and then access the command by referring to the namespace, here `sl`:

```
import scipy.linalg as sl
A = array([[1,2],[3,4]])
(eig, eigvec) = sl.eig(A) # eig and sl.eig are different objects
...
(c, d) = sl.eig(B)
```

Throughout this book, we have used many commands, objects, and functions. These were imported into the local namespace by statements such as:

```
from scipy import *
```

Importing objects in this manner does not make the module from which they are imported evident. Some examples are given in the following table (*Table 13.1*):

Libraries	Methods
numpy	array, arange, linspace, vstack, hstack, dot, eye, identity, and zeros.
scipy.linalg	solve, lstsq, eig, and det.
matplotlib.pyplot	plot, legend, and cla.
scipy.integrate	quad.
copy	copy and deepcopy.

Table 13.1: Examples of modules and corresponding imported functions

13.3.2 Modules in IPython

IPython is used in code development. A typical scenario is that you work on a file with some function or class definitions that you change within a development cycle. To load the contents of such a file into the shell, you may use `import` but the file is loaded only once. Changing the file has no effect on later imports. That is where IPython's *magic command* `run` enters the stage.

The IPython magic command – run

IPython has a special *magic command* named `run` that executes a file as if you were running it directly in Python. This means that the file is executed independently of what is already defined in IPython. This is the recommended method to execute files from within IPython when you want to test a script intended as a standalone program. You must import all you need in the executed file in the same way as if you were executing it from the command line. A typical example of running code in `myfile.py` is:

```
from numpy import array
...
a = array(...)
```

This script file is executed in Python by `exec(open('myfile.py').read())`. Alternatively, in IPython the *magic command* `run myfile` can be used if you want to make sure that the script runs independently of the previous imports. Everything that is defined in the file is imported into the IPython workspace.

13.3.3 The variable __name__

In any module, the special variable `__name__` is defined as the name of the current module. In the command line (in IPython), this variable is set to `__main__`. This fact allows the following trick:

```
# module
import ...

class ...

if __name__ == "__main__":
    # perform some tests here
```

The tests will be run only when the file is directly run, *not* when it is imported as, when imported, the variable `__name__` takes the name of the module instead of `__main__`.

13.3.4 Some useful modules

The list of useful Python modules is vast. In the following table, we have given a very short segment of such a list, focused on modules related to mathematical and engineering applications (*Table 13.2*):

Module	Description
scipy	Functions used in scientific computing
numpy	Support arrays and related methods
matplotlib	Plotting and visualization
functools	Partial application of functions
itertools	Iterator tools to provide special capabilities, such as slicing to generators
re	Regular expressions for advanced string handling
sys	System-specific functions
os	Operating system interfaces such as directory listing and file handling
datetime	Representing dates and date increments
time	Returning wall clock time
timeit	Measuring execution time
sympy	Computer arithmetic package (symbolic computations)
pickle	Pickling, a special file input and output format
shelves	Shelves, a special file input and output format
contextlib	Tools for context managers

Table 13.2: A non-exhaustive list of useful Python packages for engineering applications

We advise against the use of the mathematics module `math` and favor `numpy` instead. The reason for this is that many of NumPy's functions, such as `sin` operate on arrays, while the corresponding functions in `math` don't.

13.4 Summary

We started the book by telling you that you had to import SciPy and other useful modules. Now you fully understand what importing means. We introduced namespaces and discussed the difference between `import` and `from ... import *`. The scope of a variable was already introduced in `Section 7.2.3`: *Access to variables defined outside the local namespace*, but now you have a more complete picture of the importance of that concept.

14
Input and Output

In this chapter, we will cover some options for handling data files. Depending on the data and the desired format, there are several options for reading and writing. We will show some of the most useful alternatives.

The following topics will be covered in this chapter:

- File handling
- NumPy methods
- Pickling
- Shelves
- Reading and writing Matlab data files
- Reading and writing images

14.1 File handling

File **input and output(I/O)** is essential in a number of scenarios, for example:

- Working with measured or scanned data. Measurements are stored in files that need to be read in order to be analyzed.
- Interacting with other programs. Save results to files so that they can be imported into other applications, and vice-versa.
- Storing information for future reference or comparisons.
- Sharing data and results with others, possibly on other platforms using other software.

In this section, we will cover how to handle file I/O in Python.

14.1.1 Interacting with files

In Python, an object of the type `file` represents the contents of a physical file stored on a disk. A new object `file` may be created using the following syntax:

```
# creating a new file object from an existing file
myfile = open('measurement.dat','r')
```

The contents of the file may be accessed, for instance, with this command:

```
print(myfile.read())
```

Usage of file objects requires some care. The problem is that a file has to be closed before it can be re-read or used by other applications, which is done using the following syntax:

```
myfile.close() # closes the file object
```

It is not that simple because an exception might be triggered before the call to `close` is executed, which will skip the closing code (consider the following example). A simple way to make sure that a file will be properly closed is to use context managers. This construction, using the keyword `with`, is explained in more detail in Section 12.1.3: *Context Managers – the with statement*. Here is how it is used with files:

```
with open('measurement.dat','r') as myfile:
    ... # use myfile here
```

This ensures that the file is closed when you exit the `with` block, even if an exception is raised inside the block. The command works with context manager objects. We recommend that you read more on context managers in Section 12.1.3: *Context Managers – the with statement*. Here is an example showing why the construct `with` is desirable:

```
myfile = open(name,'w')
myfile.write('some data')
a = 1/0
myfile.write('other data')
myfile.close()
```

An exception is raised before the file is closed. The file remains open, and there is no guarantee of what data is written in the file or when it is written. Hence, the proper way to achieve the same result is this:

```
with open(name,'w') as myfile:
    myfile.write('some data')
    a = 1/0
    myfile.write('other data')
```

In that case, the file is cleanly closed just after the exception (here, `ZeroDivisionError`) is raised. Notice also that there is no need to close the file explicitly.

14.1.2 Files are iterables

A file is, in particular, iterable (see `Section 9.3`: *Iterable objects*). Files iterate their lines:

```
with open(name,'r') as myfile:
    for line in myfile:
        data = line.split(';')
        print(f'time {data[0]} sec temperature {data[1]} C')
```

The lines of the file are returned as strings. The string method `split` is a possible tool to convert the string to a list of strings; for example:

```
data = 'aa;bb;cc;dd;ee;ff;gg'
data.split(';') # ['aa', 'bb', 'cc', 'dd', 'ee', 'ff', 'gg']

data = 'aa bb cc dd ee ff gg'
data.split(' ') # ['aa', 'bb', 'cc', 'dd', 'ee', 'ff', 'gg']
```

Since the object `myfile` is iterable, we can also do a direct extraction into a list, as follows:

```
data = list(myfile)
```

14.1.3 File modes

As you can see in these examples of file handling, the function `open` takes at least two arguments. The first is obviously the filename, and the second is a string describing the way in which the file will be used. There are several such modes for opening files. The basic ones are as follows:

```
with open('file1.dat','r') as ...   # read only
with open('file2.dat','r+') as ...  # read/write
with open('file3.dat','rb') as ...  # read in byte mode
```

```
with open('file4.dat','a') as ...  # append (write to the end of the file)
with open('file5.dat','w') as ... # (over-)write the file
with open('file6.dat','wb') as ... # (over-)write the file in byte mode
```

The modes `'r'`, `'r+'`, and `'a'` require that the file exists, whereas `'w'` will create a new file if no file with that name exists. Reading and writing with `'r'` and `'w'` is most common, as you saw in previous examples.

Consider an example of opening a file and adding data at the end of the file without modifying what is already there using the append mode `'a'`. Note the line break,`\n`:

```
_with open('file3.dat','a') as myfile:
    myfile.write('something new\n')
```

14.2 NumPy methods

NumPy has built-in methods for reading and writing NumPy array data to text files. These are `numpy.loadtxt` and `numpy.savetxt`.

14.2.1 savetxt

Writing an array to a text file is simple:

```
savetxt(filename,data)
```

There are two useful parameters given as strings, `fmt`, and `delimiter`, which control the format and the delimiter between columns. The defaults are space for the delimiter and `%.18e` for the format, which corresponds to the exponential format with all digits. The formatting parameters are used as follows:

```
x = range(100) # 100 integers
savetxt('test.txt',x,delimiter=',') # use comma instead of space
savetxt('test.txt',x,fmt='%d') # integer format instead of float with e
```

14.2.3 loadtxt

Reading to an array from a text file is done with the help of the following syntax:

```
filename = 'test.txt'
data = loadtxt(filename)
```

Due to the fact that each row in an array must have the same length, each row in the text file must have the same number of elements. Similar to `savetxt`, the default values are `float` and the delimiter is a space. These can be set using the parameters `dtype` and `delimiter`. Another useful parameter is `comments`, which can be used to mark what symbol is used for comments in the data file. An example of using the formatting parameters is as follows:

```
data = loadtxt('test.txt',delimiter=';')     # data separated by semicolons

# read to integer type, comments in file begin with a hash character
data = loadtxt('test.txt',dtype=int,comments='#')
```

14.3 Pickling

The read and write methods you just saw convert data to strings before writing. Complex types (such as objects and classes) cannot be written this way. With Python's module `pickle`, you can save any object and also multiple objects to a file.

Data can be saved in plain-text (ASCII) format or using a slightly more efficient binary format. There are two main methods: `dump`, which saves a pickled representation of a Python object to a file, and `load`, which retrieves a pickled object from the file. The basic usage is like this:

```
import pickle
with open('file.dat','wb') as myfile:
    a = random.rand(20,20)
    b = 'hello world'
    pickle.dump(a,myfile)     # first call: first object
    pickle.dump(b,myfile)     # second call: second object

import pickle
with open('file.dat','rb') as myfile:
    numbers = pickle.load(myfile) # restores the array
    text = pickle.load(myfile)    # restores the string
```

Note the order in which the two objects are returned. Besides the two main methods, it is sometimes useful to serialize a Python object to a string instead of a file. This is done with `dumps` and `loads`. Consider an example of serializing an array and a dictionary:

```
a = [1,2,3,4]
pickle.dumps(a) # returns a bytes object
b = {'a':1,'b':2}
pickle.dumps(b) # returns a bytes object
```

A good example of using `dumps` is when you need to write Python objects or NumPy arrays to a database. These usually have support for storing strings, which makes it easy to write and read complex data and objects without any special modules. Besides the `pickle` module, there is also an optimized version called `cPickle`. It is written in C and is an option if you need fast reading and writing. The data produced by pickle and *cPickle* is identical and can be interchanged.

14.4 Shelves

Objects in dictionaries can be accessed by keys. There is a similar way to access particular data in a file by first assigning it a key. This is possible by using the module `shelve`:

```
from contextlib import closing
import shelve as sv
# opens a data file (creates it before if necessary)
with closing(sv.open('datafile')) as data:
    A = array([[1,2,3],[4,5,6]])
    data['my_matrix'] = A  # here we created a key
```

In `Section 14.1.1`: *Interacting with files*, we saw that the built-in command `open` generates a context manager, and we saw why this is important for handling external resources, such as files. In contrast to this command, `sv.open` does not create a context manager by itself. The command `closing` from the module `contextlib` is needed to transform it into an appropriate context manager.

Consider the following example of restoring the file:

```
from contextlib import closing
import shelve as sv
with closing(sv.open('datafile')) as data: # opens a data file
    A = data['my_matrix']  # here we used the key
    ...
```

A `shelve` object has all dictionary methods, for example, keys and values, and can be used in the same way as a dictionary. Note that changes are only written in the file after one of the methods `close` or `sync` has been called.

14.5 Reading and writing Matlab data files

SciPy has the ability to read and write data in Matlab's `.mat` file format using the module \pyth!scipy.io!. The commands are `loadmat` and `savemat`.

To load data, use the following syntax:

```
import scipy.io
data = scipy.io.loadmat('datafile.mat')
```

The variable data now contains a dictionary, with keys corresponding to the variable names saved in the .mat file. The variables are in NumPy array format. Saving to .mat files involves creating a dictionary with all the variables you want to save (variable name and value). The command is then savemat:

```
data = {}
data['x'] = x
data['y'] = y
scipy.io.savemat('datafile.mat',data)
```

This saves the NumPy arrays, x and y, in Matlab's internal file format, thereby preserving variable names.

14.6 Reading and writing images

The module PIL.Image comes with some functions for handling images. The following will read a *JPEG* image, print the shape and type, and then create a resized image, and write the new image to a file:

```
import PIL.Image as pil   # imports the Pillow module

# read image to array
im=pil.open("test.jpg")
print(im.size)    # (275, 183)
                  # Number of pixels in horizontal and vertical directions
# resize image
im_big = im.resize((550, 366))
im_big_gray = im_big.convert("L") # Convert to grayscale

im_array=array(im)

print(im_array.shape)
print(im_array.dtype)    # unint 8
# write result to new image file
im_big_gray.save("newimage.jpg")
```

PIL creates an image object that can easily be converted to a NumPy array. As an array object, images are stored with pixel values in the range *0...255* as 8-bit unsigned integers (unint8). The third shape value shows how many color channels the image has. In this case, *3* means it is a color image with values stored in this order: red im_array[:,:,0], green im_array[:,:,1], and blue im_array[:,:,2]. A grayscale image would only have one channel.

For working with images, the module PIL contains many useful basic image processing functions, including filtering, transforms, measurements, and conversion from a NumPy array to a PIL image object:

```
new_image = pil.from_array(ima_array)
```

14.7 Summary

File handling is inevitable when dealing with measurements and other sources of a larger amount of data. Also, communication with other programs and tools is done via file handling.

You learned to see a file as a Python object, like others, with important methods such as readlines and write. We showed how files can be protected by special attributes, which may allow only read or write access.

The way you write to a file often influences the speed of the process. We saw how data is stored by pickling or by using the method shelve.

15
Testing

In this chapter, we'll focus on two aspects of testing for scientific programming. The first aspect is the often difficult topic of *what to test* in scientific computing. The second aspect covers the question of *how to test*. We will distinguish between manual and automated testing. Manual testing is what is done by every programmer to quickly check that a program is doing what it should or should not. Automated testing is the refined, automated variant of that idea. We will introduce some tools available for automatic testing in general, with a view of the particular case of scientific computing.

15.1 Manual testing

During code development, you do a lot of small tests in order to test its functionality. This could be called manual testing. Typically, you would test if a given function does what it is supposed to do, by manually testing the function in an interactive environment. For instance, suppose that you implement the bisection algorithm. It is an algorithm that finds a zero (root) of a scalar non-linear function. To start the algorithm, an interval has to be given with the property that the function takes different signs on the interval boundaries (see Exercise 4 in `Section 7.10`: Exercises, for more information).

You will then test an implementation of that algorithm, typically by checking that:

- A solution is found when the function has opposite signs at the interval boundaries.
- An exception is raised when the function has the same sign at the interval boundaries.

Manual testing, as necessary as it may seem to be, is unsatisfactory. Once you have convinced yourself that the code does what it is supposed to do, you formulate a relatively small number of demonstration examples to convince others of the quality of the code. At that stage, you often lose interest in the tests made during development, and they are forgotten or even deleted. As soon as you change a detail and things no longer work correctly, you might regret that your earlier tests are no longer available.

15.2 Automatic testing

The correct way to develop any piece of code is to use automatic testing. The advantages are:

- The automated repetition of a large number of tests after every code refactoring and before any new versions are launched.
- Silent documentation of the use of the code.
- Documentation of the test coverage of your code: Did things work before a change or was a certain aspect never tested?

Changes in the program and in particular in its structure that do not affect its functionality are called code refactoring.

We suggest developing tests in parallel to coding. Good design of tests is an art of its own and there is rarely an investment that guarantees such a good pay-off in development time savings as the investment in good tests.

Now we will go through the implementation of a simple algorithm with the automated testing methods in mind.

15.2.1 Testing the bisection algorithm

Let's examine automated testing for the bisection algorithm. With this algorithm, a zero of a real-valued function is found. It is described in *Exercise 4* in `Section 7.10`: *Exercises*. An implementation of the algorithm can have the following form:

```
def bisect(f, a, b, tol=1.e-8):
    """
    Implementation of the bisection algorithm
    f real valued function
    a,b interval boundaries (float) with the property
    f(a) * f(b) <= 0
    tol tolerance (float)
    """
    if f(a) * f(b)> 0:
        raise ValueError("Incorrect initial interval [a, b]")
    for i in range(100):
        c = (a + b) / 2.
        if f(a) * f(c) <= 0:
            b = c
        else:
            a = c
```

```
        if abs(a - b) < tol:
            return (a + b) / 2
    raise Exception('No root found within the given tolerance {tol}')
```

We assume this to be stored in a file named bisection.py. As the first test case, we test that the zero of the function $f(x) = x$ is found:

```
def test_identity():
    result = bisect(lambda x: x, -1., 1.)
    expected = 0.
    assert allclose(result, expected),'expected zero not found'
test_identity()
```

In this code, you meet the Python keyword assert for the first time. It raises the exception AssertionError if its first argument returns the value False. Its optional second argument is a string with additional information. We use the function allclose in order to test for equality of floats.

Let's comment on some of the features of the test function. We use an assertion to make sure that an exception will be raised if the code does not behave as expected. We have to manually run the test in the line test_identity().

There are many tools to automate this kind of call; we will see one of those in Section 15.2.2: *Using the unittest module.*

Let's now set up a second test that checks if bisect raises an exception when the function has the same sign on both ends of the interval. For now, we will suppose that the exception raised is ValueError. In the following example, we will check the initial interval $[a, b]$. For the bisection algorithm, it should fulfill the sign condition:

```
def test_badinput():
    try:
        bisect(lambda x: x,0.5,1)
    except ValueError:
        pass
    else:
        raise AssertionError()

test_badinput()
```

In this case, an AssertionError is raised if the exception is not of the type ValueError. There are tools to simplify the preceding construction to check that an exception is raised.

Another useful test is the edge case test. Here we test arguments or user input, which are likely to create mathematically undefined situations or states of the program not foreseen by the programmer. For instance, what happens if both bounds are equal? What happens if $a > b$?

The following code is an example for such an edge test:

```
def test_equal_boundaries():
    result = bisect(lambda x: x, 0., 0.)
    expected = 0.
    assert allclose(result, expected), \
                'test equal interval bounds failed'

def test_reverse_boundaries():
    result = bisect(lambda x: x, 1., -1.)
    expected = 0.
    assert allclose(result, expected),\
                'test reverse int_erval bounds failed'

test_equal_boundaries()
test_reverse_boundaries()
```

A test checks that the program unit does what is demanded by its specification. In the preceding example, we assumed that the specifications state that in the case $a > b$ the two values should tacitly be interchanged. And that is what was tested. An alternative way would be to specify that this situation would be considered as wrong input, which the user has to correct. There, we would have tested for an appropriate exception, for example, `ValueError`.

15.2.2 Using the unittest module

The Python module `unittest` greatly facilitates automated testing. This module requires that we rewrite our previous tests to be compatible.

The first test would have to be rewritten in a `class`, as follows:

```
from bisection import bisect
import unittest

class TestIdentity(unittest.TestCase):
    def test(self):
        result = bisect(lambda x: x, -1.2, 1.,tol=1.e-8)
```

```
        expected = 0.
        self.assertAlmostEqual(result, expected)

if __name__=='__main__':
    unittest.main()
```

Let's examine the differences from the previous implementation. First, the test is now a method and a part of a class. The class must inherit from `unittest.TestCase`. The test method's name must start with `test`. Note that we may now use one of the assertion tools of the `unittest` package, namely `assertAlmostEqual`. Finally, the tests are run using `unittest.main`. We recommend writing the tests in a file separate from the code to be tested. That is why it starts with an `import`. The test passes and returns as follows:

```
Ran 1 test in 0.002s

OK
```

If we run it with a loose tolerance parameter, for example, `1.e-3`, a failure of the test will be reported:

```
F
============================================================================
FAIL: test (__main__.TestIdentity)
----------------------------------------------------------------------------
Traceback (most recent call last):
  File "<ipython-input-11-e44778304d6f>", line 5, in test
    self.assertAlmostEqual(result, expected)
AssertionError: 0.00017089843750002018 != 0.0 within 7 places
----------------------------------------------------------------------------
Ran 1 test in 0.004s
FAILED (failures=1)
```

Tests can and should be grouped together as methods of a test class, as given in the following example:

```
import unittest
from bisection import bisect

class TestIdentity(unittest.TestCase):
    def identity_fcn(self,x):
        return x
    def test_functionality(self):
        result = bisect(self.identity_fcn, -1.2, 1.,tol=1.e-8)
        expected = 0.
        self.assertAlmostEqual(result, expected)
    def test_reverse_boundaries(self):
        result = bisect(self.identity_fcn, 1., -1.)
```

```
            expected = 0.
            self.assertAlmostEqual(result, expected)
        def test_exceeded_tolerance(self):
            tol=1.e-80
            self.assertRaises(Exception, bisect, self.identity_fcn,
                                             -1.2, 1.,tol)
    if __name__=='__main__':
        unittest.main()
```

Here, in the last test we used the method unittest.TestCase.assertRaises. It tests whether an exception is correctly raised. Its first parameter is the exception type, for example, ValueError, Exception, and its second argument is the name of the function, which is expected to raise the exception. The remaining arguments are the arguments for this function.

The command unittest.main() creates an instance of the class TestIdentity and executes those methods starting with test.

15.2.3 Test setUp and tearDown methods

The class unittest.TestCase provides two special methods, setUp and tearDown, which run before and after every call to a test method. This is needed when testing generators, which are exhausted after every test. We demonstrate this by testing a program that checks the line in a file in which a given string occurs for the first time:

```
class StringNotFoundException(Exception):
    pass

def find_string(file, string):
    for i,lines in enumerate(file.readlines()):
        if string in lines:
            return i
    raise StringNotFoundException(
        f'String {string} not found in File {file.name}.')
```

We assume that this code is saved in a file named find_in_file.py.

A test has to prepare a file and open it and remove it after the test as given in the following example:

```
import unittest
import os # used for, for example, deleting files

from find_in_file import find_string, StringNotFoundException
```

```
class TestFindInFile(unittest.TestCase):
    def setUp(self):
        file = open('test_file.txt', 'w')
        file.write('bird')
        file.close()
        self.file = open('test_file.txt', 'r')
    def tearDown(self):
        self.file.close()
        os.remove(self.file.name)
    def test_exists(self):
        line_no=find_string(self.file, 'bird')
        self.assertEqual(line_no, 0)
    def test_not_exists(self):
        self.assertRaises(StringNotFoundException, find_string,
                                          self.file, 'tiger')

if __name__=='__main__':
    unittest.main()
```

Before each test `setUp` is run and after each test `tearDown` is executed.

Setting up testdata when a test case is created

The methods `setUp` and `tearDown` are executed before and after any test method of a test case. This is necessary when the test methods change the data. They guarantee that the test data is restored before the next test is executed.

However, there is also often a situation where your tests do not change the test data and you want to save time by only once setting up the data. This is done by the class method `setUpClass`.

The following code block schematically illustrates how the method `setUpClass` is used. You might also want to check `Section 8.4`: *Class attributes and class methods* again.

```
import unittest

class TestExample(unittest.Testcase):
    @classmethod
    def setUpClass(cls):
        cls.A=....
    def Test1(self):
        A=self.A
        # assert something
        ....
    def Test2(self):
```

```
A=self.A
# assert something else
```

15.2.4 Parameterizing tests

We frequently want to repeat the same test with different datasets. When using the functionalities of unittest, this requires us to automatically generate test cases with the corresponding methods injected.

To this end, we first construct a test case with one or several methods that will be used, when we later set up test methods. We'll consider the bisection method again and let's check if the values it returns are really zeros of the given function.

We first build the test case and the method that we will use for the tests as follows:

```
class Tests(unittest.TestCase):
    def checkifzero(self,fcn_with_zero,interval):
        result = bisect(fcn_with_zero,*interval,tol=1.e-8)
        function_value=fcn_with_zero(result)
        expected=0.
        self.assertAlmostEqual(function_value, expected)
```

Then we dynamically create test functions as attributes of this class:

```
test_data=[
            {'name':'identity', 'function':lambda x: x,
                                'interval' : [-1.2, 1.]},
            {'name':'parabola', 'function':lambda x: x**2-1,
                                'interval' :[0, 10.]},
            {'name':'cubic', 'function':lambda x: x**3-2*x**2,
                                'interval':[0.1, 5.]},
            ]
def make_test_function(dic):
    return lambda self :\
        self.checkifzero(dic['function'],dic['interval'])
for data in test_data:
    setattr(Tests, f"test_{data['name']}", make_test_function(data))

if __name__=='__main__':
    unittest.main()
```

In this example, the data is provided as a list of dictionaries. The function make_test_function dynamically generates a test function, which uses a particular data dictionary to perform the test with the previously defined method checkifzero. Finally, the command setattr is used to make these test functions methods of the class Tests.

15.2.5 Assertion tools

In this section, we collect the most important tools for raising an `AssertionError`. We saw the command `assert` and three tools from `unittest`, namely `assertAlmostEqual`, `assertEqual`, and `assertRaises`. The following table (Table 15.1) summarizes the most important assertion tools and the related modules:

Assertion tool and application example	Module
`assert 5==5`	–
`assertEqual(5.27, 5.27)`	`unittest.TestCase`
`assertAlmostEqual(5.24, 5.2,places = 1)`	`unittest.TestCase`
`assertTrue(5 > 2)`	`unittest.TestCase`
`assertFalse(2 < 5)`	`unittest.TestCase`
`assertRaises(ZeroDivisionError,lambda x: 1/x,0.)`	`unittest.TestCase`
`assertIn(3,{3,4})`	`unittest.TestCase`
`assert_array_equal(A,B)`	`numpy.testing`
`assert_array_almost_equal(A, B, decimal=5)`	`numpy.testing`
`assert_allclose(A, B, rtol=1.e-3,atol=1.e-5)`	`numpy.testing`

Table 15.1: Assertion tools in Python, unittest, and NumPy

15.2.6 Float comparisons

Two floating-point numbers should not be compared with the `==` comparison, because the result of a computation is often slightly off due to rounding errors. There are numerous tools to test the equality of floats for testing purposes.

First, `allclose` checks that two arrays are almost equal. It can be used in a test function, as shown:

```
self.assertTrue(allclose(computed, expected))
```

Here, `self` refers to a `unittest.Testcase` instance. There are also testing tools in the `numpy` package `testing`. These are imported by using:

```
import numpy.testing
```

Testing that two scalars or two arrays are equal is done using `numpy.testing.assert_array_allmost_equal` or `numpy.testing.assert_allclose`. These methods differ in the way they describe the required accuracy, as shown in the preceding table, *Table 15.1*.

QR factorization decomposes a given matrix into a product of an orthogonal matrix Q and an upper triangular matrix R as given in the following example:

```
import scipy.linalg as sl
A=rand(10,10)
[Q,R]=sl.qr(A)
```

Is the method applied correctly? We can check this by verifying that Q is indeed an orthogonal matrix:

```
import numpy.testing as npt
npt.assert_allclose(
                Q.T @ self.Q,identity(Q.shape[0]),atol=1.e-12)
```

Furthermore, we might perform a sanity test by checking if $A = QR$:

```
import numpy.testing as npt
npt.assert_allclose(Q @ R,A))
```

All this can be collected into the test case `unittest` as follows:

```
import unittest
import numpy.testing as npt
from scipy.linalg import qr
from scipy import *

class TestQR(unittest.TestCase):
    def setUp(self):
        self.A=rand(10,10)
        [self.Q,self.R]=qr(self.A)
    def test_orthogonal(self):
        npt.assert_allclose(
            self.Q.T @ self.Q,identity(self.Q.shape[0]),
            atol=1.e-12)
    def test_sanity(self):
        npt.assert_allclose(self.Q @ self.R,self.A)

if __name__=='__main__':
    unittest.main()
```

Note in `assert_allclose` the parameter `atol` defaults to zero, which often causes problems when working with matrices having small elements.

15.2.7 Unit and functional tests

Up to now, we have only used functional tests. A functional test checks whether the functionality is correct. For the bisection algorithm, this algorithm actually finds a zero when there is one. In that simple example, it is not really clear what a unit test is. Although it might seem slightly contrived, it is still possible to make a unit test for the bisection algorithm. It will demonstrate how unit testing often leads to more compartmentalized implementation.

So, in the bisection method, we would like to check, for instance, that at each step the interval is chosen correctly. How to do that? Note that it is absolutely impossible with the current implementation because the algorithm is hidden inside the function. One possible remedy is to run only one step of the bisection algorithm. Since all the steps are similar, we might argue that we have tested all the possible steps. We also need to be able to inspect the current bounds a and b at the current step of the algorithm. So we have to add the number of steps to be run as a parameter and change the return interface of the function. We will do that as shown:

```
def bisect(f,a,b,n=100):
    ...
    for iteration in range(n):
        ...
    return a,b
```

Note that we have to change the existing unit tests in order to accommodate that change. We may now add a unit test as shown:

```
def test_midpoint(self):
    a,b = bisect(identity,-2.,1.,1)
    self.assertAlmostEqual(a,-0.5)
    self.assertAlmostEqual(b,1.)
```

15.2.8 Debugging

Debugging is sometimes necessary while testing, in particular, if it is not immediately clear why a given test does not pass. In that case, it is useful to be able to debug a given test in an interactive session. This is, however, made difficult by the design of the class `unittest.TestCase`, which prevents easy instantiation of test case objects. The solution is to create a special instance for debugging purposes only.

Suppose that, in the previous example of the class `TestIdentity`, we want to test the method `test_functionality`. This would be achieved as follows:

```
test_case = TestIdentity(methodName='test_functionality')
```

Now this test can be run individually with:

```
test_case.debug()
```

This will run this individual test and it allows for debugging.

15.2.9 Test discovery

If you write a Python package, various tests might be spread out through the package. The module `discover` finds, imports, and runs these test cases. The basic call from the command line is:

```
python -m unittest discover
```

It starts looking for test cases in the current directory and recurses the directory tree downward to find Python objects with the `'test'` string contained in its name. The command takes optional arguments. Most important are `-s` to modify the start directory and `-p` to define the pattern to recognize the tests:

```
python -m unittest discover -s '.' -p 'Test*.py'
```

15.3 Measuring execution time

In order to take decisions on code optimization, you often have to compare several code alternatives and decide which code should be preferred based on the execution time. Furthermore, discussing execution time is an issue when comparing different algorithms. In this section, we present a simple and easy way to measure execution time.

15.3.1 Timing with a magic function

The easiest way to measure the execution time of a single statement is to use IPython's magic function `%timeit`.

The shell IPython adds additional functionality to standard Python. These extra functions are called magic functions.

As the execution time of a single statement can be extremely short, the statement is placed in a loop and executed several times. By taking the minimum measured time, you make sure that other tasks running on the computer do not influence the measured result too much.

Let's consider four alternative ways to extract nonzero elements from an array as follows:

```
A=zeros((1000,1000))
A[53,67]=10

def find_elements_1(A):
    b = []
    n, m = A.shape
    for i in range(n):
        for j in range(m):
            if abs(A[i, j]) > 1.e-10:
                b.append(A[i, j])
    return b

def find_elements_2(A):
    return [a for a in A.reshape((-1, )) if abs(a) > 1.e-10]

def find_elements_3(A):
    return [a for a in A.flatten() if abs(a) > 1.e-10]

def find_elements_4(A):
    return A[where(0.0 != A)]
```

Measuring time with IPython's magic function %timeit gives the following result:

```
In [50]: %timeit -n 50 -r 3 find_elements_1(A)
50 loops, best of 3: 585 ms per loop

In [51]: %timeit -n 50 -r 3 find_elements_2(A)
50 loops, best of 3: 514 ms per loop

In [52]: %timeit -n 50 -r 3 find_elements_3(A)
50 loops, best of 3: 519 ms per loop

In [53]: %timeit -n 50 -r 3 find_elements_4(A)
50 loops, best of 3: 7.29 ms per loop
```

The parameter −n controls how often the statement is executed before time is measured and the −r parameter controls the number of repetitions.

15.3.2 Timing with the Python module timeit

Python provides the module timeit, which can be used to measure execution time. It requires that, first, a time object is constructed. It is constructed from two strings: a string with setup commands and a string with the commands to be executed.

We take the same four alternatives as in the preceding example. The array and function definitions are written now in a string called setup_statements and four timing objects are constructed as follows:

```
import timeit
setup_statements="""
from scipy import zeros
from numpy import where
A=zeros((1000,1000))
A[57,63]=10.

def find_elements_1(A):
    b = []
    n, m = A.shape
    for i in range(n):
        for j in range(m):
            if abs(A[i, j]) > 1.e-10:
                b.append(A[i, j])
    return b

def find_elements_2(A):
    return [a for a in A.reshape((-1,)) if abs(a) > 1.e-10]

def find_elements_3(A):
    return [a for a in A.flatten() if abs(a) > 1.e-10]

def find_elements_4(A):
    return A[where( 0.0 != A)]
"""
experiment_1 = timeit.Timer(stmt = 'find_elements_1(A)',
                            setup = setup_statements)
experiment_2 = timeit.Timer(stmt = 'find_elements_2(A)',
                            setup = setup_statements)
experiment_3 = timeit.Timer(stmt = 'find_elements_3(A)',
                            setup = setup_statements)
experiment_4 = timeit.Timer(stmt = 'find_elements_4(A)',
                            setup = setup_statements)
```

The timer objects have a method repeat. It takes the two parameters repeat and number. It executes the statement of the timer object in a loop, measures the time, and repeats this experiment corresponding to the parameter repeat.

We continue the preceding example and measure execution times as shown:

```
t1 = experiment_1.repeat(3,5)
t2 = experiment_2.repeat(3,5)
t3 = experiment_3.repeat(3,5)
t4 = experiment_4.repeat(3,5)
# Results per loop in ms
min(t1)*1000/5 # 615 ms
min(t2)*1000/5 # 543 ms
min(t3)*1000/5 # 546 ms
min(t4)*1000/5 # 7.26 ms
```

In contrast to the method in the example using `timeit`, we obtain lists of all the obtained measurements. As the computing time may vary depending on the overall load of the computer, the minimal value in such a list can be considered a good approximation to the computation time necessary to execute the statement.

15.3.3 Timing with a context manager

Finally, we present the third method. It serves to show another application of a context manager. We first construct a context manager object for measuring the elapsed time as shown:

```
import time
class Timer:
    def __enter__(self):
        self.start = time.time()
        # return self
    def __exit__(self, ty, val, tb):
        end = time.time()
        self.elapsed=end-self.start
        print(f'Time elapsed {self.elapsed} seconds')
        return False
```

Recall that the __enter__ and __exit__ methods make this class a context manager. The __exit__ method's parameters ty, val, and tb are in the normal case None. If an exception is raised during execution, they take the exception type, its value, and traceback information. The return value False indicates that the exception has not been caught so far.

We'll now show the use of the context manager to measure the execution time of the four alternatives in the previous example:

```
with Timer(): find_elements_1(A)
```

This will then display a message like `Time elapsed 15.0129795074 ms.`

If the timing result should be accessible in a variable, the `enter` method must return the `Timer` instance (uncomment the `return` statement) and a `with ... as ...` construction has to be used:

```
with Timer() as t1:
    find_elements_1(A)
t1.elapsed # contains the result
```

15.4 Summary

No program development without testing! We showed the importance of well-organized and documented tests. Some professionals even start development by first specifying tests. A useful tool for automatic testing is the module `unittest`, which we explained in detail. While testing improves the reliability of code, profiling is needed to improve the performance. Alternative ways to code may result in large performance differences. We showed how to measure computation time and how to localize bottlenecks in your code.

15.5 Exercises

Ex. 1: Two matrices A, B are called similar if there exists a matrix S, such that $B = S^{-1}AS$. The matrices A and B have the same eigenvalues. Write a test checking that two matrices are similar, by comparing their eigenvalues. Is it a functional or a unit test?

Ex. 2: Create two vectors of large dimensions. Compare the execution time of various ways to compute their dot product:

- SciPy function: `v @ w`
- Generator and sum: `sum((x*y for x,y in zip(v,w)))`
- Comprehensive list and sum: `sum([x*y for x,y in zip(v,w)])`

Ex. 3: Let u be a vector. The vector v with components

$$v_i = \frac{u_i + u_{i+1} + u_{i+2}}{3}$$

is called a moving average of u. Determine which of the two alternatives to compute v is faster:

```
v = (u[:-2] + u[1:-1] + u[2:]) / 3
```

or

```
v = array([(u[i] + u[i + 1] + u[i + 2]) / 3
    for i in range(len(u)-3)])
```

16
Symbolic Computations - SymPy

In this chapter, we will give a brief introduction to using Python for symbolic computations. There is powerful software on the market for performing symbolic computations, for example, Maple™ or Mathematica™. But sometimes, it might be favorable to make symbolic calculations in the language or framework you are used to. At this stage of the book, we assume that this language is Python, so we seek a tool in Python—the module SymPy.

A complete description of SymPy, if even possible, would fill an entire book, and that is not the purpose of this chapter. Instead, we will stake out a path into this tool by examining some guiding examples, giving a flavor of the potential of this tool as a complement to NumPy and SciPy.

16.1 What are symbolic computations?

All computations we did so far in this book were so-called numeric computations. These were a sequence of operations mainly on floating-point numbers. It is the nature of numeric computations that the result is an approximation of the exact solution.

Symbolic computations operate on formulas or symbols by transforming them as taught in algebra or calculus into other formulas. The last step of these transformations might then require that numbers are inserted and a numeric evaluation is performed.

We illustrate the difference by computing this definite integral:

$$\int_0^4 \frac{1}{x^2 + x + 1}\, \mathrm{d}x$$

Symbolically this expression can be transformed by considering the primitive function of the integrand:

$$\frac{2}{\sqrt{3}}\arctan\left(\frac{2x+1}{\sqrt{3}}\right)$$

We now obtain a formula for the definite integral by inserting the integral bounds:

$$\int_0^4 \frac{1}{x^2+x+1}\,dx = \frac{\sqrt{3}}{9}\left(-\pi + 6\arctan\left(3\sqrt{3}\right)\right)$$

This is called a closed-form expression for the integral. Very few mathematical problems have a solution that can be given in a closed-form expression. It is the exact value of the integral without any approximation. Also, no error is introduced by representing real numbers as floating-point numbers, which would otherwise introduce round-off errors.

Approximation and round-off come into play at the very last moment, when this expression needs to be evaluated. The square root and the *arctan* can only be evaluated approximately by numerical methods. Such an evaluation gives the final result up to a certain (often unknown) precision:

$$\int_0^4 \frac{1}{x^2+x+1}\,dx \approx 0.9896614396123$$

On the other hand, numerical computation would directly approximate the definite integral by some approximation method, for example, Simpson's rule, and deliver a numeric result, often with an estimate of error. In Python, this is done by these commands:

```
from scipy.integrate import quad
quad(lambda x : 1/(x**2+x+1),a=0, b=4)
```

They return the value 0.9896614396122965 and an estimate for the error bound $1.1735663442283496\ 10^{-08}$.

The following diagram (*Figure 16.1*) shows the comparison of the numeric and symbolic approximations:

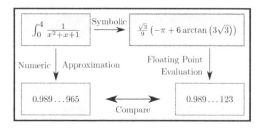

Figure 16.1: Symbolic and numeric quadrature

16.1.1 Elaborating an example in SymPy

To begin with, let's elaborate on the previous example in SymPy and explain the steps.

First, we have to import the module:

```
from sympy import *
init_printing()
```

The second command makes sure that formulas are presented in a graphical way, if possible. Then, we generate a symbol and define the integrand:

```
x = symbols('x')
f = Lambda(x, 1/(x**2 + x + 1))
```

x is now a Python object of type `Symbol` and f is a SymPy `Lambda` function (note the command starting with a capital letter).

Now we start with the symbolic computation of the integral:

```
integrate(f(x),x)
```

Depending on your working environment, the result is presented in different ways; see the following screenshot (*Figure 16.2*), which represents two different results of a SymPy formula in different environments:

Figure 16.2: Two screenshots of a SymPy presentation of formula in two different environments

We can check by differentiation whether the result is correct. To this end, we assign a name to the primitive function and differentiate with respect to x:

```
pf = Lambda(x, integrate(f(x),x))
diff(pf(x),x)
```

The result obtained will be as follows:

$$\frac{4}{3\left(\frac{2x}{3}\sqrt{3}+\frac{\sqrt{3}}{3}\right)^2+3}$$

Which can be simplified by using the following command:

```
simplify(diff(pf(x),x))
```

To

$$\frac{1}{x^2+x+1}$$

This is the result we expected.

The definite integral is obtained by using the following command:

```
pf(4) - pf(0)
```

It gives the following output after simplification with `simplify`:

$$\frac{\sqrt{3}}{9}\left(-\pi+6\arctan\left(3\sqrt{3}\right)\right)$$

To obtain a numerical value, we finally evaluate this expression to a floating-point number:

```
(pf(4)-pf(0)).evalf() # returns 0.9896614396123
```

16.2 Basic elements of SymPy

Here we introduce the basic elements of SymPy. You will find it favorable to be already familiar with classes and data types in Python.

16.2.1 Symbols – the basis of all formulas

The basic construction element to build a formula in SymPy is the symbol. As we saw in the introductory example, a symbol is created by the command `symbols`. This SymPy command generates symbol objects from a given string:

```
x, y, mass, torque = symbols('x y mass torque')
```

It is actually a short form of the following command:

```
symbol_list=[symbols(l) for l in 'x y mass torque'.split()]
```

Followed by an unpacking step to obtain variables:

```
x, y, mass, torque = symbol_list
```

The arguments of the command define the string representation of the symbol. The variable name of the symbol chosen is often identical to its string representation, but this is not required by the language:

```
row_index=symbols('i',integer=True)
print(row_index**2)   # returns i**2
```

Here, we also defined that the symbol is assumed to be an integer.

An entire set of symbols can be defined in a very compact way:

```
integervariables = symbols('i:l', integer=True)
dimensions = symbols('m:n', integer=True)
realvariables = symbols('x:z', real=True)
```

Similarly, symbols for indexed variables can be defined by using the following:

```
A = symbols('A1:3(1:4)')
```

This gives a tuple of symbols:

$$(A_{11}, \quad A_{12}, \quad A_{13}, \quad A_{21}, \quad A_{22}, \quad A_{23}).$$

The rules for the range of the indexes are those we saw earlier in this book when working with slices (see `Section 3.1.1`: *Slicing,* for more details).

16.2.2 Numbers

Python evaluates operations on numbers directly and introduces unavoidable rounding errors. These would obstruct all symbolic calculations. This is avoided when we `sympify` numbers:

```
1/3  # returns 0.3333333333333333
sympify(1)/sympify(3)  # returns '1/3'
```

The `sympify` command converts an integer to an object of type `sympy.core.numbers.Integer`.

Instead of writing **1/3** as an operation of two integers, it can also be represented directly as a rational number by `Rational(1,3)`.

16.2.3 Functions

SymPy distinguishes between defined and undefined functions. The term undefined functions (which might be a bit misleading) refers to well-defined Python objects for generic functions that have no special properties.

An example of a function with special properties is `atan` or the `Lambda` function used in the introductory example of this chapter.

Note the different names for the different implementations of the same mathematical function: `sympy.atan` and `scipy.arctan`.

Undefined functions

A symbol for an undefined function is created by giving the `symbols` command an extra class argument:

```
f, g = symbols('f g', cls=Function)
```

The same can be achieved by using the constructor `Function`:

```
f = Function('f')
g = Function('g')
```

With undefined functions, we can evaluate the general rules of calculus.

For example, let's evaluate the following expression:

$$\frac{\mathrm{d}}{\mathrm{d}x} f(xg(x))$$

This is symbolically computed in Python by using the following command:

```
x = symbols('x')
f, g = symbols('f g', cls=Function)
diff(f(x*g(x)),x)
```

When executed, the previous code returns the following as output:

$$\left(x\frac{d}{dx}g(x) + g(x) \right) \frac{d}{d\xi_1} f(\xi_1) \Bigg|_{\xi_1 = xg(x)}$$

This example shows how the product rule and the chain rule were applied.

We can even use an undefined function as a function in several variables, for example:

```
x = symbols('x:3')
f(*x)
```

which returns the following output:

$$f(x_0, x_1, x_2)$$

Note the use of the star operator to unpack a tuple to form *f* with arguments; see `Section 7.2.5`: *Variable Number of Arguments*.

By using list comprehension, we can construct a list of all partial derivatives of f:

```
[diff(f(*x),xx) for xx in x]
```

This returns a list with the elements of ∇f (the gradient of f):

$$\left[\frac{\partial}{\partial x_0} f(x_0, x_1, x_2), \quad \frac{\partial}{\partial x_1} f(x_0, x_1, x_2), \quad \frac{\partial}{\partial x_2} f(x_0, x_1, x_2) \right]$$

The command can also be rewritten by using the method `diff` of the `Function` object:

```
[f(*x).diff(xx) for xx in x]
```

Another method is Taylor series expansion:

```
x = symbols('x')
f(x).series(x,0,n=4)
```

This returns Taylor's formula, together with the rest term expressed by the Landau symbol:

$$f(0) + x\,f'(0) + \frac{x^2}{2}\frac{d}{dx}\,f'(x)\Big|_{x=0} + \frac{x^3}{6}\frac{d^2}{dx^2}\,f'(x)\Big|_{x=0} + \mathcal{O}\left(x^4\right)$$

16.2.4 Elementary functions

Examples for elementary functions in SymPy are trigonometric functions and their inverses. The following example shows how `simplify` acts on an expression which includes elementary functions:

```
x = symbols('x')
simplify(cos(x)**2 + sin(x)**2)   # returns 1
```

Here is another example of the use of elementary functions:

```
atan(x).diff(x) - 1./(x**2+1)   # returns 0
```

If you use SciPy and SymPy together, we strongly recommend that you use them in different namespaces:

```
import numpy as np
import sympy as sym
# working with numbers
x=3
y=np.sin(x)
# working with symbols
x=sym.symbols('x')
y=sym.sin(x)
```

16.2.5 Lambda functions

In `Section 7.7`: *Anonymous functions*, we saw how to define so-called anonymous functions in Python. The SymPy counterpart is the command `Lambda`. Note the difference; `lambda` is a keyword while `Lambda` is a constructor.

The command `Lambda` takes two arguments, the symbol of the function's independent variable, and a SymPy expression to evaluate the function.

Here is an example that defines air resistance (also called drag) as a function of speed:

```
C,rho,A,v=symbols('C rho A v')
# C drag coefficient, A coss-sectional area, rho density
# v speed
f_drag = Lambda(v,-Rational(1,2)*C*rho*A*v**2)
```

`f_drag` is displayed as a graphical expression:

$$\left(v \mapsto -\frac{AC}{2}\rho v^2 \right)$$

This function can be evaluated in the usual way by providing it with an argument:

```
x = symbols('x')
f_drag(2)
f_drag(x/3)
```

Which results in the expressions:

$$-2.0AC\rho \qquad -\frac{AC}{18}\rho x^2$$

It is also possible to create functions in several variables by just providing the first parameter of `Lambda` with a tuple, as follows for example:

```
x,y=symbols('x y')
t=Lambda((x,y),sin(x) + cos(2*y))
```

A call to this function can be done in two ways, either by directly providing several arguments:

```
t(pi,pi/2)   # returns -1
```

Or by unpacking a tuple or list:

```
p=(pi,pi/2)
t(*p)    # returns -1
```

Matrix objects in SymPy even make it possible to define vector-valued functions:

```
F=Lambda((x,y),Matrix([sin(x) + cos(2*y),  sin(x)*cos(y)]))
```

This enables us to compute Jacobians:

```
F(x,y).jacobian((x,y))
```

Which gives the following expression as output:

$$\begin{bmatrix} \cos{(x)} & -2\sin{(2y)} \\ \cos{(x)}\cos{(y)} & -\sin{(x)}\sin{(y)} \end{bmatrix}$$

In the case of more variables, it is convenient to use a more compact form to define the function:

```
x=symbols('x:2')
F=Lambda(x,Matrix([sin(x[0]) + cos(2*x[1]),sin(x[0])*cos(x[1])]))
F(*x).jacobian(x)
```

16.3 Symbolic linear algebra

Symbolic linear algebra is supported by SymPy's data type `matrix` which we will introduce first. Then we will present some linear algebra methods as examples for the broad spectrum of possibilities for symbolic computations in this field.

16.3.1 Symbolic matrices

We briefly met the `matrix` data type when we discussed vector-valued functions. There, we saw it in its simplest form, which converts a list of lists into a matrix. To see an example, let's construct a rotation matrix:

```
phi=symbols('phi')
rotation=Matrix([[cos(phi), -sin(phi)],
                 [sin(phi), cos(phi)]])
```

When working with SymPy matrices we have to note that the operator * performs matrix multiplications and is not acting as an elementwise multiplication, which is the case for NumPy arrays.

The previously defined rotation matrix can be checked for orthogonality by using this matrix multiplication and the transpose of a matrix:

```
simplify(rotation.T*rotation -eye(2))  # returns a 2 x 2 zero matrix
```

The previous example shows how a matrix is transposed and how the identity matrix is created. Alternatively, we could have checked whether its inverse is its transpose, which can be done as follows:

```
simplify(rotation.T - rotation.inv())
```

Another way to set up a matrix is by providing a list of symbols and a shape:

```
M = Matrix(3,3, symbols('M:3(:3)'))
```

This creates the following matrix:

$$\begin{bmatrix} M_{00} & M_{01} & M_{02} \\ M_{10} & M_{11} & M_{12} \\ M_{20} & M_{21} & M_{22} \end{bmatrix}$$

A third way to create a matrix is by generating its entries by a given function. The syntax is as follows:

```
Matrix(number of rows,number of colums, function)
```

We exemplify the preceding matrix by considering a Toeplitz matrix. It is a matrix with constant diagonals. Given a $2n - 1$ data vector a, its elements are defined as:

$$T_{ij} := a_{i-j+(n-1)} \ \text{ for } i, j = 0, \ldots, n - 1$$

In SymPy, the matrix can be defined by directly making use of this definition:

```
def toeplitz(n):
    a = symbols('a:'+str(2*n))
    f = lambda i,j: a[i-j+n-1]
    return Matrix(n,n,f)
```

Executing the previous code gives `toeplitz(5)`:

$$\begin{bmatrix} a_4 & a_3 & a_2 & a_1 & a_0 \\ a_5 & a_4 & a_3 & a_2 & a_1 \\ a_6 & a_5 & a_4 & a_3 & a_2 \\ a_7 & a_6 & a_5 & a_4 & a_3 \\ a_8 & a_7 & a_6 & a_5 & a_4 \end{bmatrix}.$$

We can see clearly the desired structures; all elements along the subdiagonals and superdiagonals are the same. We can access matrix elements by the indexes and slices according to the Python syntax introduced in `Section 3.1.1`: *Slicing*:

```
M[0,2]=0  # changes one element
M[1,:]=Matrix(1,3,[1,2,3]) # changes an entire row
```

16.3.2 Examples for linear algebra methods in SymPy

The basic task in linear algebra is to solve linear equation systems:

$$Ax = b$$

Let's do this symbolically for a 3×3 matrix:

```
A = Matrix(3,3,symbols('A1:4(1:4)'))
b = Matrix(3,1,symbols('b1:4'))
x = A.LUsolve(b)
```

The output of this relatively small problem is already merely readable, which can be seen in the following graphical expression:

$$
\begin{bmatrix}
\dfrac{1}{A_{11}}\left(-\dfrac{A_{12}}{A_{22}-\frac{A_{12}A_{21}}{A_{11}}}\left(b_2 - \dfrac{\left(A_{23}-\frac{A_{13}A_{21}}{A_{11}}\right)\left(b_3 - \frac{\left(A_{32}-\frac{A_{12}A_{31}}{A_{11}}\right)\left(b_2-\frac{A_{21}b_1}{A_{11}}\right)}{A_{22}-\frac{A_{12}A_{21}}{A_{11}}} - \frac{A_{31}b_1}{A_{11}}\right)}{A_{33}-\frac{\left(A_{23}-\frac{A_{13}A_{21}}{A_{11}}\right)\left(A_{32}-\frac{A_{12}A_{31}}{A_{11}}\right)}{A_{22}-\frac{A_{12}A_{21}}{A_{11}}}-\frac{A_{13}A_{31}}{A_{11}}} - \dfrac{A_{21}b_1}{A_{11}}\right) - \dfrac{A_{13}\left(b_3 - \frac{\left(A_{32}-\frac{A_{12}A_{31}}{A_{11}}\right)\left(b_2-\frac{A_{21}b_1}{A_{11}}\right)}{A_{22}-\frac{A_{12}A_{21}}{A_{11}}}-\frac{A_{31}b_1}{A_{11}}\right)}{A_{33}-\frac{\left(A_{23}-\frac{A_{13}A_{21}}{A_{11}}\right)\left(A_{32}-\frac{A_{12}A_{31}}{A_{11}}\right)}{A_{22}-\frac{A_{12}A_{21}}{A_{11}}}-\frac{A_{13}A_{31}}{A_{11}}} + b_1\right) \\[4em]
\dfrac{1}{A_{22}-\frac{A_{12}A_{21}}{A_{11}}}\left(b_2 - \dfrac{\left(A_{23}-\frac{A_{13}A_{21}}{A_{11}}\right)\left(b_3 - \frac{\left(A_{32}-\frac{A_{12}A_{31}}{A_{11}}\right)\left(b_2-\frac{A_{21}b_1}{A_{11}}\right)}{A_{22}-\frac{A_{12}A_{21}}{A_{11}}} - \frac{A_{31}b_1}{A_{11}}\right)}{A_{33}-\frac{\left(A_{23}-\frac{A_{13}A_{21}}{A_{11}}\right)\left(A_{32}-\frac{A_{12}A_{31}}{A_{11}}\right)}{A_{22}-\frac{A_{12}A_{21}}{A_{11}}}-\frac{A_{13}A_{31}}{A_{11}}} - \dfrac{A_{21}b_1}{A_{11}}\right) \\[4em]
\dfrac{b_3 - \frac{\left(A_{32}-\frac{A_{12}A_{31}}{A_{11}}\right)\left(b_2-\frac{A_{21}b_1}{A_{11}}\right)}{A_{22}-\frac{A_{12}A_{21}}{A_{11}}} - \frac{A_{31}b_1}{A_{11}}}{A_{33}-\frac{\left(A_{23}-\frac{A_{13}A_{21}}{A_{11}}\right)\left(A_{32}-\frac{A_{12}A_{31}}{A_{11}}\right)}{A_{22}-\frac{A_{12}A_{21}}{A_{11}}}-\frac{A_{13}A_{31}}{A_{11}}}
\end{bmatrix}
$$

Again, the use of `simplify` command helps us to detect canceling terms and to collect common factors:

```
simplify(x)
```

Which will result in the following output, which looks much better:

$$x = \begin{bmatrix} \dfrac{A_{12}A_{23}b_3 - A_{12}A_{33}b_2 - A_{13}A_{22}b_3 + A_{13}A_{32}b_2 + A_{22}A_{33}b_1 - A_{23}A_{32}b_1}{A_{11}A_{22}A_{33} - A_{11}A_{23}A_{32} - A_{12}A_{21}A_{33} + A_{12}A_{23}A_{31} + A_{13}A_{21}A_{32} - A_{13}A_{22}A_{31}} \\[2ex] \dfrac{-A_{11}A_{23}b_3 + A_{11}A_{33}b_2 + A_{13}A_{21}b_3 - A_{13}A_{31}b_2 - A_{21}A_{33}b_1 + A_{23}A_{31}b_1}{A_{11}A_{22}A_{33} - A_{11}A_{23}A_{32} - A_{12}A_{21}A_{33} + A_{12}A_{23}A_{31} + A_{13}A_{21}A_{32} - A_{13}A_{22}A_{31}} \\[2ex] \dfrac{A_{11}A_{22}b_3 - A_{11}A_{32}b_2 - A_{12}A_{21}b_3 + A_{12}A_{31}b_2 + A_{21}A_{32}b_1 - A_{22}A_{31}b_1}{A_{11}A_{22}A_{33} - A_{11}A_{23}A_{32} - A_{12}A_{21}A_{33} + A_{12}A_{23}A_{31} + A_{13}A_{21}A_{32} - A_{13}A_{22}A_{31}} \end{bmatrix}$$

Symbolic computations become very slow when increasing matrix dimensions. For dimensions bigger than 15, memory problems might even occur.

The next figure (*Figure 16.3*) illustrates the differences in CPU time between symbolically and numerically solving a linear system:

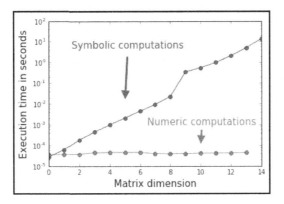

Figure 16.3: CPU time for numerically and symbolically solving a linear system

16.4 Substitutions

Let's first consider a simple symbolic expression:

```
x, a = symbols('x a')
b = x + a
```

What happens if we set x = 0 ? We observe that b did not change. What we did was that we changed the Python variable x. It now no longer refers to the symbol object but to the integer object 0. The symbol represented by the string 'x' remains unaltered, and so does b.

Instead, altering an expression by replacing symbols with numbers, other symbols, or expressions is done by a special substitution method, which can be seen in the following code:

```
x, a = symbols('x a')
b = x + a
c = b.subs(x,0)
d = c.subs(a,2*a)
print(c, d)    # returns (a, 2a)
```

This method takes one or two arguments. The following two statements are equivalent:

```
b.subs(x,0)
b.subs({x:0})   # a dictionary as argument
```

Dictionaries as arguments allow us to make several substitutions in one step:

```
b.subs({x:0, a:2*a})   # several substitutions in one
```

As items in dictionaries have no defined order—we can never know which would be the first—there is a need for ensuring that permuting the items would not affect the substitution result. Therefore in SymPy, substitutions are first made within the dictionary and then on the expression. This is demonstrated by the following example:

```
x, a, y = symbols('x a y')
b = x + a
b.subs({a:a*y, x:2*x, y:a/y})
b.subs({y:a/y, a:a*y, x:2*x})
```

Both substitutions return the same result:

$$\frac{a^2}{y} + 2x$$

A third alternative to defining multiple substitutions is by using a list of old-value/new-value pairs instead:

```
b.subs([(y,a/y), (a,a*y), (x,2*x)])
```

It is also possible to substitute entire expressions for others:

```
n, alpha = symbols('n alpha')
b = cos(n*alpha)
b.subs(cos(n*alpha), 2*cos(alpha)*cos((n-1)*alpha)-cos((n-2)*alpha))
```

To illustrate substitutions of matrix elements, we take the 5×5 Toeplitz matrix again:

$$T = \begin{bmatrix} a_4 & a_3 & a_2 & a_1 & a_0 \\ a_5 & a_4 & a_3 & a_2 & a_1 \\ a_6 & a_5 & a_4 & a_3 & a_2 \\ a_7 & a_6 & a_5 & a_4 & a_3 \\ a_8 & a_7 & a_6 & a_5 & a_4 \end{bmatrix}$$

Consider the substitution `T.subs(T[0,2],0)`. It changes the symbol object at position `[0, 2]`, which is the symbol a_2. It also occurs at two other places, which are automatically affected by this substitution.

The given expression is the resulting matrix:

$$\begin{bmatrix} a_4 & a_3 & 0 & a_1 & a_0 \\ a_5 & a_4 & a_3 & 0 & a_1 \\ a_6 & a_5 & a_4 & a_3 & 0 \\ a_7 & a_6 & a_5 & a_4 & a_3 \\ a_8 & a_7 & a_6 & a_5 & a_4 \end{bmatrix}$$

Alternatively, we can create a variable for this symbol and use it in the substitution:

```
a2 = symbols('a2')
T.subs(a2,0)
```

As a more complex example for substitution, let's consider how to turn the Toeplitz matrix into a tridiagonal Toeplitz matrix. This can be done in the following ways:

First, we generate a list of those symbols that we want to substitute; and then we use the `zip` command to generate a list of pairs. Finally, we substitute by giving a list of old-value/new-value pairs as described previously:

```
symbs = [symbols('a'+str(i)) for i in range(19) if i < 3 or i > 5]
substitutions=list(zip(symbs,len(symbs)*[0]))
T.subs(substitutions)
```

This gives the following matrix as a result:

$$\begin{bmatrix} a_4 & a_3 & 0 & 0 & 0 \\ a_5 & a_4 & a_3 & 0 & 0 \\ 0 & a_5 & a_4 & a_3 & 0 \\ 0 & 0 & a_5 & a_4 & a_3 \\ 0 & 0 & 0 & a_5 & a_4 \end{bmatrix}$$

16. 5 Evaluating symbolic expressions

In the context of scientific computing, there is often the need to first make symbolic manipulations and then convert the symbolic result into a floating-point number.

The central tool for evaluating a symbolic expression is `evalf`. It converts symbolic expressions to floating-point numbers by using the following:

```
pi.evalf()   # returns 3.14159265358979
```

The data type of the resulting object is `Float` (note the capitalization), which is a SymPy data type that allows floating-point numbers with an arbitrary number of digits (arbitrary precision).

The default precision corresponds to 15 digits, but it can be changed by giving `evalf` an extra positive integer argument

specifying the desired precision in terms of the numbers of digits:

```
pi.evalf(30)   # returns  3.14159265358979323846264338328
```

A consequence of working with arbitrary precision is that numbers can be arbitrarily small, that is, the limits of the classical floating-point representation are broken; see `Section 2.2.2`: *Floating-point numbers*.

Interestingly enough, evaluating a SymPy function with an input of type `Float` returns a `Float` with the same precision as the input. We demonstrate the use of this fact in a more elaborated example from numerical analysis.

16.5.1 Example: A study on the convergence order of Newton's method

An iterative method that iterates x_n is said to converge with order q with $1 < q \in \mathbb{N}$ if there exists a positive constant C such that

$$\lim_{n \to \infty} \frac{|x_{n+1} - x_n|}{|x_n - x_{n-1}|^q} = C$$

Newton's method, when started with a good initial value, has order $q = 2$, and for certain problems, even $q = 3$. Newton's method when applied to the problem $\arctan(x) = 0$ gives the following iteration scheme:

$$x_{n+1} = x_n - \frac{f(x_n)}{f'(x_n)} = x_n - \arctan(x_n)(x_n^2 - 1)$$

Which converges cubically; that is, $q = 3$.

This implies that the number of correct digits triples from iteration to iteration. To demonstrate cubic convergence and to numerically determine the constant C is hardly possible with the standard 16-digit `float` data type.

The following code uses SymPy together with high-precision evaluation instead and takes the study on cubic convergence to the extreme:

```
import sympy as sym
x = sym.Rational(1,2)
xns=[x]

for i in range(1,9):
    x = (x - sym.atan(x)*(1+x**2)).evalf(3000)
    xns.append(x)
```

The result is depicted in the next figure (*Figure 16.4*), which shows that the number of correct digits triples from iteration to iteration:

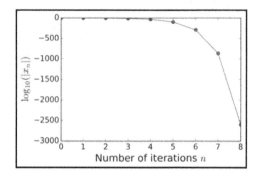

Figure 16.4: A study on the convergence of Newton's method applied to $\arctan(x) = 0$

This extreme precision requirement (3,000 digits!) enables us to evaluate seven terms of the preceding sequence to demonstrate cubic convergence in the following way:

```
import numpy as np
# Test for cubic convergence
print(np.array(np.abs(np.diff(xns[1:]))/np.abs(np.diff(xns[:-1]))**3,
            dtype=np.float64))
```

The result is a list of seven terms that let us assume that $C = 2/3$:

```
[ 0.41041618,  0.65747717,  0.6666665,   0.66666667,  0.66666667,  0.66666667,
0.66666667]}
```

16.5.2 Converting a symbolic expression into a numeric function

As we have seen, the numerical evaluation of symbolic expressions is done in three steps: first, we do some symbolic computations and then we substitute values by numbers and do an evaluation to a floating-point number with `evalf`.

The reason for symbolic computations is often that we want to make parameter studies. This requires that the parameter is modified within a given parameter range. This requires that a symbolic expression is eventually turned into a numeric function.

A study on the parameter dependency of polynomial coefficients

We demonstrate a symbolic/ numeric parameter study by an interpolation example to introduce the SymPy command `lambdify`.

Let's consider the task to interpolate the data $x = [0, t, 1]$ and $y = [0, 1, -1]$. Here, t is a free parameter, which we will vary over the interval $[-0.4, 1.4]$.

The quadratic interpolation polynomial has coefficients depending on this parameter:

$$y(x) = a_2(t)x^2 + a_1(t)x + a_0$$

Using SymPy and the monomial approach described in *Exercise 3* in `Section 4.11`: *Exercises* gives us the closed formula for these coefficients:

```
t=symbols('t')
x=[0,t,1]
# The Vandermonde Matrix
V = Matrix([[0, 0, 1], [t**2, t, 1], [1, 1,1]])
y = Matrix([0,1,-1]) # the data vector
a = simplify(V.LUsolve(y)) # the coefficients
# the leading coefficient as a function of the parameter
a2 = Lambda(t,a[0])
```

We obtain a symbolic function for the leading coefficient a_2 of the interpolation polynomial:

$$\left(t \mapsto \frac{t+1}{t(t-1)}\right)$$

Now it is time to turn the expression into a numeric function, for example, to make a plot. This is done by the function `lamdify`. This function takes two arguments, the independent variable, and a SymPy function.

For our example in Python, we can write:

```
leading_coefficient = lambdify(t,a2(t))
```

This function can now be plotted, for example, by the following commands:

```
import numpy as np
import matplotlib.pyplot as mp
t_list= np.linspace(-0.4,1.4,200)
ax=mp.subplot(111)
```

```
lc_list = [leading_coefficient(t) for t in t_list]
ax.plot(t_list, lc_list)
ax.axis([-.4,1.4,-15,10])
ax.set_xlabel('Free parameter $t$')
ax.set_ylabel('$a_2(t)$')
```

Figure 16.5 is the result of this parameter study, we can clearly see the singularities due to multiple interpolation points (here at $t = 0$ or $t = 1$):

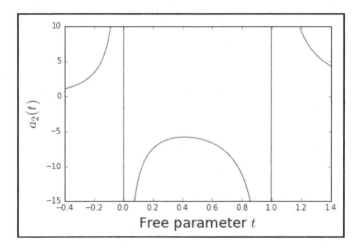

Figure 16.5: The dependency of a polynomial coefficient on the location of an interpolation point

16.6 Summary

In this chapter, you were introduced to the world of symbolic computations and you got a glimpse of the power of SymPy. By following the examples, you learned how to set up symbolic expressions, how to work with symbolic matrices, and you saw how to make simplifications. Working with symbolic functions and transforming them into numerical evaluations, finally, established the link to scientific computing and floating-point results. You experienced the strength of SymPy as you used its full integration into Python with its powerful constructs and legible syntax.

Consider this last chapter as an appetizer rather than a complete menu. We hope you became hungry for future fascinating programming challenges in scientific computing and mathematics.

17
Interacting with the Operating System

This section is an add-on to the introduction to Python. It puts Python into the context of the operating system on your computer and shows how Python is used in a command window, also called a console. We demonstrate how system commands and a Python command interact with each other and how you make a new application.

Among many other operating systems and various *dialects*, there are three main operating systems in use on desktop computers and notebooks: Windows 10, macOS, and Linux. In this chapter, we discuss how to use Python within the Linux world. All examples are tested in the widely distributed Ubuntu environment. The principles presented here apply also to the other big operating systems. The presentation is nevertheless restricted to Linux as a completely freely accessible environment.

First, we assume we have written and tested a Python program and want to run it now from a console window directly instead of from a Python shell such as IPython.

In this chapter, we cover the following topics:

- Running a Python program in a Linux shell
- The module `sys`
- How to execute Linux commands from Python

17.1 Running a Python program in a Linux shell

When you open a terminal window with the terminal app, you obtain a window with a command prompt; see *Figure 17.1*:

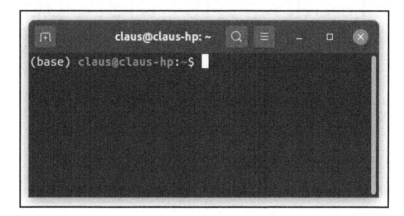

Figure 17.1: A terminal window in Ubuntu 20.04

The terminal windows come with a command prompt, often prefixed by the username and the computer's name followed by the directory name. This depends on the individual settings.

To execute the Python commands written in a file named `myprogram.py`, you have two choices:

- Executing the command `python myprogram.py`
- Executing the command `myprogram.py` directly

The second variant needs some preparation. First, you have to give permission to execute that file, and secondly, you have to tell the system which command is needed to execute that file. The permission to execute that file is given by the command:

```
chmod myprogram.py o+x
```

`chmod` stands for changing the file mode. The command is followed by the filename and finally the desired new modes, here `o+x`.

The modes that are given in that example stand for "give (+) the owner (o) rights to execute (x) that file." We suppose that you are the owner of the file and that it is in the current directory.

Then, we have to find the location of the command `python` on our computer. This is done by running the command:

```
which python
```

If you installed Python via Anaconda as described in `Section 1.1`: *Installation and configuration instructions*, you will get information about the location of the command `python` on your system, for example, `/home/claus/anaconda3/bin/python`.

This information has to be written in the first line of a Python script to tell the system by which program the text file can be transformed into an executable. Here is an example:

```
#! /home/claus/anaconda3/bin/python
a=3
b=4
c=a+b
print(f'Summing up {a} and {b} gives {c}')
```

The first line in Python's view is just a comment and ignored. But Linux takes the rest of the first line after the so-called *shebang* combination, `#!`, as the command needed to transform the file into an executable. Here, it learns to use the command `python` located in the directory `/home/claus/anaconda3/bin/` for that purpose.

Instead of defining the location of the Python interpreter by an absolute path, we can define it also by a logical path, which would make the code more portable. You can give it to a colleague on a Linux system without any modification:

```
#! /usr/bin/env  python   # a logical path to Python (mind the blank)
```

Now you can execute the example code in the console directly; see *Figure 17.2*:

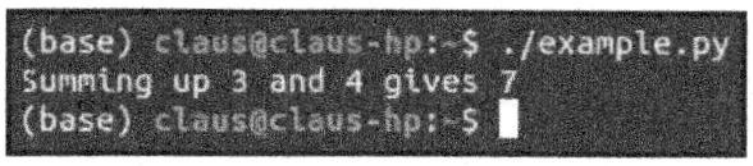

Figure 17.2: Executing the example file example.py in a Linux terminal

We have to prefix the command with `./`, which tells the operating system that it should look in the current directory to find that command. If this prefix is not present, Linux expects the file `example.py` in one of the directories listed in the search path.

In the next section, we will show how to provide a Python program with arguments given directly from the command line.

17.2 The module sys

The module `sys` provides tools to communicate from a Python script with system commands. We can provide the Python script as a command directly from the command line with arguments and we can output the results to the console.

17.2.1 Command-line arguments

To illustrate the use of command-line arguments, we consider the following piece of code, which we save in a file called `demo_cli.py`:

```python
#! /usr/bin/env  python
import sys
text=f"""
You called the program{sys.argv[0]}
with the {len(sys.argv)-1} arguments, namely {sys.argv[1:]}"""
print(text)
```

After giving execution permissions to the file by `chmod o+x demo_cli.py`, we can execute it in the shell with arguments; see *Figure 17.3*:

```
(base) claus@claus-hp:~$ ./demo_cli.py 1 2 17


You called the  program ./demo_cli.py
with the 3 arguments, namely ['1', '2', '17']
```

Figure 17.3: Executing a Python script with three arguments on a terminal command line

The three arguments given in the console are accessible in the Python script via the list `sys.argv`. The first element in this list—the element with index 0—is the name of the script. The other elements are the given arguments as strings.

Arguments are given to the call of the Python script. They should not be confounded with user input during the execution of a script.

17.2.2 Input and output streams

In the preceding example, we used the command `print` to display the generated message in the terminal (or even in the Python shell). A priory input to the script is obtained via arguments and the variable `sys.argv`. The counterpart to `print` is the command `input`, which prompts for data from the terminal (or from the Python shell).

In `Section 14.1`: *File handling*, we saw how to provide a script with data and how to output data from a script by the use of file objects and related methods. The module `sys` makes it possible to treat the keyboard as a file object for input (for example, `readline`, `readlines`) and the console as a file object for output (for example, `write`, `writelines`).

The information flow is organized in UNIX by three streams:

- The standard input stream: `STDIN`
- The standard output stream: `STDOUT`
- The standard error stream: `STDERR`

These streams correspond to file objects that can be accessed in Python by `sys.stdin`, `sys.stdout`, and `sys.stderr`.

To have an example, we consider a little script, `pyinput.py`, which sums up some numbers:

```
#!/usr/bin/env python3
from numpy import *
import sys

# Terminate input by CTRL+D
a=array(sys.stdin.readlines()).astype(float)
print(f'Input: {a}, Sum {sum(a)}'
```

The statement `sys.stdin.readlines()` establishes a generator. The command `array` iterates this generator until the user inputs an end-of-input symbol, which is `CTRL-D` on Linux systems or `CTRL-Z` on Windows systems. See the screenshot in *Figure 17.4*:

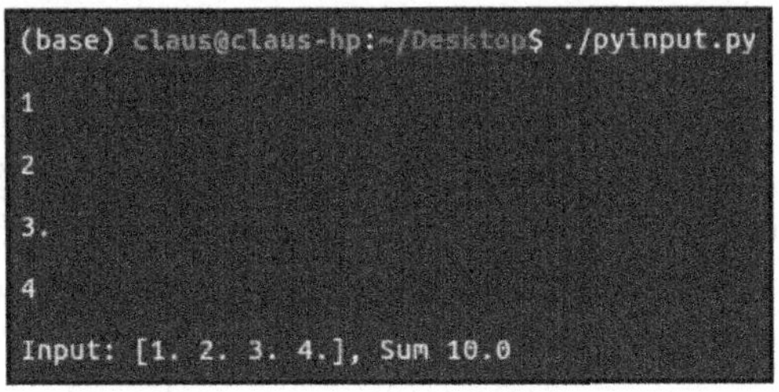

```
(base) claus@claus-hp:~/Desktop$ ./pyinput.py

1

2

3.

4

Input: [1. 2. 3. 4.], Sum 10.0
```

Figure 17.4: Screenshot of the terminal execution of a script using sys.stdin.
Note, the given end-of-input symbol CTRL-D is not visible

Redirecting streams

The standard input is expecting a data stream from the keyboard. But the input can be redirected from a file instead. This is done by using the redirection symbol < in Linux. We demonstrate this by using the same script as previously, but now a data file, `intest.txt`, provides the script with data; see *Figure 17.5*:

```
(base) claus@claus-hp:~/Desktop$ ./pyinput.py < intest.txt
Input: [1. 2. 3. 4.], Sum 10.0
```

Figure 17.5: Screenshot to demonstrate the redirection of input (sys.stdin)

No modification in the script itself is required. It can be used in either way.

The same holds for outputs. By default the output is displayed in the terminal, but also here there is the option to redirect the output to a file. In that case, the redirect symbol is >; see *Figure 17.6*:

```
(base) claus@claus-hp:~/Desktop$ ./pyinput.py < intest.txt > result.txt
```

Figure 17.6: Screenshot of a redirected input and redirected output

Now, a file with the name `result.txt` is created and the output of the script is written to it. If there was already a file with this name, its content is overwritten. If instead the output should be appended to an already-existing file, the redirection symbol >> has to be used.

Finally, it might sometimes be desired to separate the output from an error or warning message. That is the reason why Linux provides two stream channels for output, `sys.stdout` and `sys.stderr`. By default, both refer to the same place, the terminal. But with the use of redirection symbols, error messages can, for example, be written into a file while the main output is displayed on the screen or vice versa.

To demonstrate this, we modify the example `pyinput.py` to generate an error message in case no input was provided:

```
#!/usr/bin/env python3
from numpy import *
import sys

# Terminate input by CTRL+D
a=array(sys.stdin.readlines()).astype(float)
print(f'Input: {a}, Sum {sum(a)}')
if a.size == 0:
    sys.stderr.write('No input given\n')
```

A typical call of this script in a terminal window with redirected input and error output is presented in *Figure 17.7*:

```
(base) claus@claus-hp:~/Desktop$ ./pyinput.py <intest2.txt 2> error.txt

Input: [], Sum 0.0
```

Figure 17.7: Screenshot of a terminal window with redirection of stdin and stderr

In the case of an empty input file, an error message is written into the file `error.txt` while the output is in the terminal window.

Error messages are those from uncaught exceptions, even syntax errors and text explicitly written to `sys.stderr`.

In *Table 17.1*, the different redirection situations are summarized:

Task	Python Object	Redirect Symbol	Alt. Symbol
Data input	sys.stdin	<	
Data output	sys.stdout	>	1>
Data output append to file	sys.stdout	>>	1>>
Error output	sys.stderr	2>	
Error output append to file	sys.stderr	2>>	
All output	sys.stdout, sys.stderr	&>	
All output append to file	sys.stdout, sys.stderr	&>>	

Table 17.1: Summary of different redirection scenarios

Building a pipe between a Linux command and a Python script

In the last section, we saw how to redirect the input and output of Python programs to files. The data flow between different Python programs or between a Python program and a Linux command goes, in that case, via a file. If the data is not used elsewhere or should be saved for later use, this is a tedious process: creating, naming, and deleting a file just for directly passing information from one piece of code to another. The alternative is to use a Linux **pipe** that lets the data flow in a direct stream from one command to another.

Let's start with a pure Linux example and then apply the pipe construction to Python.

The Linux command `ifconfig` displays a lot of information about the actual network configuration of a Linux computer. Among this information, you find the IP number(s), which are the current network addresses in use. To automatically find out whether a computer, for example, a notebook, is connected via a certain network unit to the home network instead of to a foreign network, you would like to scan the output of `ifconfig` for a line containing the identifier for the network card, for example, `wlp0s20f3`, and some lines below for a string with the network prefix, for example, `192.168`. If this string is found, the output should be just the line with this string; that is, a line count would return `1`. If the computer is not connected to the home network, the line count returns `0`.

We use three commands:

- `ifconfig` for the entire lengthy network information.
- `grep` for finding lines containing a certain pattern. The line and, if required by the parameter `-A`, some following lines are displayed.
- `wc` for doing various countings on a file. The argument `-l` specifies that lines should be counted.

The output of these commands is directly piped into the next command. This is done by using the pipe symbol `|`:

```
ifconfig|grep -A1 wlp0s20f3 | grep 192.168|wc -l
```

This command line displays just `1` on the screen when executed in the home network. All the intermediate output is passed directly to the next command without displaying anything and without the use of any files to park temporarily the information until the next command reads it. The standard output, `stdout`, of one command becomes the standard input, `stdin`, of the next.

This also applies directly to Python scripts.

We continue the previous example by demonstrating a Python script in the pipe. Here we simply use Python to generate a nice message:

```
#!/usr/bin/env python3

import sys

count = sys.stdin.readline()[0]
status = '' if count == '1' else 'not'

print(f"I am {status} at home")
```

Now, we can extend the pipe by adding this script; see the screenshot in *Figure 17.8*:

Figure 17.8: A command chain with five pipes and a Python script

In this example, we executed a chain of Linux programs and a Python script in the terminal window. Alternatively, it is possible to let the Python script call the UNIX commands. That will be demonstrated in the next section.

17.3 How to execute Linux commands from Python

We saw in the last section how to execute a Python command from the Linux terminal. In this section, we consider the important case of how to execute Linux commands within a Python program.

17.3.1 The modules subprocess and shlex

To execute system commands within Python, we need to import the module subprocess first. The high-level tool provided by this module is run. With this tool, you quickly access Linux commands within Python and can process their output.

The more sophisticated tool is Popen, which we will shortly present when explaining how to mimic Linux pipes in Python.

A complete process: subprocess.run

We demonstrate this tool with the most standard and simple UNIX command, `ls`—the command for listing the content of a directory. It comes with various optional arguments; for example, `ls -l` displays the list with extended information.

To execute this command within a Python script, we use `subprocess.run`. The simplest usage is using only one argument, a list with the Linux command split into several text strings:

```
import subprocess as sp
res = sp.run(['ls','-l'])
```

The module `shlex` provides a special tool for performing this split:

```
_import shlex
command_list = shlex.split('ls -l') # returns ['ls', '-l']
```

It also respects empty spaces in filenames and does not use those as separators.

The command `run` displays the result of the Linux command and the `subprocess.CompletedProcess` object `res`.

To execute UNIX commands in this way is quite useless. Mostly, you want to process the output. Therefore, the output has to be made available to the Python script. For this, the optional parameter `capture_output` has to be set to `True`. By this, the `stdout` and `stderr` streams of the UNIX command become available as attributes of the return object:

```
import subprocess as sp
import shlex
command_list = shlex.split('ls -l') # returns ['ls', '-l']
res = sp.run(command_list, capture_output=True)
print(res.stdout.decode())
```

Note, the method `decode` is used here to decode a byte string to a standard string format.

If the Linux command returns an error, the attribute `res.returncode` gets a nonzero value, and `res.stderr` contains the error message.

The Python way would be that an error is raised instead. This can be achieved by setting the optional parameter `check` to `True`:

```
import subprocess as sp
import shlex
command ='ls -y'
command_list = shlex.split(command) # returns ['ls', '-y']
```

```
try:
    res = sp.run(command_list, capture_output=True, check=True)
    print(res.stdout.decode())
except sp.CalledProcessError:
  print(f"{command} is not a valid command")
```

Creating processes: subprocess.Popen

What happens when you apply `subprocess.run` on a Linux command that starts a process that requires user input to terminate?

A simple example of such a program is `xclock`. It opens a new window displaying a clock until the window is closed by the user.

As the command `subprocess.run` creates a `CompletedProcess` object, the following Python script:

```
import subprocess as sp
res=sp.run(['xclock'])
```

starts a process and waits until it ends, that is, until somebody closes the window with the clock; see *Figure 17.9*:

Figure 17.9: The xclock window

This makes a difference to `subprocess.Popen`. It creates a `_Popen` object. The process itself becomes a Python object. It need not be completed to become an accessible Python object:

```
import subprocess as sp
p=sp.Popen(['xclock'])
```

The process is completed by either a user action on the clock window or by explicitly terminating the process with:

```
p.terminate()
```

With `Popen`, we can construct Linux pipes in Python. The following script:

```
import subprocess as sp_
p1=sp.Popen(['ls', '-l'],stdout=sp.PIPE)
cp2=sp.run(['grep','apr'], stdin=p1.stdout, capture_output=True)
print(cp2.stdout.decode())
```

Corresponds to the UNIX pipe:

```
ls -l |grep 'apr
```

It displays all files in a directory last accessed in April.

The module `subprocess` has an object `PIPE` that takes the output of the first process `p1`. It is then passed as `stdin` to the command `run`. This command then returns a `CompletedProcess` object `cp2` with the attribute `stdout` of type `bytes`. Finally, calling the method `decode` allows a nice print of the results.

Alternatively, the same could be achieved by using two `Popen` processes. The second also uses a pipe that can be displayed through the method `communicate`:

```
import subprocess as sp
p1=sp.Popen(['ls', '-l'],stdout=sp.PIPE)
p2=sp.Popen(['grep','apr'], stdin=p1.stdout, stdout=sp.PIPE)
print(p2.communicate()[0].decode)
```

The method `communicate` returns a tuple with the output on `stdout` and `stderr`.

17.4 Summary

In this chapter, we demonstrated the interaction of a Python script with system commands. Either a Python script can be called in a way as if it would be a system command or a Python script can itself create system processes. The chapter is based on Linux systems such as Ubuntu and serves only as a demonstration of concepts and possibilities. It allows putting scientific computing tasks in an application context, where often different software have to be combined. Even hardware components might come into play.

18
Python for Parallel Computing

This chapter covers parallel computing and the module `mpi4py`. Complex and time-consuming computational tasks can often be divided into subtasks, which can be carried out simultaneously if there is capacity for it. When these subtasks are independent of each other, executing them in parallel can be especially efficient. Situations where subtasks have to wait until another subtask is completed are less suited for parallel computing.

Consider the task of computing an integral of a function by a quadrature rule:

$$\int_a^b f(x)\mathrm{d}x \approx \sum_{i=0}^{n} \frac{1}{2}(f(x_i) + f(x_{i+1}))\,(x_{i+1} - x_i)$$

with $a = x_0 < x_1 < \cdots < x_n = b$. If the evaluation of f is time-consuming and n is large , it would be advantageous to split the problem into two or several subtasks of smaller size:

$$\int_a^b f(x)\mathrm{d}x \approx \underbrace{\sum_{i=0}^{n/2-1} \frac{1}{2}(f(x_i) + f(x_{i+1}))\,(x_{i+1} - x_i)}_{\text{Subtask 1}} + \underbrace{\sum_{i=n/2}^{n} \frac{1}{2}(f(x_i) + f(x_{i+1}))\,(x_{i+1} - x_i)}_{\text{Subtask 2}}$$

We can use several computers and give each of them the necessary information so that they can perform their subtasks, or we can use a single computer with a so-called multicore architecture.

Once the subtasks are accomplished the results are communicated to the computer or processor that controls the entire process and performs the final additions.

We will use this as a guiding example in this chapter while covering the following topics:

- Multicore computers and computer clusters
- Message passing interface (MPI)

18.1 Multicore computers and computer clusters

Most of the modern computers are multicore computers. For example, the laptop used when writing this book has an Intel® i7-8565U processor that has four cores with two threads each.

What does this mean? Four cores on a processor allow performing four computational tasks in parallel. Four cores with two threads each are often counted as eight CPUs by system monitors. For the purposes of this chapter only the number of cores matters.

These cores share a common memory—the RAM of your laptop—and have individual memory in the form of cache memory:

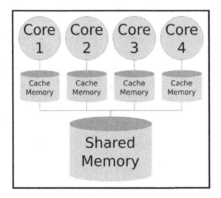

Figure 18.1: A multicore architecture with shared and local cache memory

The cache memory is used optimally by its core and is accessed at high speed, while the shared memory can be accessed by all cores of one CPU. On top, there is the computer's RAM memory and finally, the hard disk, which is also shared memory.

In the next section, we will see how a computational task can be distributed to individual cores and how results are received and further processed, for example, being stored in a file.

A different setting for parallel computing is the use of a computer cluster. Here, a task is divided into parallelizable subtasks that are sent to different computers, sometimes even over long distances. Here, communication time can matter substantially. The use of such a computer cluster makes sense only if the time for processing subtasks is large in relation to communication time.

18.2 Message passing interface (MPI)

Programming for several cores or on a computer cluster with distributed memory requires special techniques. We describe here *message passing* and related tools standardized by the MPI standard. These tools are similar in different programming languages, such as C, C++, and FORTRAN, and are realized in Python by the module `mpi4py`.

18.2.1 Prerequisites

You need to install this module first by executing the following in a terminal window:

```
conda install mpi4py
```

The module is imported by adding the following line to your Python script:

```
import mpi4py as mpi
```

The execution of a parallelized code is done from a terminal with the command `mpiexec`. Assuming that your code is stored in the file `script.py`, executing this code on a computer with a four-core CPU is done in the terminal window by running the following command:

```
mpiexec -n 4 python script.py
```

Alternatively, to execute the same script on a cluster with two computers, run the following in a terminal window:

```
mpiexec --hostfile=hosts.txt python script.py
```

You have to provide a file `hosts.txt` containing the names or IP addresses of the computers with the number of their cores you want to bind to a cluster:

```
# Content of hosts.txt
192.168.1.25 :4 # master computer with 4 cores
192.168.1.101:2 # worker computer with 2 cores
```

The Python script, here `script.py`, has to be copied to all computers in the cluster.

18.3 Distributing tasks to different cores

When executed on a multicore computer, we can think of it that `mpiexec` copies the given Python script to the number of cores and runs each copy. As an example, consider the one-liner script `print_me.py` with the command `print("Hello it's me")`, that, when executed with `mpiexec -n 4 print_me.py`, generates the same message on the screen four times, each sent from a different core.

In order to be able to execute different tasks on different cores, we have to be able to distinguish these cores in the script.

To this end, we create a so-called communicator instance, which organizes the communication between the *world*, that is, the input and output units like the screen, the keyboard, or a file, and the individual cores. Furthermore, the individual cores are given identifying numbers, called a rank:

```
from mpi4py import MPI
comm=MPI.COMM_WORLD  # making a communicator instance
rank=comm.Get_rank() # querrying for the numeric identifyer of the core
size=comm.Get_size() # the total number of cores assigned
```

The communicator attribute size refers to the total number of processes specified in the statement `mpiexec`.

Now we can give every core an individual computational task, as in the next script, which we might call `basicoperations.py`:

```
from mpi4py import MPI
comm=MPI.COMM_WORLD # making a communicator instance
rank=comm.Get_rank() # querrying for the numeric identifyer of the core
size=comm.Get_size() # the total number of cores assigned
a=15
b=2
if rank==0:
    print(f'Core {rank} computes {a}+{b}={a+b}')
if rank==1:
    print(f'Core {rank} computes {a}*{b}={a*b}')
if rank==2:
    print(f'Core {rank} computes {a}**{b}={a**b}')
```

This script is executed in the terminal by entering the following command:

```
mpiexec -n 3 python basicoperations.py
```

We obtain three messages:

```
Core 0 computes 15+2=17
Core 2 computes 15**2=225
Core 1 computes 15*2=3
```

All three processes got their individual tasks, which were executed in parallel. Clearly, printing the result to the screen is a bottleneck as the screen is shared by all three processes.

In the next section, we see how communication between the processes is done.

18.3.1 Information exchange between processes

There are different ways to send and receive information between processes:

- Point-to-point communication
- One-to-all and all-to-one
- All-to-all

In this section, we will introduce point-to-point, one-to-all, and all-to-one communication.

Speaking to a neighbor and letting information pass along a street this way is an example from daily life of the first communication type from the preceding list, while the second can be illustrated by the daily news, spoken by one person and broadcast to a big group of listeners.One-to-all and all-to-one communication

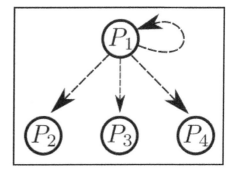

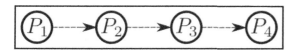

Figure 18.2: Point-to-point communication and one-to-all communication

In the next subsections, we will study these different communication types in a computational context.

18.3.2 Point-to-point communication

Point-to-point communication directs information flow from one process to a designated receiving process. We first describe the methods and features by considering a ping-pong situation and a telephone-chain situation and explain the notion of blocking.

Point-to-point communication is applied in scientific computing, for instance in random-walk or particle-tracing applications on domains that are divided into a number of subdomains corresponding to the number of processes that can be carried out in parallel.

The ping-pong example assumes that we have two processors sending an integer back and forth to each other and increasing its value by one.

We start by creating a communicator object and checking that we have two processes available:

```
from mpi4py import MPI
comm=MPI.COMM_WORLD # making a communicator instance
rank=comm.Get_rank() # querying for the numeric identifier of the core
size=comm.Get_size() # the total number of cores assigned
if not (size==2):
    raise Exception(f"This examples requires two processes. \
                    {size} processes given.")
```

Then we send information back and forth between the two processes:

```
count = 0
text=['Ping','Pong']
print(f"Rank {rank} activities:\n===================")
while count < 5:
    if rank == count%2:
        print(f"In round {count}: Rank {rank} says {text[count%2]}""
                "and sends the ball to rank {(rank+1)%2}")
        count += 1
        comm.send(count, dest=(rank+1)%2)
    elif rank == (count+1)%2:
        count = comm.recv(source=(rank+1)%2)
```

Information is sent by the method `send` of the communicator. Here, we provided it with the information that we want to send, along with the destination. The communicator takes care that the destination information is translated to a hardware address; either one core of the CPU in your machine or that of a host machine.

The other machine receives the information by the communicator method `comm.recv`. It requires information on where the information is expected from. Under the hood, it tells the sender that the information has been received by freeing the information buffer on the data channel. The sender awaits this signal before it can proceed.

The two statements `if rank == count%2` and `elif rank == (count+1)%2` ensure that the processors alternate their sending and receiving tasks.

Here is the output of this short script that we saved in a file called `pingpong.py` and executed with the following:

```
mpiexec -n 2 python pingpong.py
```

In the terminal, this produces the following output:

```
Rank 0 activities:
===================
In round 0: Rank 0 says Ping and sends the ball to rank 1
In round 2: Rank 0 says Ping and sends the ball to rank 1
In round 4: Rank 0 says Ping and sends the ball to rank 1
Rank 1 activities:
===================
In round 1: Rank 1 says Pong and sends the ball to rank 0
In round 3: Rank 1 says Pong and sends the ball to rank 0
```

What types of data can be sent or received? As the commands `send` and `recv` communicate data in binary form, they `pickle` the data first (see `Section 14.3`: *Pickling*). Most of the Python objects can be pickled, but not `lambda` functions for instance. It is also possible to pickle buffered data such as NumPy arrays, but a direct send of buffered data is more efficient, as we'll see in the next subsection.

Note that there might be reasons for sending and receiving functions between processes. As the methods `send` and `recv` only communicate references to functions, the references have to exist on the sending and receiving processors. Therefore the following Python script returns an error:

```python
from mpi4py import MPI
comm=MPI.COMM_WORLD # making a communicator instance
rank=comm.Get_rank() # querying for the numeric identifier of the core
size=comm.Get_size() # the total number of cores assigned

if rank==0:
    def func():
        return 'Function called'
    comm.send(func, dest=1)
if rank==1:
```

```
        f=comm.recv(source=0)     # <<<<<< This line reports an error
        print(f())One-to-all and all-to-one communication
```

The error message thrown by the statement `recv` is `AttributeError: Can't get attribute 'func'`. This is caused by the fact that `f` refers to the function `func`, which is not defined for the processor with rank 1. The correct way is to define this function for both processors:

```
from mpi4py import MPI
comm=MPI.COMM_WORLD # making a communicator instance
rank=comm.Get_rank() # querying for the numeric identifier of the core
size=comm.Get_size() # the total number of cores assigned

def func():
    return 'Function called'
if rank==0:
    comm.send(func, dest=1)
if rank==1:
    f=comm.recv(source=0)
    print(f())
```

18.3.3 Sending NumPy arrays

The commands `send` and `recv` are high-level commands. That means they do under-the-hood work that saves the programmer time and avoids possible errors. They allocate memory after having internally deduced the datatype and the amount of buffer data needed for communication. This is done internally on a lower level based on C constructions.

NumPy arrays are objects that themselves make use of these C-buffer-like objects, so when sending and receiving NumPy arrays you can gain efficiency by using them in the lower-level communication counterparts `Send` and `Recv` (mind the capitalization!).

In the following example, we send an array from one processor to another:

```
from mpi4py import MPI
comm=MPI.COMM_WORLD # making a communicator instance
rank=comm.Get_rank() # querying for the numeric identifier of the core
size=comm.Get_size() # the total number of cores assigned
import numpy as np

if rank==0:
    A = np.arange(700)
    comm.Send(A, dest=1)
```

```
if rank==1:
    A = np.empty(700, dtype=int)   # This is needed for memory allocation
                                   # of the buffer on Processor 1
    comm.Recv(A, source=0)         # Note, the difference to recv in
                                   # providing the data.
    print(f'An array received with last element {A[-1]}')
```

It is important to note, that on both processors, memory for the buffer has to be allocated. Here, this is done by creating on Processor 0 an array with the data and on Processor 1 an array with the same size and datatype but arbitrary data.

Also, we see a difference in the command recv in the output. The command Recv returns the buffer via the first argument. This is possible as NumPy arrays are mutable.

18.3.4 Blocking and non-blocking communication

The commands send and recv and their buffer counterparts Send and Recv are so-called blocking commands. That means a command send is completed when the corresponding send buffer is freed. When this will happen depends on several factors such as the particular communication architecture of your system and the amount of data that is to be communicated. Finally, the command send is considered to be freed when the corresponding command recv has got all the information. Without such a command recv, it will wait forever. This is called a deadlock situation.

The following script demonstrates a situation with the potential for deadlock. Both processes send simultaneously. If the amount of data to be communicated is too big to be stored the command send is waiting for a corresponding recv to empty the pipe, but recv never is invoked due to the waiting state. That's a deadlock.

```
from mpi4py import MPI
comm=MPI.COMM_WORLD # making a communicator instance
rank=comm.Get_rank() # querrying for the numeric identifier of the core
size=comm.Get_size() # the total number of cores assigned


if rank==0:
    msg=['Message from rank 0',list(range(101000))]
    comm.send(msg, dest=1)
    print(f'Process {rank} sent its message')
    s=comm.recv(source=1)
    print(f'I am rank {rank} and got a {s[0]} with a list of \
          length {len(s[1])}')
if rank==1:
    msg=['Message from rank 1',list(range(-101000,1))]
    comm.send(msg,dest=0)
```

```
        print(f'Process {rank} sent its message')
        s=comm.recv(source=0)
        print(f'I am rank {rank} and got a {s[0]} with a list of \
            length {len(s[1])}')
```

Note that executing this code might not cause a deadlock on your computer as the amount of data communicated is very small.

The straightforward remedy to avoid a deadlock, in this case, is to swap the order of the commands `recv` and `send` on *one* of the processors:

```
from mpi4py import MPI
comm=MPI.COMM_WORLD # making a communicator instance
rank=comm.Get_rank() # querrying for the numeric identifier of the core
size=comm.Get_size() # the total number of cores assigned


if rank==0:
    msg=['Message from rank 0',list(range(101000))]
    comm.send(msg, dest=1)
    print(f'Process {rank} sent its message')
    s=comm.recv(source=1)
    print(f'I am rank {rank} and got a {s[0]} with a list of \
        length {len(s[1])}')
if rank==1:
    s=comm.recv(source=0)
    print(f'I am rank {rank} and got a {s[0]} with a list of \
        length {len(s[1])}')
  msg=['Message from rank 1',list(range(-101000,1))]
    comm.send(msg,dest=0)
    print(f'Process {rank} sent its message')
    print(f'I am rank {rank} and got a {s[0]} with a list of \
        length {len(s[1])}')
```

18.3.5 One-to-all and all-to-one communication

When a complex task depending on a larger amount of data is divided into subtasks, the data also has to be divided into portions relevant to the related subtask and the results have to be assembled and processed into a final result.

Let's consider as an example the scalar product of two vectors $u, v \in \mathbb{R}^N$ divided into m subtasks:

$$u \cdot v = \sum_{i=1}^{N} u_i v_i = \sum_{j=0}^{m-1} \underbrace{\sum_{i=1+jN_m}^{(j+1)N_m} u_i v_i}_{\text{subtask } j} + \sum_{i=mN_m+1}^{N} u_i v_i$$

with $N_m = \text{int}(N/m)$. All subtasks perform the same operations on portions of the initial data, the results have to be summed up, and possibly any remaining operations have to be carried out.

We have to perform the following steps:

1. Creating the vectors u and v
2. Dividing them into m subvectors with a balanced number of elements, that is, N_m elements if N is divisible by m, otherwise some subvectors have more elements
3. Communicating each subvector to "its" processor
4. Performing the scalar product on the subvectors on each processor
5. Gathering all results
6. Summing up the results

Steps 1, 2, and *6* are run on one processor, the so-called *root* processor. In the following example code, we choose the processor with rank 0 for these tasks. *Steps 3, 4,* and *5* are executed on all processors, including the root processor. For the communication in *Step 3*, mpi4py provides the command scatter, and for recollecting the results the command gather is available.

Preparing the data for communication

First, we will look into *Step 2*. It is a nice exercise to write a script that splits a vector into m pieces with a balanced number of elements. Here is one suggestion for such a script, among many others:

```
def split_array(vector, n_processors):
  # splits an array into a number of subarrays
  # vector one dimensional ndarray or a list
  # n_processors integer, the number of subarrays to be formed
```

```
n=len(vector)
n_portions, rest = divmod(n,n_processors) # division with remainder
# get the amount of data per processor and distribute the res on
# the first processors so that the load is more or less equally
# distributed
# Construction of the indexes needed for the splitting
counts = [0]+ [n_portions + 1 \
            if p < rest else n_portions for p in range(n_processors)]
counts=numpy.cumsum(counts)
start_end=zip(counts[:-1],counts[1:]) # a generator
slice_list=(slice(*sl) for sl in start_end) # a generator comprehension
return [vector[sl] for sl in slice_list] # a list of subarrays
```

As this chapter is one of the last in this book we have seen a lot of tools that can be used for this code. We worked with NumPy's cumulative sum, cumsum. We used the generator zip, unpacking arguments by the operator *, and generator comprehension. We also tacitly introduced the data type slice, which allows us to do the splitting step in the last line in a very compact way.

The commands – scatter and gather

Now we are ready to look at the entire script for our demo problem, the scalar product:

```
from mpi4py import MPI
import numpy as np

comm = MPI.COMM_WORLD
rank = comm.Get_rank()
nprocessors = comm.Get_size()
import splitarray as spa

if rank == 0:
    # Here we generate data for the example
    n = 150
    u = 0.1*np.arange(n)
    v = - u
    u_split = spa.split_array(u, nprocessors)
    v_split = spa.split_array(v, nprocessors)
else:
    # On all processor we need variables with these names,
    # otherwise we would get an Exception "Variable not defined" in
    # the scatter command below
    u_split = None
    v_split = None
# These commands run now on all processors
u_split = comm.scatter(u_split, root=0) # the data is portion wise
```

```
                                         # distributed from root
v_split = comm.scatter(v_split, root=0)
# Each processor computes its part of the scalar product
partial_dot = u_split@v_split
# Each processor reports its result back to the root
partial_dot = comm.gather(partial_dot,root=0)

if rank==0:
    # partial_dot is a list of all collected results
    total_dot=np.sum(partial_dot)
    print(f'The parallel scalar product of u and v'
        f'on {nprocessors} processors is {total_dot}.\n'
        f'The difference to the serial computation is \
        {abs(total_dot-u@v)}')
```

If this script is stored in a file `parallel_dot.py` the command for execution with five processors is the following:

```
mexec -n 5 python parallel_dot.py
```

The result in this case is as follows:

```
The parallel scalar product of u and v on 5 processors is -11137.75.
The difference to the serial computation is 0.0
```

This example demonstrates the use of `scatter` to send out specific information to each processor. To use this command the root processor has to provide a list with as many elements as available processors. Each element contains the data to be communicated to one of the processors including the root processor.

The reversing process is `gather`. When all processors completed this command the root processor is provided with a list with as many elements as available processors, each containing the resulting data of its corresponding processor.

In the final step, the root processor again works alone by postprocessing this result list. The example above it sums all list elements and displays the result.

The art of parallel programming is to avoid bottlenecks. Ideally, all processors should be busy and should start and stop simultaneously. That is why the workload is distributed more or less equally to the processors by the script `splitarray` that we described previously. Furthermore, the code should be organized in such a way that the start and end periods with the root processor working alone are short compared to the computationally intense part carried out by all processors simultaneously.

A final data reduction operation – the command reduce

The parallel scalar product example is typical for many other tasks in the way how results are handled: the amount of data coming from all processors is reduced to a single number in the last step. Here, the root processor sums up all partial results from the processors. The command `reduce` can be efficiently used for this task. We modify the preceding code by letting `reduce` do the gathering and summation in one step. Here, the last lines of the preceding code are modified in this way:

```
........ modification of the script above .....
# Each processor reports its result back to the root
# and these results are summed up
total_dot = comm.reduce(partial_dot, op=MPI.SUM, root=0)

if rank==0:
    print(f'The parallel scalar product of u and v'
          f' on {nprocessors} processors is {total_dot}.\n'
          f'The difference to the serial computation \
          is {abs(total_dot-u@v)}')
```

Other frequently applied reducing operations are:

- `MPI.MAX` or `MPI.MIN`: The maximum or minimum of the partial results
- `MPI.MAXLOC` or `MPI.MINLOC`: The argmax or argmin of the partial results
- `MPI.PROD`: The product of the partial results
- `MPI.LAND` or `MPI.LOR`: The logical and/logical or of the partial results

Sending the same message to all

Another collective command is the broadcasting command `bcast`. In contrast to `scatter` it is used to send the same data to all processors. Its call is similar to that of `scatter`:

```
data = comm.bcast(data, root=0)
```

but it is the total data and not a list of portioned data that is sent. Again, the root processor can be any processor. It is the processor that prepares the data to be broadcasted.

Buffered data

In an analogous manner, `mpi4py` provides the corresponding collective commands for buffer-like data such as NumPy arrays by capitalizing the command: `scatter/Scatter`, `gather/Gather`, `reduce/Reduce`, `bcast/Bcast`.

18.4 Summary

In this chapter, we saw how to execute copies of the same script on different processors in parallel. Message passing allows the communication between these different processes. We saw *point-to-point* communication and the two different distribution type collective communications *one-to-all* and *all-to-one*. The commands presented in this chapter are provided by the Python module `mpi4py`, which is a Python wrapper to realize the MPI standard in C.

Having worked through this chapter, you are now able to work on your own scripts for parallel programming and you will find that we described only the most essential commands and concepts here. Grouping processes and tagging information are only two of those concepts that we left out. Many of these concepts are important for special and challenging applications, which are far too particular for this introduction.

19
Comprehensive Examples

In this chapter, we will present some comprehensive and longer examples together with a brief introduction to the theoretical background and the examples' complete implementation. Here, we want to show you how the concepts defined in this book are used in practice.

The following topics are covered in this chapter:

- Polynomials
- The polynomial class
- Spectral clustering
- Solving initial value problems

19.1 Polynomials

First, we will demonstrate the power of the Python constructs presented so far by designing a class for polynomials.

Note that this class differs conceptually from the class `numpy.poly1d`.

We will give some theoretical background, which will lead us to a list of requirements, and then we will give the code, with some comments.

19.1.1 Theoretical background

A polynomial $p(x) = a_n x^n + a_{n-1} x^{n-1} + \cdots + a_1 x + a_0$ is defined by its degree, representation, and coefficients. The polynomial representation shown in the preceding equation is called a *monomial representation*. In this representation, the polynomial is written as a linear combination of monomials x^i.

Alternatively, the polynomial can be written in:

- *Newton representation* with the coefficients c_i and n points, $x_0, \cdots, x_{n-1}$:

$$p(x) = c_0 + c_1(x - x_0) + c_2(x - x_0)(x - x_1) + c_n(x - x_0) \cdots (x - x_{n-1})$$

- *Lagrange representation* with the coefficients y_i and $n+1$ points, $x_0, \cdots, x_{n-1}$:

$$p(x) = y_0 l_0(x) + y_1 l_1(x) + \cdots + y_n l_n(x)$$

with the cardinal functions:

$$l_i(x) = \Pi_{j=0, j \neq i}^n \frac{x - x_i}{x_j - x_i}$$

There are infinitely many representations, but we restrict ourselves here to these three typical ones.

A polynomial can be determined from interpolation conditions:

$$p(x_i) = y_i \quad i = 0, \ldots, n$$

with the given distinct values x_i and arbitrary values y_i as input. In the Lagrange formulation, the interpolation polynomial is directly available, as its coefficients are the interpolation data. The coefficients for the interpolation polynomial in Newton representation can be obtained by a recursion formula, called the divided differences formula:

$$c_{i,0} = y_i$$

and

$$c_{i,j} = \frac{c_{i+1,j-1} - c_{i,j-1}}{x_{i+j} - x_i}$$

We then obtain the coefficients by $c_i := c_{0,i}$.

The coefficients of the interpolation polynomial in monomial representation are obtained by solving a linear system:

$$\begin{bmatrix} x_0^n & x_0^{n-1} & \cdots & x_0^1 & x_0^0 \\ x_1^n & x_1^{n-1} & \cdots & x_1^1 & x_1^0 \\ & & \vdots & & \\ x_n^n & x_n^{n-1} & \cdots & x_n^1 & x_n^0 \end{bmatrix} \begin{bmatrix} a_n \\ a_{n-1} \\ \vdots \\ a_0 \end{bmatrix} = \begin{bmatrix} y_0 \\ y_1 \\ \vdots \\ y_n \end{bmatrix}.$$

A matrix that has a given polynomial p (or a multiple of it) as its characteristic polynomial is called a *companion matrix*. The eigenvalues of the companion matrix are the zeros (roots) of the polynomial. An algorithm for computing the zeros of p can be constructed by first setting up its companion matrix and then computing the eigenvalues with `scipy.linalg.eig`. The companion matrix for a polynomial in Newton representation reads as follows:

$$\begin{bmatrix} x_0 & & & & & -c_{0,0} \\ 1 & x_1 & & & & -c_{0,1} \\ & 1 & x_2 & & & -c_{0,2} \\ & & \ddots & \ddots & & \vdots \\ & & & 1 & x_{n-2} & -c_{0,n-2} \\ & & & & 1 & x_{n-1} - c_{0,n-1} \end{bmatrix}$$

19.1.2 Tasks

We can now formulate some programming tasks:

1. Write a class called `PolyNomial` with the attributes `points`, `degree`, `coeff`, and `basis`, where:

   - `points` is a list of tuples (x_i, y_i).
   - `degree` is the degree of the corresponding interpolation polynomial.
   - `coeff` contains the polynomial coefficients.
   - `basis` is a string stating which representation is used.

2. Provide the class with a method for evaluating the polynomial at a given point.
3. Provide the class with a method called `plot` that plots the polynomial over a given interval.

4. Write a method called __add__ that returns a polynomial that is the sum of two polynomials. Be aware that only in the monomial case the sum can be computed by just summing up the coefficients.
5. Write a method that computes the coefficients of the polynomial represented in a monomial form.
6. Write a method that computes the polynomial's companion matrix.
7. Write a method that computes the zeros of the polynomial by computing the eigenvalues of the companion matrix.
8. Write a method that computes the polynomial that is the ith derivative of the given polynomial.
9. Write a method that checks whether two polynomials are equal. Equality can be checked by comparing all coefficients (zero leading coefficients should not matter).

19.1.3 The polynomial class

Let's now design a polynomial base class based on a monomial formulation of the polynomial. The polynomial can be initialized either by giving its coefficients with respect to the monomial basis or by giving a list of interpolation points, as follows:

```python
import scipy.linalg as sl
import matplotlib.pyplot as mp

class PolyNomial:
    base='monomial'
    def __init__(self,**args):
        if 'points' in args:
            self.points = array(args['points'])
            self.xi = self.points[:,0]
            self.coeff = self.point_2_coeff()
            self.degree = len(self.coeff)-1
        elif 'coeff' in args:
            self.coeff = array(args['coeff'])
            self.degree = len(self.coeff)-1
            self.points = self.coeff_2_point()
        else:
            self.points = array([[0,0]])
            self.xi = array([1.])
            self.coeff = self.point_2_coeff()
            self.degree = 0
```

The method __init__ of the new class uses the construction `**args` as discussed in Section 7.2.5: *Variable number of arguments*. If no arguments are given, a zero polynomial is assumed. If the polynomial is given by interpolation points, the method used to compute the coefficients by solving a Vandermonde system is given as follows:

```
def point_2_coeff(self):
    return sl.solve(vander(self.x),self.y)
```

From k given coefficients, k interpolation points are constructed by:

```
def coeff_2_point(self):
    points = [[x,self(x)] for x in linspace(0,1,self.degree+1)]
    return array(points)
```

The command `self(x)` does a polynomial evaluation, which is done by providing a method __call__:

```
def __call__(self,x):
    return polyval(self.coeff,x)
```

(See also the example for the method __call__ in Section 8.1.5: *Special methods*.) Here, this method uses the NumPy command `polyval`. As a next step, we just add for convenience two methods, which we decorate with the `property` decorator (see also Section 7.8: *Functions as decorators*):

```
@property
def x(self):
    return self.points[:,0]
@property
def y(self):
    return self.points[:,1]
```

Let's explain what is going on here. We define a method to extract the x values of the data, which were used to define the polynomial. Similarly, a method to extract the y values of the data is defined. With the `property` decorator, the result of calling the method is presented as if it were just an attribute of the polynomial. There are two coding alternatives:

1. We use a method call:

   ```
   def x(self):
       return self.points[:,0]
   ```

   This gives access to the x values by the call: `p.x()`.

2. We use the `property` decorator. It permits us to access the x values simply by using this statement: `p.x`. We choose here the second variant.

It is always a good practice to define a __repr__ method (see also `Section 8.1.5`: *Special methods.*). At least for a quick check of the results, this method is useful:

```
def __repr__(self):
    txt  = f'Polynomial of degree {self.degree} \n'
    txt += f'with coefficients {self.coeff} \n in {self.base} basis.'
    return txt
```

We now provide a method for plotting the polynomial, as follows:

```
margin = .05
plotres = 500
def plot(self,ab=None,plotinterp=True):
    if ab is None: # guess a and b
        x = self.x
        a, b = x.min(), x.max()
        h = b-a
        a -= self.margin*h
        b += self.margin*h
    else:
        a,b = ab
    x = linspace(a,b,self.plotres)
    y = vectorize(self.__call__)(x)
    mp.plot(x,y)
    mp.xlabel('$x$')
    mp.ylabel('$p(x)$')
    if plotinterp:
        mp.plot(self.x, self.y, 'ro')
```

Note the use of the command `vectorize` (see `Section 4.8`: *Functions acting on arrays*). The method __call__ is specific to the monomial representation and has to be changed if a polynomial is represented in another way. This is also the case for the computation of the polynomial's companion matrix:

```
def companion(self):
    companion = eye(self.degree, k=-1)
    companion[0,:] -= self.coeff[1:]/self.coeff[0]
    return companion
```

Once the companion matrix is available, the zeros of the polynomial are given by its eigenvalues:

```
def zeros(self):
    companion = self.companion()
    return sl.eigvals(companion)
```

To this end, the module `scipy.linalg` has to be imported first as `sl`.

19.1.4 Usage examples of the polynomial class

Let's give some usage examples.

First, we create a polynomial instance from the given interpolation points:

```
p = PolyNomial(points=[(1,0),(2,3),(3,8)])
```

The polynomial's coefficients with respect to the monomial basis are available as an attribute of p:

```
p.coeff # returns array([ 1., 0., -1.]) (rounded)
```

This corresponds to the polynomial $p(x) = 1x^2 + 0x - 1$. The default plot of the polynomial, obtained by `p.plot((-3.5,3.5))`, results in the following figure (*Figure 19.1*):

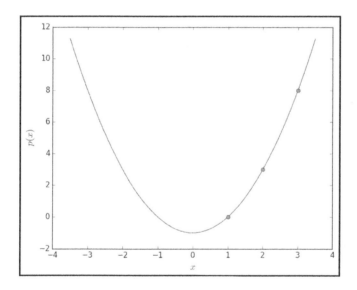

Figure 19.1: Result of the polynomial plot method

Finally, we compute the zeros of the polynomial, which in this case are two real numbers:

```
pz = p.zeros() # returns array([-1.+0.j, 1.+0.j])
```

The result can be verified by evaluating the polynomial at these points:

```
p(pz) # returns array([0.+0.j, 0.+0.j])
```

19.1.5 Newton polynomial

The class `NewtonPolyNomial` defines a polynomial described with respect to the Newton basis. We let it inherit some common methods from the polynomial base class, for example, `polynomial.plot`, `polynomial.zeros`, and even parts of the __init__ method, by using the command `super` (see Section 8.5: *Subclasses and inheritance*):

```
class NewtonPolynomial(PolyNomial):
    base = 'Newton'
    def __init__(self,**args):
        if 'coeff' in args:
            try:
                self.xi = array(args['xi'])
            except KeyError:
                raise ValueError('Coefficients need to be given'
                'together with abscissae values xi')
        super(NewtonPolynomial, self).__init__(**args)
```

Once the interpolation points are given, the computation of the coefficients is performed by:

```
def point_2_coeff(self):
    return array(list(self.divdiff()))
```

We used divided differences for computing the Newton representation of the polynomial, which is programmed as a generator here (see Section 9.3.1: *Generators* and Section 9.4: *List-filling patterns*):

```
def divdiff(self):
    xi = self.xi
    row = self.y
    yield row[0]
    for level in range(1,len(xi)):
        row = (row[1:] - row[:-1])/(xi[level:] - xi[:-level])
        if allclose(row,0): # check: elements of row nearly zero
            self.degree = level-1
            break
        yield row[0]
```

Let's briefly check how this works:

```
# here we define the interpolation data: (x,y) pairs
pts = array([[0.,0],[.5,1],[1.,0],[2,0.]])

pN = NewtonPolynomial(points=pts) # this creates an instance of the
                                  # polynomial class
pN.coeff # returns the coefficients array([0. , 2. , -4. , 2.66666667])
print(pN)
```

The function `print` executes the method `__repr__` of the base class and returns the following text:

```
Polynomial of degree 3
  with coefficients [ 0.     2.    -4.      2.66666667]
  in Newton basis.
```

The polynomial evaluation is different from the corresponding method of the base class. The method `NewtonPolyNomial.__call__` needs to override `Polynomial.__call__`:

```
def __call__(self,x):
    # first compute the sequence 1, (x-x_1), (x-x_1)(x-x_2),...
    nps = hstack([1., cumprod(x-self.xi[:self.degree])])
    return self.coeff@nps
```

Finally, we give the code for the companion matrix, which overrides the corresponding method of the parent class, as follows:

```
def companion(self):
    degree = self.degree
    companion = eye(degree, k=-1)
    diagonal = identity(degree,dtype=bool)
    companion[diagonal] = self.x[:degree]
    companion[:,-1] -= self.coeff[:degree]/self.coeff[degree]
    return companion
```

Note the use of Boolean arrays. The exercises will further build on this foundation.

19.2 Spectral clustering

An interesting application of eigenvectors is for clustering data. Using the eigenvectors of a matrix derived from a distance matrix, unlabeled data can be separated into groups. Spectral clustering methods get their name from the use of the spectrum of this matrix. A distance matrix for n elements (for example, the pairwise distance between data points) is an $n \times n$ symmetric matrix. Given such an $n \times n$ distance matrix M with distance values m_{ij}, we can create the Laplacian matrix of the data points as follows:

$$L = I - D^{-1/2} M D^{-1/2}$$

Here, I is the identity matrix and D is the diagonal matrix containing the row sums of M:

$$D = \mathrm{diag}(d_i), d_i = \sum_j m_{ij}$$

The data clusters are obtained from the eigenvectors of *L*. In the simplest case of data points with only two classes, the first eigenvector (that is, the one corresponding to the largest eigenvalue) is often enough to separate the data.

Here is an example of simple two-class clustering. The following code creates some 2D data points and clusters them based on the first eigenvector of the Laplacian matrix:

```python
import scipy.linalg as sl

# create some data points
n = 100
x1 = 1.2 * random.randn(n, 2)
x2 = 0.8 * random.randn(n, 2) + tile([7, 0], (n, 1))
x = vstack((x1, x2))

# pairwise distance matrix
M = array([[ sqrt(sum((x[i] - x[j])**2))
            for i in range(2*n)]
            for j in range(2 * n)])

# create the Laplacian matrix
D = diag(1 / sqrt( M.sum(axis = 0) ))
L = identity(2 * n) - dot(D, dot(M, D))

# compute eigenvectors of L
S, V = sl.eig(L)
# As L is symmetric the imaginary parts
# in the eigenvalues are only due to negligible numerical errors S=S.real
V=V.real
```

The eigenvector corresponding to the largest eigenvalue gives the grouping (for example, by thresholding at 0) and can be shown with:

```python
largest=abs(S).argmax()
plot(V[:,largest])
```

The following figure (*Figure 19.2*) shows the result of spectral clustering of a simple two-class dataset:

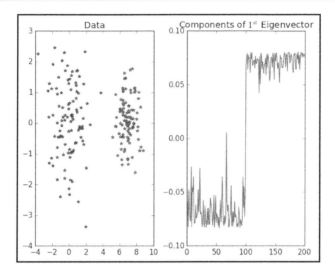

Figure 19.2: The result of a simple two-class clustering

For more difficult datasets and more classes, one usually takes the *k* eigenvectors corresponding to the *k* largest eigenvalues and then clusters the data with some other method, but using the eigenvectors instead of the original data points. A common choice is the *k*-means clustering algorithm, which is the topic of the next example.

The eigenvectors are used as input to *k*-means clustering, as follows:

```
import scipy.linalg as sl
import scipy.cluster.vq as sc
# simple 4 class data
x = random.rand(1000,2)
ndx = ((x[:,0] < 0.4) | (x[:,0] > 0.6)) & \
                ((x[:,1] < 0.4) | (x[:,1] > 0.6))
x = x[ndx]
n = x.shape[0]

# pairwise distance matrix
M = array([[ sqrt(sum((x[i]-x[j])**2)) for i in range(n) ]
            for j in range(n)])

# create the Laplacian matrix
D = diag(1 / sqrt( M.sum(axis=0) ))
L = identity(n) - dot(D, dot(M, D))

# compute eigenvectors of L
_,_,V = sl.svd(L)
```

```
k = 4
# take k first eigenvectors
eigv = V[:k,:].T

# k-means
centroids,dist = sc.kmeans(eigv,k)
clust_id = sc.vq(eigv,centroids)[0]
```

Note that we computed the eigenvectors here using the singular value decomposition sl.svd. As *L* is symmetric, the result is the same as if we had used sl.eig, but svd gives the eigenvectors already ordered corresponding to the ordering of the eigenvalues. We also used throw-away variables. svd returns a list with three arrays, the left and right singular vectors, U and V, and the singular values, S, as follows:

```
U, S, V = sl.svd(L)
```

As we do not need U and S here, we can throw them away when unpacking the return value of svd:

```
_, _, V = sl.svd(L)
```

The result can be plotted using:

```
for i in range(k):
    ndx = where(clust_id == i)[0]
    plot(x[ndx, 0], x[ndx, 1],'o')
axis('equal')
```

The following figure shows the result of spectral clustering of a simple *multiclass dataset*:

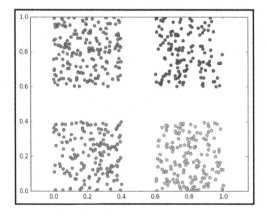

Figure 19.3: An example of the spectral clustering of a simple four-class dataset

19.3 Solving initial value problems

In this section, we will consider the mathematical task of numerically solving a system of ordinary equations for given initial values:

$$y'(t) = f(t, y) \qquad y(t_0) = y_0 \in \mathbb{R}^n.$$

The solution to this problem is a function y. A numerical method computes approximations, $y_i \approx y(t_i)$ at discrete communications points, t_i, within the interval of interest $[t_0, t_e]$. We collect the data that describes the problem in a class as follows:

```
class IV_Problem:
    """
    Initial value problem (IVP) class
    """
    def __init__(self, rhs, y0, interval, name='IVP'):
        """
        rhs 'right hand side' function of the ordinary differential
                                        equation f(t,y)
        y0 array with initial values
        interval start and end value of the interval of independent
        variables often initial and end time
        name descriptive name of the problem
        """
        self.rhs = rhs
        self.y0 = y0
        self.t0, self.tend = interval
        self.name = name
```

The differential equation:

$$y'(t) = \begin{pmatrix} y_1'(t) \\ y_2'(t) \end{pmatrix} = \begin{pmatrix} y_2(t) \\ g/l \sin y_1(t) \end{pmatrix} \quad \text{with} \quad y_0 = \begin{pmatrix} \pi/2 \\ 0 \end{pmatrix}$$

describes a mathematical pendulum; y_1 is its angle with respect to the vertical axis, g is the gravitation constant, and l is its length. The initial angle is $\pi/2$ and the initial angular velocity is zero.

The pendulum problem becomes an instance of the problem class, as follows:

```
def rhs(t,y):
    g = 9.81
    l = 1.
    yprime = array([y[1], g / l * sin(y[0])])
    return yprime

pendulum = IV_Problem(rhs, array([pi / 2, 0.]), [0., 10.] ,
                      'mathem. pendulum')
```

There might be different views on the problem at hand, leading to a different design of the class. For example, one might want to consider the interval of independent variables as a part of a solution process instead of the problem definition. The same holds when considering initial values. They might, as we did here, be considered a part of the mathematical problem, while other authors might want to allow variation of initial values by putting them as a part of the solution process.

The solution process is modeled as another class:

```
class IVPsolver:
    """
    IVP solver class for explicit one-step discretization methods
    with constant step size
    """
    def __init__(self, problem, discretization, stepsize):
        self.problem = problem
        self.discretization = discretization
        self.stepsize = stepsize
    def one_stepper(self):
        yield self.problem.t0, self.problem.y0
        ys = self.problem.y0
        ts = self.problem.t0
        while ts <= self.problem.tend:
            ts, ys = self.discretization(self.problem.rhs, ts, ys,
                                         self.stepsize)
            yield ts, ys
    def solve(self):
        return list(self.one_stepper())
```

We continue by first defining two discretization schemes:

* *Explicit Euler method*:

```
def expliciteuler(rhs, ts, ys, h):
    return ts + h, ys + h * rhs(ts, ys)
```

- *Classical Runge-Kutta four-stage method (RK4):*

```
def rungekutta4(rhs, ts, ys, h):
    k1 = h * rhs(ts, ys)
    k2 = h * rhs(ts + h/2., ys + k1/2.)
    k3 = h * rhs(ts + h/2., ys + k2/2.)
    k4 = h * rhs(ts + h, ys + k3)
    return ts + h, ys + (k1 + 2*k2 + 2*k3 + k4)/6.
```

With these, we can create instances to obtain the corresponding discretized versions of the pendulum ODE:

```
pendulum_Euler = IVPsolver(pendulum, expliciteuler, 0.001)
pendulum_RK4 = IVPsolver(pendulum, rungekutta4, 0.001)
```

We can solve the two discrete models and plot the solution and the angle difference:

```
sol_Euler = pendulum_Euler.solve()
sol_RK4 = pendulum_RK4.solve()
tEuler, yEuler = zip(*sol_Euler)
tRK4, yRK4 = zip(*sol_RK4)
subplot(1,2,1), plot(tEuler,yEuler),\
        title('Pendulum result with Explicit Euler'),\
        xlabel('Time'), ylabel('Angle and angular velocity')
subplot(1,2,2), plot(tRK4,abs(array(yRK4)-array(yEuler))),\
        title('Difference between both methods'),\
        xlabel('Time'), ylabel('Angle and angular velocity')
```

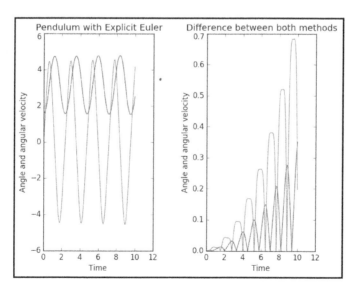

Figure 19.4: Pendulum simulation with the explicit Euler method and comparison with the results of the more accurate Runge–Kutta 4 method

It is worthwhile discussing alternative class designs. What should be put in separate classes, what should be bundled into the same class?

- We strictly separated the mathematical problem from the numerical method. Where should the initial values go? Should they be part of the problem or part of the solver? Or should they be left as input parameters for the solve method of the solver instance? One might even design the program so that it allows several possibilities. The decision to use one of these alternatives depends on the future use of this program. Looping over various initial values as in parameter identification would be eased by leaving the initial values as input parameters for the solve method. On the other hand, simulating different model variants with the same initial values would make coupling the initial values to the problem preferable.

- We presented for simplicity only solvers with a constant and given step size. Is the design of the IVPsolver class appropriate for a future extension of adaptive methods, where a tolerance rather than a step size is given?

- We suggested earlier using a generator construction for the stepping mechanism. Adaptive methods need to reject steps from time to time. Is this need conflicting with the design of the stepping mechanism in IVPsolver.onestepper?

- We encourage you to check the design of the two SciPy tools for solving initial values, namely scipy.integrate.ode and scipy.integrate.odeint.

19.4 Summary

Most of what we explained in this book was bundled into the three longer examples in this chapter. These examples mimic code development and give prototypes, which you are encouraged to alter and confront with your own ideas.

You saw that code in scientific computing can have its own flavor due to its strong relationship with mathematically defined algorithms and that it is often wise to keep the relationship between code and formula visible. Python has techniques for this, as you have seen.

19.5 Exercises

Ex. 1: Implement a method __add__ that constructs a new polynomial $p + q$ by adding two given polynomials p and q. In monomial form, polynomials are added by just adding the coefficients, whereas in Newton form, the coefficients depend on the abscissas x_i of the interpolation points. Before adding the coefficients of both polynomials, the polynomial q has to get new interpolation points with the property that their abscissas x_i coincide with those of p, and the method __changepoints__ has to be provided for that. It should change the interpolation points and return a new set of coefficients.

Ex. 2: Write conversion methods to convert a polynomial from Newton form into monomial form and vice versa.

Ex. 3: Write a method called add_point that takes a polynomial q and a tuple (x, y) as parameters and returns a new polynomial that interpolates self.points and (x, y).

Ex. 4: Write a class called LagrangePolynomial that implements polynomials in Lagrange form and inherits as much as possible from the polynomial base class.

Ex. 5: Write tests for the polynomial class.

Subscribe to our online digital library for full access to over 7,000 books and videos, as well as industry-leading tools to help you plan your personal development and advance your career. For more information, please visit our website.

Why subscribe?

- Spend less time learning and more time coding with practical eBooks and Videos from over 4,000 industry professionals

- Improve your learning with Skill Plans built especially for you

- Get a free eBook or video every month

- Fully searchable for easy access to vital information

- Copy and paste, print, and bookmark content

Did you know that Packt offers eBook versions of every book published, with PDF and ePub files available? You can upgrade to the eBook version at www.packt.com and as a print book customer, you are entitled to a discount on the eBook copy. Get in touch with us at customercare@packtpub.com for more details.

At www.packt.com, you can also read a collection of free technical articles, sign up for a range of free newsletters, and receive exclusive discounts and offers on Packt books and eBooks.

Other Books You May Enjoy

If you enjoyed this book, you may be interested in these other books by Packt:

Learn Amazon SageMaker

Julien Simon

ISBN: 978-1-80020-891-9

- Create and automate end-to-end machine learning workflows on Amazon Web Services (AWS)

- Become well-versed with data annotation and preparation techniques

- Use AutoML features to build and train machine learning models with AutoPilot

- Create models using built-in algorithms and frameworks and your own code

- Train computer vision and NLP models using real-world examples

- Cover training techniques for scaling, model optimization, model debugging, and cost optimization

- Automate deployment tasks in a variety of configurations using SDK and several automation tools

Python Data Cleaning Cookbook

Michael Walker

ISBN: 978-1-80056-566-1

- Find out how to read and analyze data from a variety of sources

- Produce summaries of the attributes of data frames, columns, and rows

- Filter data and select columns of interest that satisfy given criteria

- Address messy data issues, including working with dates and missing values

- Improve your productivity in Python pandas by using method chaining

- Use visualizations to gain additional insights and identify potential data issues

- Enhance your ability to learn what is going on in your data

- Build user-defined functions and classes to automate data cleaning

Packt is searching for authors like you

If you're interested in becoming an author for Packt, please
visit authors.packtpub.com and apply today. We have worked with thousands of
developers and tech professionals, just like you, to help them share their insight with the
global tech community. You can make a general application, apply for a specific hot topic
that we are recruiting an author for, or submit your own idea.

Leave a review - let other readers know what you think

Please share your thoughts on this book with others by leaving a review on the site that you
bought it from. If you purchased the book from Amazon, please leave us an honest review
on this book's Amazon page. This is vital so that other potential readers can see and use
your unbiased opinion to make purchasing decisions, we can understand what our
customers think about our products, and our authors can see your feedback on the title that
they have worked with Packt to create. It will only take a few minutes of your time, but is
valuable to other potential customers, our authors, and Packt. Thank you!

References

1. M. Abramowitz and I.A. Stegun, *Handbook of Mathematical Functions with Formulas, Graphs, and Mathematical Tables*, U.S. Department of Commerce, 2002. ISBN: 9780486612720.

2. *Anaconda – Continuum Analytics Download page*. URL: `https://www.continuum.io/downloads`.

3. Michael J. Cloud, Moore Ramon E., and R. Baker Kearfott, *Introduction to Interval Analysis*, Society for Industrial and Applied Mathematics (SIAM), 2009. ISBN: 0-89871-669-1.

4. *Python Decorator Library*. URL: `http://wiki.python.org/moin/PythonDecoratorLibrary`.

5. Z. Bai E. Anderson, C. Bischof, S. Blackford, J. Demmel, J. Dongarra, J. Du Croz, A. Greenbaum, S. Hammarling, A. McKenney, and D. Sorensen, *LAPACK Users' Guide*, SIAM, 1999. ISBN: 9780898714470.

6. *fraction – Rational Numbers Library*. URL: `http://docs.python.org/library/fractions.html`.

7. Claus Führer, Jan Erik Solem, and Olivier Verdier, *Computing with Python*, Pearson, 2014. ISBN: 978-0-273-78643-6.

8. *functools – Higher order functions and operations on callable objects*. URL: `http://docs.python.org/library/functools.html`.

9. *Python Generator Tricks*. URL: `http://linuxgazette.net/100/pramode.html`.

10. G.H. Golub and C.F.V. Loan, *Matrix computations*, Johns Hopkins studies in the mathematical sciences. Johns Hopkins University Press, 1996. ISBN: 9780801854149.

11. Ernst Hairer and Gerhard Wanner, *Analysis by its history*, Springer, 1995.

12. *Python versus Haskell*. URL: `http://wiki.python.org/moin/PythonVsHaskell`.

13. *The IEEE 754-2008 standard.* URL: `http://en.wikipedia.org/wiki/IEEE_754-2008`.

14. *Interval arithmetic.* URL: `http://en.wikipedia.org/wiki/Interval_arithmetic`.

15. *IPython: Interactive Computing.* URL: `http://ipython.org/`.

16. H.P. Langtangen, *Python scripting for computational science* (Texts in computational science and engineering), *Springer*, 2008. ISBN:9783540739159.

17. H.P. Langtangen, *A Primer on Scientific Programming with Python* (Texts in Computational Science and Engineering), Springer, 2009. ISBN: 9783642024740.

18. D. F. Lawden, *Elliptic Functions and Applications*, Springer, 1989. ISBN: 9781441930903.

19. M. Lutz, *Learning Python: Powerful Object-Oriented Programming*, O'Reilly, 2009. *ISBN: 9780596158064.*

20. *NumPy Tutorial – Mandelbrot Set Example.* URL: `http://www.scipy.org/Tentative_NumPy_Tutorial/Mandelbrot_Set_Example`.

21. *matplotlib. URL:* `http://matplotlib.sourcefciteorge.net`.

22. *Standard: Memoized recursive Fibonacci in Python.* URL: `http://ujihisa.blogspot.se/2010/11/memoized-recursive-fibonacciin-python.html`.

23. *Matplotlib mplot3d toolkit.* URL: `http://matplotlib.sourceforge.net/mpl_toolkits/mplot3d`.

24. James M. Ortega and Werner C. Rheinboldt, *Iterative solution of nonlinear equations in several variables*, SIAM, 2000. ISBN: 9780898714616.

25. *pdb – The Python Debugger,* documentation: `http://docs.python.org/library/pdb.html`.

26. Fernando Pérez and Brian E. Granger. IPython: a System for Interactive Scientific Computing." In: Comput. Sci. Eng. 9.3 (May 2007), pp. 21–29. URL: `http://ipython.org`.

27. Michael J.D. Powell. "An efficient method for finding the minimum of a function of several variables without calculating derivatives." In: Computer Journal 7 (2 1964), pp. 155–162. `doi:10.1093/comjnl/7.2.155`.

28. Timothy Sauer, *Numerical Analysis*, Pearson, 2006.

29. L.F. Shampine, R.C. Allen, and S. Pruess, *Fundamentals of Numerical Computing*, John Wiley, 1997. ISBN: 9780471163633.

30. Jan Erik Solem, *Programming Computer Vision with Python*, O'Reilly Media, 2012. URL: `http://programmingcomputervision.com`.

31. *Python Documentation – Emulating numeric types.* URL: `http://docs.python.org/reference/datamodel.html#emulating-numeric-types`.

32. *Sphinx: Python Documentation Generator*. URL: `http://sphinx.pocoo.org/`.

33. J. Stoer and R. Bulirsch, *Introduction to numerical analysis. Texts in applied mathematics*, Springer, 2002. ISBN: 9780387954523.

34. *Python Format String Syntax*. URL: `http://docs.python.org/library/string.html#format-string-syntax`.

35. S. Tosi, *Matplotlib for Python Developers*, Packt Publishing, 2009. ISBN: 9781847197900.

36. Lloyd N. Trefethen and David Bau, *Numerical Linear Algebra*, SIAM: Society for Industrial and Applied Mathematics, 1997. ISBN: 0898713617.

37. *visvis – The object oriented approach to visualization*. URL: `http://code.google.com/p/visvis/`.

38. The full list of built-in exceptions can be found at `http://docs.python.org/library/exceptions.html`

Index

Made in the USA
Coppell, TX
03 January 2022

70744055R00216